Palgrave Studies in Risk, Crime and Society

Series editors
Kieran McCartan
Dept of Criminology
University of the West of England
Bristol, United Kingdom

Philip N. S. Rumney
University of the West of England
Bristol, United Kingdom

Nicholas Ryder
University of the West of England
Bristol, United Kingdom

Risk is a major contemporary issue which has widespread implications for theory, policy, governance, public protection, professional practice and societal understandings of crime and criminal justice. The potential harm associated with risk can lead to uncertainty, fear and conflict as well as disproportionate, ineffective and ill-judged state responses to perceived risk and risky groups. Risk, Crime and Society is a series featuring monographs and edited collections which examine the notion of risk, the risky behaviour of individuals and groups, as well as state responses to risk and its consequences in contemporary society. The series will include critical examinations of the notion of risk and the problematic nature of state responses to perceived risk. While Risk, Crime and Society will consider the problems associated with 'mainstream' risky groups including sex offenders, terrorists and white collar criminals, it welcomes scholarly analysis which broadens our understanding of how risk is defined, interpreted and managed. Risk, Crime and Society examines risk in contemporary society through the multi-disciplinary perspectives of law, criminology and socio-legal studies and will feature work that is theoretical as well as empirical in nature.

More information about this series at
http://www.springer.com/series/14593

Hazel Kemshall • Kieran McCartan
Editors

Contemporary Sex Offender Risk Management, Volume II

Responses

palgrave
macmillan

Editors
Hazel Kemshall
Community and Criminal Justice
De Montfort University
Leicester, United Kingdom

Kieran McCartan
Dept of Criminology
University of the West of England
Bristol, United Kingdom

Palgrave Studies in Risk, Crime and Society
ISBN 978-3-319-63572-9   ISBN 978-3-319-63573-6   (eBook)
DOI 10.1007/978-3-319-63573-6

Library of Congress Control Number: 2017955322

This Palgrave Macmillan imprint is published by Springer Nature
The registered company is Springer International Publishing AG
The registered company address is: Gewerbestrasse 11, 6330 Cham, Switzerland

Preface

Sexual harm continues to be one of the most pressing global social problems (UNICEF, 2014), and arguably we are at a tipping point where resources to combat it are continually outstripped. The 'growth industry' of sex offender management within a climate of diminishing resources has focused research, policy, and practice attention on increasing effectiveness, efficiency, and impact of interventions. All the chapters presented in this volume are characterised by a focus on alternative or emerging approaches to work with sexual offenders, and, in particular, how to gain greater effectiveness in offence reduction and sexual harm prevention. The chapters presented here offer critical reviews of existing practice, alternative responses, and innovatory approaches that can be replicated 'on the ground'.

Ashmore-Hills, Burrell, and Tonkin, in Chapter 1, present an innovatory approach to combating prolific serial sexual offenders through the use of Behavioural Crime Linkage (BCL), a form of behavioural analysis which identifies behavioural similarities across multiple crimes. They describe the usefulness of this approach to law enforcement agencies when investigating sexual crime. In addition to its utility in crime investigation, Ashmore-Hills et al. also explore its role in primary, secondary, and tertiary prevention, particularly in identifying sexual offenders early in their offending cycle and preventing further crimes. The chapter has a practical focus and will particularly benefit those operating in law enforcement.

Wilson and Sandler, in Chapter 2, explore risk assessment in some detail, providing an overview of actuarial risk assessment instruments. They critically assess the utility of actuarial risk assessment tools, particularly with reference to the contentious areas of civil commitment and preventive sentencing. They cogently argue for the combination of psychologically meaningful factors with actuarial risk assessment factors to provide more comprehensive and robust risk assessment tools. Chapter 3 by **Case** takes an alternative view of risk assessment tools, challenging the claims of the risk prevention paradigm, and critically reviewing the major risk assessment tools for assessing youth in England and Wales. He argues that reductionism and de-individualisation are unhelpful negative consequences of our over-preoccupation with risk prevention and risk prediction. He concludes by examining the more recent English juvenile justice risk assessment tool 'AssetPlus' and the prosocial ethos rather than risk focus embedded within it.

Hilder identifies larger-scale challenges to risk assessment and risk management in Chapter 4 reviewing current issues in the assessment and management of serious sexual offenders who travel between the Member States of the European Union. Current levels of travel, particularly for 'sexual tourism' and to avoid vetting and barring, in addition to those EU nationals who have previous convictions in Home Member States who then reside and work in another Member State make this a significant and growing issue. Drawing on a project examining current EU wide procedures and the practices of individual Member States she identifies the key issues which prevent effective assessment, information exchange, and management of this cohort across the EU. Whilst a number of EU legislative arrangements do enable information exchange, management, and monitoring across borders, effectiveness is reduced by varied understandings of risk, rehabilitation, multi-agency working, privacy, and data protection rights across Member States. The implications for a post-Brexit UK are also explored.

International and globalised sexual crime is also enabled by online offending. In Chapter 5, **Brennan, Meridian, and Perkins** present a clear exposition of current knowledge on different types of online sex offending behaviour, including use of child sexual exploitation material, online solicitation behaviour, and use of the Internet for international perpetrators of sexual abuse. They recognise the growing problem for law enforcement and related agencies in dealing with ever-increasing caseloads, and they consider the utility of risk assessment tools for online offending, and their potential role in case prioritisation.

Gerald Zeng and Chu Chi Meng, in Chapter 6, outline current practice with youth who sexually offend in Singapore, with an important focus on rehabilitation. They offer a practical demonstration of the meshing of risk prevention with the Good Lives model in order to illustrate a comprehensive and holistic approach to the treatment and management of youth who sexually offend. Their approach is developmentally sensitive, and rooted in a commitment to research and evaluation.

Hulley, in Chapter 7, pursues the role of Good Lives in more detail, and outlines her recent research into desistance-based practice with sexual offenders. Her small-scale but in-depth study provides useful insights into the practice of police officers working with sex offenders in the community. Her research importantly shows that sex offenders managed within a strengths-based paradigm are more likely to have a positive relationship with their supervising officer and are more likely to achieve the necessary positive identity change to achieve a non-offending lifestyle. Hulley also considers the role of Active Risk Management System (ARMS) in promoting a strengths-based approach to supervision within policing.

McCartan, Kemshall, and Hoggett, in Chapter 8 extend these issues by considering the role of the sex offender register and disclosure in the community management of sexual offenders. They argue that a different approach is required to deal effectively with the ever-increasing caseload, and to promote rehabilitation, desistance, and reductions in sexual crime. An increased understanding of desistance processes for sexual offenders, and a greater focus on effective practice is advocated in order to make better use of diminishing resources. The chapter concludes with tips for improving current practice.

Hazel Kemshall

May 2017   Kieran McCartan

Contents

List of Contributors

Leah Ashmore-Hill is a police crime intelligence researcher based in the United Kingdom. Prior to this, she was the Network Facilitator for the Crime Linkage International Research Network (C-LINK). Leah holds an MSc in Forensic Mental Health Research (2015) from the Institute of Psychiatry, King's College, London. Leah's primary research interests include crime intelligence analysis, investigative psychology, and forensic mental health.

Maggie Brennan is a lecturer in the Schools of Applied Psychology and Criminology, University College Cork, Ireland. She is the director of the recently established Research Cluster on Online Sexual Violence and Prevention at University College, Cork. Her primary research interest relates to online child sexual offending—to the role of Child Sexual Exploitation Material (CSEM) and online technologies in the offending process, and the impact of this exploitation on victims. A major focus of Maggie's work is the development of novel approaches to the assessment, management, and prevention of online child sexual offences, with an emphasis on the development of enhancements for front-line domain practice. Her recent research includes work to develop models of online child sexual offending behaviour, as well as decision-support technologies for public protection professionals involved in the risk assessment and management of CSEM offences. Maggie is a serving member of the Europol EC3 Academic Advisory Network (EC3AAN) and Interpol Specialist Group on Crimes Against Children.

Amy Burrell is a lecturer in Forensic Psychology at Coventry University, UK. Previous roles include Research Fellow at the Jill Dando Institute of Crime Science and Training Manager at Perpetuity Training. Her PhD focused on linking robbery offences using crime scene behaviour with several of the studies published in peer review journals, including *Psychology, Crime, & Law* and the *Journal of Investigative Psychology and Offender Profiling*. She is a founding member of the Crime Linkage International Network (C-LINK); a Leverhulme Trust funded research project which brought academics and practitioners from seven countries together to collaborate on research to link serial sexual offences. She was also a co-convenor of a British Academy funded conference entitled 'Using behavioural science to target prolific criminals'. Her research interests include crime linkage, robbery, security risk management, violence in the night-time economy, and victimology.

Stephen Case is a professor and criminologist in the Department of Social Sciences at Loughborough University. He specialises in youth justice issues, particularly the implementation of 'children first', 'positive' practice models that challenge the negative, risk-based approaches of post Crime and Disorder Act youth justice. Stephen has written three youth justice texts: 'Contemporary Youth Justice' (Case 2017, Routledge), 'Positive Youth Justice: Children First, Offenders Second' (Haines and Case 2015, Policy Press) and 'Understanding Youth Offending: Risk Factor Research, Policy and Practice' (Case and Haines 2009, Willan). He has published numerous academic articles in multi-disciplinary, international journals, including *Youth Justice, Children and Society*, the *Howard Journal*, and the *Journal of Substance Use*. Professor Case has conducted research for the Youth Justice Board, the Leverhulme Trust, the Home Office, the Welsh Government, the National Institute for Health and Social Care Research and the Wales Office for Research and Development, including leading the national evaluation of the Welsh Government's youth inclusion strategy 'Extending Entitlement'.

Sarah Hilder is a senior lecturer and researcher in Criminology at Nottingham Trent University. Her research and teaching expertise has centred on working with victims, domestic abuse, issues of social justice, sex offender rehabilitation, supervision, and surveillance. Prior to an academic career, she worked for the National Probation Service as both a main grade and then Senior Probation Officer in various capacities from 1993 to 2004, where her work included the management of Court and Victim Services, domestic abuse perpetrator programmes, and work with high-risk violent and sexual offenders. Sarah has published academic work on risk assessment and safety planning in situations of domestic abuse, multi-agency working, desistance work, sexual exploitation and female gang members, sexual offending, and cross border information exchanges on serious violent or sexual offenders travelling across the EU community. She is well versed in comparative victim and criminal justice work across the European Union having worked as a senior researcher on two major EU-funded projects from 2010 to 2015.

Joanne Hulley has recently completed her doctoral thesis, which explored desistance from sexual offending, and was conducted at the University of Sheffield. She has since been teaching at various universities including University Centre Doncaster and Sheffield Hallam University. Joanne's research interests include various aspects of sexual offending, strengths-based treatment approaches, community supervision, and desistance.

Hazel Kemshall is currently Professor of Community and Criminal Justice at De Montfort University. She has research interests in risk assessment and management of offenders, effective work in multi-agency public protection, and implementing effective practice with high-risk offenders. She has completed research for the Economic and Social Research Council, the Home Office, Ministry of Justice, the Scottish Government, the Risk Management Authority, and the European Union. She was appointed to the Parole Board Review Committee in 2011, and is a Board Member of the Risk Management Authority Scotland. She has over 100 publications on risk, including *Understanding Risk in Criminal Justice* (2003, Open University Press), and *Understanding the Community Management of High Risk* (2008). Hazel led the Serious Offending by Mobile European Criminals (SOMEC) EU project investigating information exchange and management systems for serious violent and sexual offenders who travel across the 28 EU states.

Kieran McCartan is Associate Professor in Criminology at the University of the West of England (UWE), Adjunct Associate Professor in Criminology at Queensland University of Technology, and a visiting research fellow at the University of Huddersfield. He has been the leader of the Social Science Research Group since 2013 and joint coordinator of the Sexual Violence Research Network since 2014 at UWE. McCartan has a track record of researching, publishing, and presenting on the sex offender register, sex offender disclosure, public health approaches to preventing sexual abuse, sex offender reintegration and management, as well as the related public/practitioner/policy debates on these issues. He has extensive experience of working in the UK and internationally xiv List of Contributors

(Ireland, Netherlands, Latvia, the USA, Canada, Australia); received funding from research councils (including ESRC and Leverhulme), government agencies (including Ministry of Justice, Cabinet Office, and Bristol City Council) and charities (including ANROWS and Circles UK); published widely in academic and professional arenas; and taken part in extensive media interviews. He is on the editorial board of *Sexual Abuse*; the International Representative on the ATSA executive board; a lead blogger on the SAJRT and the NOTA Prevention Blogs; a member of the ATSA Prevention Committee, the NOTA Research Committee and the NOTA Prevention Committee; a Trustee of Circles South West; a grants reviewer for ESRC and NSVRC; and the only international expert research advisor to Bravehearts (Australia). McCartan has over 40 academic publications (including journal articles, books, book chapters, and external research reports); 25+ practitioner/professional articles; 65+ blogs and online publications; generated over half a million pounds in external research funding; given 100+ external presentations nationally and internationally (including conference papers and invited keynotes); and taken part in over 25 media interviews (including ABC *Lateline*, Australia; *Points West*, BBC England; *Nolan Live*, BBC Northern Ireland; BBC International; and TV Live Asia).

Chi Meng is currently Deputy Director and the Senior Principal Clinical and Forensic Psychologist at the Rehabilitation and Protection Group, Ministry of Social and Family Development, Singapore (MSF). At MSF, he provides assessment and treatment services to the courts, child protection services, probations services, as well as youth correctional institutions. He also heads the Centre for Research on Rehabilitation and Protection, as well as the Centre for Evaluation at the Rehabilitation and Protection Group. Presently, he is overseeing two longitudinal studies on youth offenders and children-in-care, respectively, as well as several evaluation initiatives. In addition, he is an adjunct associate professor with the Department of Psychology, National University of Singapore.

Hannah Merdian is Senior Lecturer in Clinical and Forensic Psychology and Programme Lead for bsc Psychology with Clinical Psychology at the University of Lincoln. She is on the Board of the International Organisation for the Treatment of Sexual Offenders, the Research Committee of the National Organisation for the Treatment of Abusers, and is Associate Editor of the *Journal of Sexual Aggression*. She and Derek Perkins (West London Mental Health NHS Trust) are co-directors of the onlineprotect research group on Internet-related sexual offending.

Derek Perkins is a clinical and forensic psychologist based at Broadmoor Hospital and a Professor of Forensic Psychology at Royal Holloway University of London. He has set up and evaluated sex offender treatment services in prison, mental health, and community settings, and has published on forensic psychology, sexual offending, and personality disorder. He and Hannah Merdian (University of Lincoln) are co-directors of onlineprotect, which researches and provides training in relation to Internet-related sex offending.

Jeffrey Sandler is a researcher whose interests include female sex offenders, public policies designed to manage sex offenders, and sex offender risk assessment.

Matthew Tonkin is a lecturer in Criminology at the University of Leicester. He is a founding member of the Crime Linkage International Network (www.crimelinkage.org), a collaborative group of academics and law enforcement practitioners who have a professional interest in enhancing the practice of crime linkage. Tonkin has published extensively in the area of investigative psychology, including publications on crime linkage, offender profiling, and geographical profiling.

Robin J. Wilson ABPP is a researcher, educator, and board-certified clinical psychologist who has worked with persons with sexual and social behaviour problems in hospital, correctional, and private practice settings for more than 30 years. He has worked in Corrections (in Canada), Sexual Offender Civil Commitment (in Florida), and has provided consultation on assessment, treatment, and risk management to state, provincial, national, and international stakeholder groups. Wilson is an assistant clinical professor [adjunct], Department of Psychiatry and Behavioural Neurosciences at McMaster University in Hamilton, Ontario and a Professor of Forensic Practice at the Humber College Institute of Technology & Advanced Learning in Toronto. He provides supervisory services to hospital-based programmes working with persons with intellectual disabilities who have sexual behaviour issues. He is also a frequent consultant to the legal and judicial system, having served as an expert witness in many Court proceedings and as a member of law enforcement panels regarding community risk management.

Gerald Zeng is currently a senior manager and senior research specialist at Rehabilitation and Protection Group, Ministry of Social and Family Development, Singapore (MSF). At MSF, he conducts research on rehabilitation and organisational well-being, and is currently involved in a longitudinal study on youth offenders as well as a panel study on the well-being of officers working at MSF. Gerald is also an adjunct research fellow at the Social Science Research Centre at the National University of Singapore.

List of Figures

1

Behavioural Crime Linkage and Multi-Agency Working

L. Ashmore-Hills, A. Burrell, and M. Tonkin

Introduction

There is much evidence to suggest that the majority of crime is committed by a minority of prolific serial offenders. These offenders pose a substantial risk to society, exerting significant financial costs on the justice system and invoking a disproportionate fear of crime amongst the general public. Developing methods to more effectively bring serial offenders to justice is therefore a priority for law enforcement. Behavioural Crime Linkage (BCL) has been proposed as one method that might help in this regard. BCL is a form of behavioural analysis (practiced by law enforcement

L. Ashmore-Hills (✉)
Police Crime Intelligence Researcher, Midlands, UK

A. Burrell
Coventry University, Coventry, UK

M. Tonkin
University of Leicester, Leicester, UK

© The Author(s) 2017
H. Kemshall, K. McCartan (eds.), *Contemporary Sex Offender Risk Management,*
Volume II, Palgrave Studies in Risk, Crime and Society,
DOI 10.1007/978-3-319-63573-6_1

agencies around the world) that seeks to identify similarities in offender crime scene behaviour across two or more crimes. By linking crimes in this way, it can allow the evidence collected across multiple investigations to be combined. Not only does this potentially increase the quantity and quality of evidence available with which to convict offenders, but it also feeds into risk assessment and helps the police to work in a more efficient way (thereby saving time and money). This chapter will introduce the concept of BCL, highlighting the different scenarios in which it is used during live police investigations and giving an overview of empirical research in the area. The chapter will also explore how BCL relates to the concept of primary, secondary, and tertiary prevention, focusing in particular on how BCL can help to identify serial offenders early in their offending cycle, thereby preventing future offending and reducing the impact of crime on victims and society as a whole. The chapter will also discuss how BCL fits within the wider criminal justice process and how BCL can support the work of other criminal justice agencies.

The Risks Posed by Serial Sex Offending

Recent years have witnessed a dramatic increase in the number of recorded sexual crimes (Office for National Statistics, 2015a, b, 2016a, b).[1] While it is difficult to determine the true extent of serial sexual offending (due to many sexual offences not being reported; Kelly et al. 2005), research by Lisak and Miller (2002) has suggested that the majority of *undetected* rapists commit more than one sexual crime (an average of 5.8 rapes each). Although studies primarily using *detected* recidivism measures have suggested the rate of sexual recidivism to be relatively low (13.7%; Hanson and Morton-Bourgon 2004), research focusing on serial sexual offenders has nevertheless demonstrated that the mean number of repeat sexual crimes range from three to five (Winter et al. 2013; Deslauriers-Varin and Beauregard 2013, 2014), with some offenders having committed as many as 65 sexual offences (Woodhams and Labuschagne 2012a). This trend towards serial sexual offending fits within a broader pattern, whereby the majority of crime is committed by a minority of prolific offenders (Innes et al. 2005;

Bennett and Davis 2004; Farrington and West 1993). Such prolific offending has significant human and financial costs for society. Between 2012 and 2015, for example, a sample of 2093 serial offenders in London cost society over £163 million (Snelling 2015). Consequently, it has become a global priority for law enforcement to develop cost-effective, evidence-based, and intelligence-led approaches to tackling the risk of serial offending, particularly serial sexual offending (College of Policing 2016; Association of Chief Police Officers 2009). Indeed, by targeting prolific serial offenders, the police can maximise crime clearance rates while minimising investigative effort (because the apprehension of just a small number of prolific offenders will lead to a significant reduction in crime; Karn 2013).

Investigative Risk Assessment

Given the significant harm prolific offenders impose on society, it is not surprising that methods have been developed to aid the identification and management of these individuals. In the criminal justice system, the term 'risk assessment' is commonly associated with identifying and managing 'sexual', 'serious violent', or other 'dangerous' offenders (e.g. Home Office 2014; Kemshall 2001) and a wealth of actuarial, statistical, and technological approaches have been developed to support these processes (Brown 2014). However, the scope of risk-based decision making in criminal justice is much broader. For example, Woodhams (2008) discusses the concept of 'investigative risk assessment' and argues that this is a core function of the police analyst. She considers the continuous pressure police analysts face when prioritising their workload, especially in an economic climate which directs focus towards cost-effective policing (Karn 2013; Neyroud 2010). Woodhams (2008) argues that there are two ways in which analyst caseloads can be prioritised: first, by establishing whether the offender is a serial offender (which gives an indication of the offender's capability to impact on a large number of victims); and second, by predicting the likelihood that an offender is going to increase their use of physical violence during their assault. In this chapter we will largely focus on the first of these methods.

Preventing the Development of a Series

Identifying potential patterns of serial sexual offending at an early stage is important to help reduce the number of victims and apprehend perpetrators (Her Majesty's Inspectorate of Constabulary (HMIC) and Her Majesty's Inspectorate of the Crown Prosecution Service (HMICPS) 2012). In 2012, HMIC and HMICPS found evidence that long series of offences were often identified retrospectively when an officer identified similarities between cases which had been allocated to different investigative teams. This raised the question of why these series were not identified earlier, an issue for which police have received criticism in the past (e.g. the John Worboys case which was referred to the Independent Police Complaints Commission (IPCC) after the offender attacked seven women between being identified as a suspect in an allegation of sexual assault and his subsequent arrest six months later (IPCC 2010)). Therefore, the recommendation from HMIC and HMICPS (2012) was that investigators should consider any reported instances of stranger rape to potentially be part of a series. Given the time and resources involved for police organisations to implement such a recommendation, a cost-effective and evidence-based method for investigating potential serial sexual offences is warranted (Rainbow 2015). If successful, this could provide opportunities for primary (i.e. preventing future offences from taking place by applying proactive strategies learned from previous series), secondary (i.e. interrupting/halting a series), and tertiary (i.e. efficient apprehension and treatment to lessen the long-term negative impact of offending) prevention against the risk of serial sexual offending.

Behavioural Crime Linkage (BCL)

It has been established that a key priority for law enforcement agencies dealing with serial sexual offences is to reduce repeat offending by identifying a series as soon as possible to halt its progress. This is indeed the core objective of the Serious Crime Analysis Section (SCAS)[2] of the National Crime Agency (NCA) in the UK (Rainbow and Webb 2016).

The most objective way to identify offences committed by the same individual is to recover matching physical trace evidence (such as DNA) from several crime scenes (Grubin et al. 2001). However, as offenders are becoming increasingly forensically aware, this is becoming a difficult task for investigating officers (Beauregard and Bouchard 2010). Furthermore, even when physical evidence is available, it can take a long time to process the information and involves a significant financial cost for law enforcement agencies (Craik and Patrick 1994; Santtila et al. 2005). The combination of these difficulties has presented an opportunity for new methods to be developed that may assist law enforcement agencies to detect offenders committing multiple sexual crimes. BCL is one method that may assist in the detection and prosecution of serial sexual offenders, particularly when there is an absence of physical trace material left at the crime scene. In this way, BCL is a method that can be used to help support the analyst to prioritise their workload (i.e. conduct their 'investigative risk assessment'). The primary focus of BCL is to identify serial offences; however, this chapter will also highlight how BCL can feed into analytically predicting the risk of a serial offender.

Assumptions of BCL

There are different types of BCL tasks with operationally distinct roles and objectives (to be discussed later in the chapter). However, regardless of which task is being undertaken, the theoretical assumptions underpinning BCL remain the same (Woodhams and Bennell 2015a). For crimes to be successfully and accurately linked, the offender must repeat certain elements of their offending behaviour across their offences. This is referred to as the 'Offender Consistency Hypothesis' (Canter 1995) or the assumption of 'behavioural consistency' (Woodhams et al. 2007). In other words, a series of sexual offences committed by the same individual must involve salient behaviours that are common across their offences in order for a practitioner to identify behavioural similarity (and therefore potentially link the crimes as a series). This is not to say that the crimes will be committed with perfect consistency, but that they will be more consistent with each other than a comparison of two crimes committed by different offenders (Bennell et al. 2009). At the same time, if all offenders committed sexual offences in the same way, it would not be possible to differentiate between series committed by separate offenders. Therefore, the second assumption is that an offender's offence behaviours will also be identifiably different from those of another offender (Woodhams and Grant 2006); that is, their series can be distinguished from other series based on the offender's crime scene behaviour. This is referred to as 'differentiation' (Bennell and Canter 2002) or 'behavioural distinctiveness' (Woodhams et al. 2007). The assumptions of behavioural consistency and distinctiveness are rooted in the study of non-criminal personality psychology (see Woodhams and Bennell 2015b for a review).

BCL in Practice

BCL is a practice used in many countries, including but not limited to the UK, the Netherlands, Belgium, Finland, the USA, Canada, South Africa, Japan, Australia, and New Zealand. Broadly speaking, BCL aims to identify crimes that have been committed by the same individual by analysing the behavioural similarity and distinctiveness of crime scene behaviour across offences (Woodhams and Bennell 2015a; Woodhams et al. 2007). It is conducted predominantly by police staff (typically crime/intelligence analysts) and sometimes by Behavioural Investigative Advisors (BIAs). Whilst this chapter will focus on the use of BCL in investigations of serial sexual offences, it is important to note that this practice is also used for many other crime types, including murder (Pakkanen et al. 2012; Santtila et al. 2008), arson (Ellingwood et al. 2013; Santtila et al. 2004), vehicle crime (Davies et al. 2012; Santtila et al. 2004), robbery (Burrell et al. 2012; Woodhams and Toye 2007), and burglary (Bennell and Jones 2005; Bouhana et al. 2016; Tonkin et al. 2012).

BCL is an umbrella term used to describe distinct operational tasks. A plethora of terms have been used interchangeably in the literature to refer to BCL tasks, such as *comparative case analysis, crime linkage, case linkage, case linkage analysis,* and *crime linkage analysis.* However, in practice there are at least three distinct tasks that an analyst may be requested to complete, and practitioners urge that these operational distinctions be reflected in modern literature (Rainbow 2015; Rainbow and Webb 2016). The three linkage task scenarios are outlined below.

Scenario 1

The first linkage scenario has attracted much of the research activity in the field (Rainbow 2015). In this scenario, the practitioner is provided with an index crime and asked to search large databases to find other crimes that are behaviourally similar and that may potentially be linked to the index crime under consideration (Rainbow and Webb 2016). In Fig. 1.1 the potentially linked crimes are represented by black dots. In this scenario, the analyst does not provide a definite statement as to whether the crimes are linked or not; rather, she/he simply identifies the behavioural similarities and differences between the index crime and other offences identified (Rainbow 2015). The decision as to whether the crimes are indeed classed as linked or not is left to the Senior Investigating Officer (SIO) or whoever else requested the analysis. This task is commonly known as *Comparative Case Analysis (CCA),* and is an example of *reactive crime linkage* (Woodhams et al. 2007) because the practitioner performs the task in response to a specific operational request.

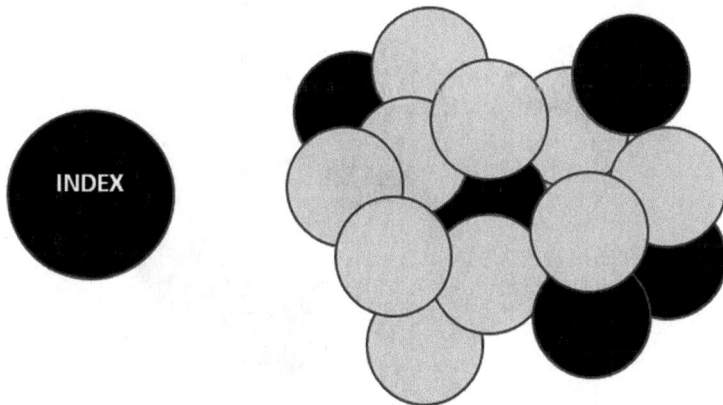

Fig. 1.1 BCL scenario 1

Scenario 2

In scenario 2 the practitioner proactively searches large police or national crime databases for potentially linked crimes. The potentially linked crime series in Fig. 1.2 are indicated using different colours to represent offence series committed by different offenders. This task is conducted without the prior request of a specific investigating officer, and is therefore an example of a *proactive crime linkage* task (Woodhams et al. 2007). This task may be manually conducted by analysts in regional police units in order to provide the force with information about potentially linked offence patterns emerging during wider daily scanning and crime pattern analysis duties (Bunch 2015).

Scenario 3

In scenario 3 the analyst is presented with a set of predetermined offences by an investigating officer and asked to provide an opinion as to whether these crimes were committed by the same offender or not. In Fig. 1.3 the predetermined set of crimes consists of 10 offences, each represented by a grey dot. This type of analysis is conducted by BIAs in the UK, and is

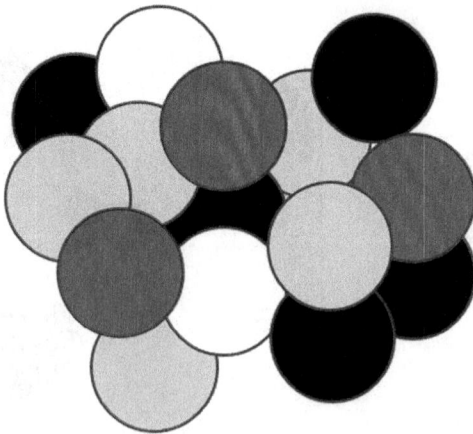

Fig. 1.2 BCL scenario 2

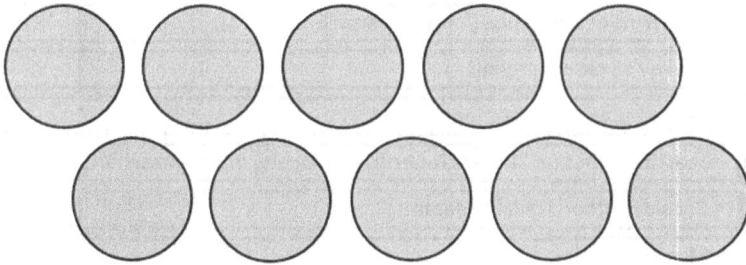

Fig. 1.3 BCL scenario 3

also known as *Crime Linkage Analysis (CLA;* Rainbow and Webb 2016; Rainbow 2015). Scenario 3 is another example of a *reactive crime linkage* task (Woodhams et al. 2007).

With regard to investigative risk assessment, the identification of a potential series (in any of the above scenarios) will justify the prioritisation of these cases within the analyst's workload (Woodhams 2008). By prioritising these cases, pooling resources, and conducting further in-depth analytical work (e.g. checking when a suspect was in custody against offences in the series), it is possible that the work of the analyst will help to generate leads for the investigative team.

The Procedure of Behaviourally Linking Crimes in Practice

Despite the aforementioned operationally distinct BCL tasks, there are some general basic steps that analysts take to approach such tasks (see Fig. 1.4):

Step 1: First, the analyst must set the terms of reference with the SIO. This step establishes the aims and objectives of the analysis and clearly lays out what the investigative team require from the analysis.

Step 2: Next, the analyst will need to review all the materials and latest developments in the case(s) of interest. This step applies to all cases brought to the analyst or BIA by the SIO, or any

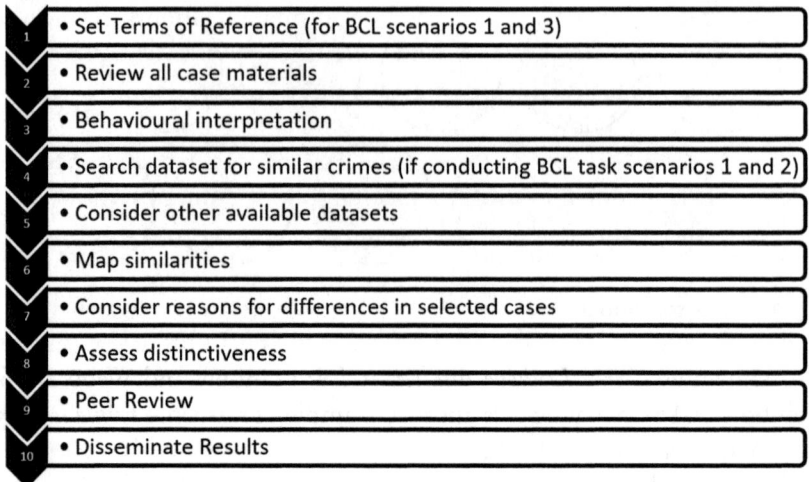

Fig. 1.4 Stages of the BCL task (information collated from Rainbow and Webb 2016; Woodhams and Bennell 2015a)

cases proactively identified by the analyst themselves. The quantity and nature of case materials will vary depending on the type of crime and availability of evidence, but may include sources such as victim statements, witness accounts, recorded footage, forensic examinations, and post-mortem reports (Woodhams and Bennell 2015a). If the analyst is working at a national level, they may also wish to review any work carried out by regional force analysts relating to the case(s) of interest, as these will incorporate local knowledge of the area and supplementary information (Rainbow and Webb 2016).

Step 3: Following familiarisation with the case materials, the analyst will then conduct a behavioural interpretation of the case(s) of interest. This interpretation involves identifying salient behavioural features of the case. One approach to this task is known as *thematic analysis,* or *dimensional behavioural linking* (Winter et al. 2013), and involves identifying the overarching offence style or theme present in a given crime. For example, a sexual offender may engage in a range of behaviours (such as kissing and hugging the victim) that indicate that the offender is trying to establish a pseudo-intimate relationship with the victim (e.g. Canter and Heritage 1990). An alternative approach to identifying salient behavioural features of the case is known as *exact match searching* or *multivariate behavioural linkage* (Winter et al. 2013), whereby comparative databases are used to ascertain how common the salient behaviours are for the specific crime type, both in combination and individually (e.g. Bennell et al. 2009; Woodhams and Labuschagne 2012a). In either approach, the analyst is aiming to identify and explain which features of the case are prominent and distinctive. This is an important task, as it will later feed in to the analyst's data searches or the SIO's later consideration of new cases in the local area (Rainbow and Webb 2016).

Step 4:   At this point in the process, an analyst conducting CCA (BCL scenario 1) or proactive linkage (BCL scenario 2) will search large crime databases for other cases that appear to be behaviourally similar. When investigating sexual offences in the UK (and many other countries), this will involve searching crimes stored on the Violent Crime Linkage Analysis System (ViCLAS; see Collins et al. 1998). ViCLAS is a database that stores records of serious crimes committed in a given country (typically, stranger sexual offences and sexual homicides), including the crime scene behaviour engaged in by the offender. Analysts can use the ViCLAS database to search for other offences within their country that share behavioural characteristics, and it is used to support the process of BCL in Belgium, the Czech Republic, France, Germany, Ireland, the Netherlands, New Zealand, Switzerland, and the UK (Wilson and Bruer 2017).

Step 5:   Analysts may also make use of other databases to inform their search findings. For example, where an offender is known for one or more of the cases under analysis, the analyst may want to search databases for details of any periods of incarceration that would rule out that offender's involvement in cases returned in the similarity search (Yaraskovitch 2017 cited in Santos 2017, p. 158).

Step 6: When the analyst has completed their search, they will need to map the behavioural similarities between cases. Analysts may make use of current statistical methodologies or visual mapping for this task. In terms of the latter, this might involve creating a matrix listing all offences identified during step 4 and the behaviours present in those crimes. Each column would correspond to a given crime, and there would be row for each salient behavioural feature identified in step 3 (e.g. see Fig. 1.5). Craik and Patrick (1994) refer to this as a salient points chart.

Step 7: Where there are differences between cases, the analyst will consider if there are any potential explanations for these. In particular, the analyst will consider the impact of situational factors (e.g. the behaviours displayed by the victim or the location of the offence), the context in which the behaviours

	Crime 1	Crime 2	Crime 3
Behavioural Feature 1	✓	✓	
Behavioural Feature 2			✓
Behavioural Feature 3	✓	✓	✓
Behavioural Feature 4	✓		

Note. ✓ = The behavioural feature was present in the crime

Fig. 1.5 Behavioural matrix listing crimes and their salient behavioural features

are being exhibited, the maturation of the offender's offence behaviours, or whether the offence was interrupted. For example, an analyst might be faced with two sexual offences, one in which the victim was violently beaten and the other in which the victim was not. On the surface, these two crimes appear quite behaviourally different. However, if one considers that the victim fought back and resisted in the first offence but was compliant in the second, then the behavioural differences are perhaps not that meaningful and the analyst may still conclude that the same person could be responsible.

Step 8:   Next, the distinctiveness of behaviours across crimes must be considered. This involves considering how common or how rare the specific behaviours, or combination of behaviours, are in general within the crime type under analysis. Knowledge of base rates for salient behaviours will be needed at this stage to inform the practitioner's decision making (Woodhams et al. 2007). Often, these base rates will be calculated from large crime databases, such as ViCLAS, by law enforcement agencies.

Step 9:   For in-house quality assurance, analysts in some units will then submit their analysis for peer review by one (or perhaps several) of their peers.

Step 10:   Once approved, the final written report is issued to the SIO. The final report will directly address the task set out in the terms of reference, and will include a clear and evidence-based conclusion.

Behaviours

Recent research has focused on which behavioural variables should be used by practitioners to successfully complete the BCL analysis process. As outlined above, there are two approaches used by practitioners to search for behaviourally similar offences: grouping behaviours into domains/themes (dimensional behavioural linking; Winter et al. 2013), or matching individual behavioural variables (multivariate behavioural linkage; Winter et al. 2013). Regardless of the approach, the variables included in such research have encompassed a wide range of offender behaviours perpetrated by sexual offenders, including behaviours designed to gain and maintain control over the victim (e.g. how the victim was approached, whether a weapon was used and how, the use of violence, gagging or binding the victim), behaviours associated with exiting the crime scene or evading capture (e.g. wearing gloves, a mask or a disguise, giving a false name, blindfolding the victim, or taking forensic precautions such as using a condom), sexual behaviours (e.g. whether the victim was penetrated and how, whether the offender ejaculated, if and how clothing was removed), target selection variables (e.g. the time and day of the offence, the age and gender of the victim, whether the victim was physically or mentally impaired) and behaviours which are not directly necessary for the offence to be successfully completed (e.g. the offender complimenting the victim, showing concern, or revealing personal information about himself/herself).

In addition to the above behavioural variables, analysts may make use of other information such as the geographical proximity (sometimes referred to as inter-crime distance) and the temporal proximity of offences to filter their cases under analysis. However, it should be noted that many research studies of BCL within the arena of sexual offending have not utilised geographical behaviour. This is because, in order to produce a sample of sufficient size to justify meaningful statistical analysis, sexual offences are gathered from national databases. As explained by Woodhams (2008), this artificially inflates the geographical distance between unlinked crimes and can lead one to over-estimate the potential linkage accuracy when using geographical behaviour to support BCL. Furthermore, research (with serial robbery) has found the value of inter-crime distance to link series diminishes when working in a smaller geographical area (i.e. a local rather than police force level) (Burrell et al. 2012). This suggests that if geographical factors were taken into consideration in a BCL analysis task, the output would need to be interpreted with care.

As highlighted earlier in this chapter, BCL is conducted in many countries around the world. An important consideration is that the distinctiveness of behaviours used to inform BCL decisions might vary between countries. For example, Woodhams and Labuschagne (2012b) found variations between South Africa and other countries in terms of how rape victims were approached, the use of physical violence, types of sexual acts, and some verbal behaviours. Consequently, what might be behaviourally distinctive in one country could be common in another, and therefore the evidence base and practice of BCL needs to accommodate cultural differences (Woodhams and Labuschagne 2012b). Similarly, society evolves over time, and what might have appeared abnormal or rare previously could now be common practice. For example, if anal penetration is becoming more common in consensual sexual relationships (e.g. Aral et al. 2005), this could translate to non-consensual contexts, and so what was once a rare behaviour in rape might lose its distinctiveness as a linking factor. Overall, these considerations highlight the importance of analysts being able to establish current base rates and correctly interpret the contexts in which behaviours are useful for linkage decisions (Alrajeh 2016; Rainbow 2015; Rainbow and Webb 2016).

Empirical Research into BCL with Sexual Offences

In a wider context of policing austerity where the resources available to support investigations are being drastically cut, there is a growing recognition/demand for evidence-based practice (see Sherman 2013, for a review). Consequently, it is clear that there is a need for research to identify if and how empirically-based methods for BCL can function most effectively. A growing body of research has sought to test the underlying theoretical assumptions of BCL (behavioural consistency and distinctiveness) and to develop statistical methods that might ultimately be used to support the linking of crimes in practice. This research has focused on a wide range of person- and property-oriented crimes (see Tonkin 2015, for a review), but this chapter will focus solely on research into serial sexual offences.

At the time of writing, there are at least 11 published articles that have examined BCL with sexual offences (and many more that have examined issues of relevance to BCL). These studies have utilised a range of methodologies, including the use of statistical methods that identify the underlying themes of sexual offending behaviour (e.g. Santtila et al. 2005), studies that have compared the degree of behavioural similarity in linked versus unlinked crime pairs (e.g. Bennell et al. 2009; Woodhams and Labuschagne 2012a), and studies that have developed and tested computerised systems that generate crime linkage predictions (e.g. Yokota et al. 2007). It is beyond the scope of this chapter to provide a complete overview of the BCL research on sexual offending; instead, we will highlight several examples that illustrate the main methodological approaches adopted. Those interested in more comprehensive reviews are directed to Bennell et al. (2014) and Woodhams and Bennell (2015a).

The first example we will illustrate is that of Santtila et al. (2005), who examined a sample of 43 serial stranger rape offences committed in Finland. For each offence, a range of dichotomous variables were coded, indicating the presence or absence of different offence features. The 16 most consistent and distinctive variables were then selected using Chi-square tests and entered into a Multidimensional Scaling (MDS) analysis. The MDS analysis created a visual plot of the variables such that those occurring close together on the plot were variables that frequently co-occurred at a crime scene, whereas those variables plotted far apart very rarely co-occurred at the crime scene. The rationale behind such an approach is that it allows the researcher to identify clusters of behavioural variables that share the same underlying meaning. By interpreting these variable clusters, the researcher can then infer what the underlying thematic structure is for a given offence type.

In Santtila et al. (2005), four behavioural styles or themes of rape were identified. The sexually hostile rapist approached his victim outdoors and engaged in a range of sexual behaviours (including multiple penetrative acts). The physically hostile rapist committed his offences outdoors, manually gagged the victim, and inflicted wounds on the victim. The rapist with an expressive involvement style removed the victim's clothing to reveal her breasts, revealed information about himself, and verbally threatened the victim not to report the offence. In the deceptive involvement style, the offender utilised a confidence approach that got the victim to accompany the offender voluntarily to a secluded place (often an apartment). The victim was usually under the influence of alcohol and targeted initially in a restaurant.

Having identified these four behavioural themes, two methods were used to examine whether BCL was possible. In the first method, a visual plot was produced (using MDS) that plotted the 43 rape cases in terms of behavioural similarity, with those most similar plotted close together. Over 40% of the time another case belonging to the same series would have been found among the top five most similar cases, and nearly 60% of the time within the top 10 most similar cases. These findings provide support for the idea that similarity in offender crime scene behaviour can be used to identify potentially linked offences.

This study also used discriminant function analysis to further investigate the potential for BCL. Summary scores were calculated for each offence, indicating the extent to which the four different themes were present in that crime. These scores were then used to predict the crimes series that each offence was most likely to belong to. A 25.6% accuracy rate was achieved, which was significantly above the 8.3% rate of accuracy that one would expect to achieve through chance. These findings further support the potential for using offender crime scene behaviour to identify linked rape series.

Another approach to investigating BCL is illustrated by the study of Woodhams and Labuschagne (2012a). In this study, 22 rape series from South Africa were examined, containing a total of 119 offences. From these crimes, both linked crime pairs (containing two crimes committed by the same serial offender) and unlinked crime pairs (containing two crimes committed by different offenders) were created. The rationale behind such an approach was that if there is support for the assumptions of BCL, we would expect to see a higher level of behavioural similarity for linked crime pairs compared to unlinked crime pairs. Using a variety of statistical approaches, it was found that linked crimes were indeed more similar in terms of offender behaviour than unlinked crimes, thereby providing support for the assumptions of BCL. These findings support the potential for using BCL with sexual offences.

The final example of BCL research that we will describe in detail is that of Yokota et al. (2007). In this study, Yokota and colleagues describe the development and evaluation of a computerised system, the Behavioural Investigative Support System (BISS), that can generate BCL predictions. This system records behavioural information relating to solved sexual offences committed in Japan and can be used to make predictions for incoming ('target') incidents. As a target incident occurs, the BISS compares the behavioural features of that crime to the features of other crimes stored on the database (identifying both similarities and differences). The BISS then calculates a probability score for each offender stored on the database that indicates the predicted likelihood that the target crime was committed by that offender. The various offenders can then be rank-ordered in terms of their probability score.

To evaluate the success of the BISS when generating BCL predictions, Yokota et al. (2007) selected an individual offence from 81 serial sexual offenders to act as target incidents. These offences were selected specifically because the crimes were solved and the researchers knew that the 81 offenders responsible for these crimes had also committed other crimes stored on the database. Consequently, if the BISS were functioning successfully, it should prioritise the correct offender towards the top of the rank-ordered list (ideally rank number one). In 24 out of 81 trials (29.6%), the correct offender was ranked number one in the list and the median rank was four. Consequently, in half the trials the correct offender was ranked within the top four prioritised offenders, which is impressive given that there were a total of 868 offenders stored on the database. Furthermore, when geographical information was used alongside traditional modus operandi behaviour to make predictions, the hit rate increased to 55.6%, meaning that a rank of one was achieved in 45 out of 81 trials.

Despite promising findings indicating support for the assumptions of BCL, there are a number of limitations to the literature. One primary limitation is that the data used by research is not always reflective of that which would be used to link crimes during live police investigations (Woodhams and Labuschagne 2012a is an exception). For example, the majority of research has focused on samples containing solved serial offences only, and has selected just two crimes per offender for analysis (see Tonkin 2015). In reality, the databases from which practitioners would be expected to conduct BCL will contain a mixture of solved and unsolved offences, as well as both serial and one-off crimes, and series length will vary significantly (with some series containing just two crimes and other series containing many more). Such heterogeneity has historically not been recognised in BCL research, which means that there are questions regarding how applicable existing research is to police practice. Despite these problems though, researchers and practitioners are working together to produce research that is much more relevant to police practice. A prime example of this is the collaborative group of academics and practitioners in the Crime Linkage International Network (C-LINK). C-LINK is conducting research into BCL with sexual offences that aims to sample more realistic data, thereby overcoming the limitations mentioned above. C-LINK is discussed in greater detail later in this chapter. But first, we will discuss BCL in relation to the concept of primary, secondary, and tertiary risk prevention.

BCL in Relation to Risk and Risk Assessment

Sexual offences pose unique difficulties for investigative teams, as often the only evidence available is the account of the victim against that of the alleged offender (Greenfield 1997). Furthermore, sexual offences are deemed amongst the most difficult offence type for a suspect to confess to, due to the resulting profound legal and social condemnations (Home Office 2013). This results in sexual offences being notoriously difficult to prosecute (Kelly et al. 2005), which further increases the human and financial risks of sexual offending to society. However, (if successful) BCL can help to mitigate these difficulties. This is because the successful identification of a series allows the evidence collected across multiple investigations to be combined, which can lead to a greater quality and quantity of evidence with which to identify (e.g. Yokota et al. 2007) and prosecute the offender (Grubin et al. 2001; Woodhams and Labuschagne 2012a). This helps to halt repeat offending as quickly as possible, thereby preventing a series escalating (secondary prevention). Furthermore, an enhanced ability to catch and convict serial sexual offenders has a number of benefits for victims dealing with the lasting negative impact, including providing closure in the criminal justice system (thereby providing tertiary prevention).

There are further benefits of BCL. The successful identification of a crime series allows multiple investigations to be combined under a single investigative team, which is more cost-effective than investigating the crimes separately because it reduces the duplication of work and responsibilities (Woodhams et al. 2007). Furthermore, by subsuming multiple crimes into a single investigation, they can be submitted for prosecution at the same time, thereby further reducing the financial impact of tackling serial sexual offending. Ultimately, this means that more resources are available to support the prevention of future sexual offences (thereby facilitating primary prevention).

It is also worth considering how BCL outputs might feed into multi-agency offender risk management. For example, if an offender is apprehended and convicted for multiple offences, as identified by the BCL analyses, this increases the amount of information available about that offender for use in predictive analytical risk assessment processes. This is especially pertinent if the BCL analysis has identified a pattern of crime scene behaviour which has been demonstrated to be associated with 'high-risk' or 'dangerous' offenders (e.g. Lehmann et al. 2016; McLean and Beak 2012). For example, sadistic offence behaviours are associated with 'increasers' (offenders who escalate their violence over time) (Hazelwood et al. 1989). In addition, specific behaviours displayed from the first offence in a series—such as binding and transporting the victim—have been associated with 'increasers' rather than 'non-increasers' (Warren et al. 1991). Offenders termed as 'increasers' have also been found to commit significantly more rapes (Warren et al. 1999). This illustrates the potential, given further research and validation, for information about particular behaviours identified within a series to contribute to the predictive assessment of an offender's relative risk.

While BCL has the potential to enhance the successful investigation, detection, and prosecution of serial sexual offenders, it can also have a detrimental impact on these tasks if incorrect linkages are made. That is, incorrect linkages can lead to unnecessary restructuring of police investigative teams, which wastes both time and resources, and in severe cases may result in a sexual offender remaining undetected and free to commit further offences that might otherwise have been prevented (Grubin et al. 2001). Incorrect BCL can also lead to miscarriages of justice, whereby individuals are prosecuted for crimes that they have not committed (Snook et al. 2012). Thus, there is a fine balance between the potential benefits of BCL and the potentially disastrous outcomes if erroneous conclusions are reached.

Multi-Agency Working

In order to maximise the success of risk assessment and investigative techniques such as BCL, effective multi-agency working is crucial. Just as the offender risk assessment process is informed and enhanced by accessing a wealth of information (e.g. age, gender, criminal history, and the like), often via a range of partnership organisations, accurate BCL is dependent on access to reliable, up-to-date data. For example, SCAS analysts conducting CCA of sexual offences in the UK will receive requests from SIOs to proactively search the country's entire serious crime database to identify any other offences that share significant similarities with the index offence of interest. In this situation, there are therefore two organisations involved: SCAS of the NCA and a police constabulary in the UK. As seen in the steps outlined in Fig. 1.4, the agencies need to collaborate at multiple stages of the BCL process. The involvement of multi-agency working in the BCL task brings its own set of unique challenges. The first challenge for practitioners is to establish a meaningful method of communication that allows the aims, objectives, and terms of reference for the analysis (step 1 of the process) to be clearly outlined. This is not always easy when the analysts providing the output and the SIO requesting the analysis are in different geographical locations, have very different rules and regulations to which they are working, different pressures and priorities, and/or diverse knowledge and experience from which they draw. It is, however, vitally important that the analyst has a clear understanding of what the 'customer' (the SIO) is asking of them and, vice versa, that the SIO has clear and realistic expectations of what the analysis will provide and what it will not provide (Martin and Walsh 2016).

The second challenge facing analysts involves the ease with which they can access complementary information via data sharing agreements. As previously discussed, the analyst may need to search other databases for complementary information that can inform an analytical or linkage decision (Rainbow and Webb 2016). The ability to do so, however, relies on effective multi-agency working, joined up data systems, and flexible data sharing agreements. Unfortunately, these do not always exist, which creates significant problems for analysts conducting BCL in some countries. To progress with this area, it is important to remember that operational risk is dynamic (College of Policing 2013), and so it would not be sufficient to simply provide 'data dumps' of information at sporadic (or even regular) intervals. Instead, comprehensive, on-going partnership working is needed to provide real-time access to live systems in order to facilitate analysis.

A third challenge facing practitioners is the volume and quality of data being collected at crime scenes. There are two primary considerations for practitioners. The first is that the large computerised databases storing this behavioural information provide effective support to analysts. The second is that the quality of the analysis is directly affected by the quality of the behavioural data being inputted to these databases. It is imperative that the right data is recorded accurately. However, in order to illustrate what this consideration requires of police professionals attending crime scenes, CCA utilising ViCLAS data necessitates collecting and inputting data relating to 100 questions per offence, with over 700 behavioural sub-variables (Rainbow and Webb 2016). Finding a way to maximise data collected whilst retaining data quality is therefore imperative.

A fourth challenge relates to receiving timely feedback. In any domain of activity, receiving timely feedback is absolutely vital if that person/ organisation is to make improvements in the future. The same is true of analytical units conducting BCL; unless these units receive feedback from their 'customers' that explicitly states what was useful/not useful in the analytical product they provided and how future analysis might be improved, it will be difficult for these units to develop their procedures and practices. While there are clearly some attempts to provide feedback, it is clear from our discussions with practitioners that this is not happening universally and, even where it is happening, that feedback could be much more extensive. Thus, there are areas in which multi-agency working within the context of BCL could be significantly improved. Such improvements will ultimately be of benefit to the whole criminal justice system, as well as helping to more effectively protect the public.

Research to Practice

In addition to multi-agency work within police practice, academics and practitioners are also working closely together to tackle real-world problems in crime analysis. However, bridging the gap between research and practice can be challenging. This is often linked to fundamental differences in working practices. For example, Canter and Youngs (2009) outline a number of differences between researchers and police in terms of how they approach information (data versus evidence), methodologies (scientific versus due process), explanations of human actions (groups of cases versus individual cases), attitude to knowledge (publication versus secrecy), and temporal perspective (long-term versus short term), all of which can act as a barrier to progress. However, effective researcher–practitioner collaborations are key to delivering impact in research and developing evidence-based interventions in practice (Sullivan et al. 2013).

One example of a practitioner–researcher collaboration is C-LINK (www.crimelinkage.org). C-LINK brought together academics and practitioners from seven countries (the UK, the Netherlands, South Africa, Belgium, Finland, Canada, and the USA) to collaborate on several large-scale research projects on BCL. One of the initial findings of the network was that academics and practitioners overlapped in terms of their expectations and knowledge base (e.g. many academics have previously held practitioner roles and many practitioners hold advanced degrees). However, the partnership of academics and practitioners was still essential for a number of reasons. First, the collaboration allowed for the collection of a large sample of sexual offences (>3,000 cases), which represents one of the biggest and most ecologically valid datasets used for BCL research. C-LINK also brought together expertise which would be difficult to gain in a smaller or purely academic or practitioner research team. For example, academic partners were able to contribute statistical expertise (e.g. on Bayesian analysis and Receiver Operating Characteristic analysis), whereas analyst partners could support the development and effective implementation of a uniform coding dictionary and facilitate access to data (Tonkin et al., 2017; Woodhams et al., under review). After the success of C-LINK, further collaborative work has been brokered by members of the network, including developing a prototype of a software engineered intelligent crime linkage support tool to aid SCAS analysts' decision-making processes (Alrajeh 2016). This project, and further planned work, represents an important next step in the BCL research field, as outlined below.

Next Steps

Developing decision-support tools (based on the research conducted thus far on BCL) can assist practitioners to analyse—in a quick and efficient manner—the vast quantities of crime scene information stored on police databases, highlighting those offences that are most behaviourally similar (and therefore most likely to be linked). While the performance of such tools would need to be evaluated and it is important to point out that these tools support (and do not replace) analysts, there are a number of potential benefits to their use. First, computerized tools can process large volumes of information in a quick and efficient manner (more quickly than a human analyst would be able to). At a time when police resources are being cut, any process that can potentially increase analytical efficiency is of significant value. Second, computerised BCL support tools would be based on empirical research (and could be updated as new findings emerge). The importance of evidence-based practice is recognised amongst criminal justice agencies around the world (see Sherman 2013, for a review); thus the use of BCL decision-support tools would help criminal justice agencies to adhere to the principles of evidence-based practice.

Conclusions

Present day UK policing aims to prevent crime and protect the public using evidence-based methods that provide value for money (College of Policing 2016). As a result, police analysts need to ensure they prioritise their workload effectively to maximise their potential to support the identification and apprehension of serial offenders (Woodhams 2008). This chapter argued that BCL is one way to support such 'investigative risk assessment'. The core function of BCL is to establish whether crimes can be grouped into offending series with the view to pooling resources and information together to maximise the chances of apprehending an offender and halting the progress of a series. However, it can also function to support primary, secondary, and tertiary prevention approaches through the provision of resources and intelligence. Furthermore, this could subsequently support predictive offender risk assessment processes (e.g. identifying behaviours associated with a high risk of reoffending and/or the likelihood of escalating violence). Multi-agency working has been highlighted as key to the advancement of BCL knowledge and practice, although there is a continued emphasis on the need to improve the scope and consistency of partnership working. Finally, although the area of BCL has developed rapidly over the last 10–15 years, there are still many un/under-explored areas. In particular, future work that develops, implements, and evaluates the use of BCL decision-support tools is vital.

Notes

1. Although these figures require careful interpretation in light of the greater willingness of victims of historical sexual offences to report their victimisation to the police (the 'Yewtree Effect'; Office for National Statistics 2015a, b) and improvements to the police recording of sexual offences (Her Majesty's Inspectorate of Constabulary 2014) and crime statistics (Public Administration Select Committee 2014).
2. SCAS has a national remit for assisting police investigations in the UK relating to stranger sexual offences and murders with a sexual element.

References

Alrajeh, D. (2016, October). *Using computer science techniques to enhance practitioner decision-making.* Presentation at the Using Behavioural Science to Target Prolific Criminals Conference, British Academy, London.

Aral, S. O., Patel, A., Holmes, K. K., & Foxman, B. (2005). Temporal trends in sexual behaviors and sexually transmitted disease history among 18- to 39-year old Seattle, Washington, residents: Results of random digit-dial surveys. *Sexually Transmitted Diseases, 32*(11), 710–717.

Association of Chief Police Officers. (2009). *Tackling perpetrators of violence against women and girls: ACPO review for the Home Secretary.* Available at: http://webarchive.nationalarchives.gov.uk/+/.../FINAL_MASTERViolence%20Review.doc. Accessed 15 Nov 2016.

Beauregard, E., & Bouchard, M. (2010). Cleaning up your act: Forensic awareness as a detection avoidance strategy. *Journal of Criminal Justice, 38*(6), 1160–1166. doi:10.1016/j.jcrimjus.2010.09.004.

Bennell, C., & Canter, D. V. (2002). Linking commercial burglaries by modus operandi: Tests using regression and ROC analysis. *Science and Justice, 42,* 153–164. doi:10.1016/S1355-0306(02)71820-0.

Bennell, C., & Jones, N. J. (2005). Between a ROC and a hard place: A method for linking serial burglaries using an offender's modus operandi. *Journal of Investigative Psychology and Offender Profiling, 2*(1), 23–41.

Bennell, C., Jones, N. J., & Melnyk, T. (2009). Addressing problems with traditional crime linking methods using receiver operating characteristic analysis. *Legal and Criminological Psychology, 14*(2), 293–310. doi:10.1348/135532508X349336.

Bennell, C., Mugford, R., Ellingwood, H., & Woodhams, J. (2014). Linking crimes using behavioural clues: Current levels of linking accuracy and strategies for moving forward. *Journal of Investigative Psychology and Offender Profiling, 11*(1), 29–56. doi:10.1002/jip.1395.

Bennett, D., & Davis, M. R. (2004, November). *The Australian forensic reference group: A multidisciplinary collaborative approach to profiling violent crime.* Paper presented at the Australian Institute of Criminology International Conference, Melbourne.

Bouhana, N., Johnson, S. D., & Porter, M. (2016). Consistency and specificity in burglars who commit prolific residential burglary: Testing the core assumptions underpinning behavioural crime linkage. *Legal and Criminological Psychology, 21*(1), 77–94. doi:10.1111/lcrp.12050.

Brown, M. (2014). New penology. In J. S. Albanese (Ed.), *Encyclopedia of criminology and criminal justice* (pp. 3283–3290). New York: Springer Science.

Bunch, D. (2015, June). *Linking acquisitive crime in the West Midlands: An analyst's perspective.* Presentation at the British Psychological Society Linking Acquisitive Crime Seminar Series, Birmingham.

Burrell, A., Bull, R., & Bond, J. (2012). Linking personal robbery offences using offender behaviour. *Journal of Investigative Psychology and Offender Profiling, 9*(3), 201–222. doi:10.1002/jip.1365.

Canter, D. (1995). Psychology of offender profiling. In R. Bull & D. Carson (Eds.), *Handbook of psychology in legal contexts* (pp. 343–355). Chichester: Wiley.

Canter, D. V., & Heritage, R. (1990). A multivariate model of sexual offence behaviour: Developments in offender profiling. *The Journal of Forensic Psychiatry, 1*(2), 185–212. doi:10.1080/09585189008408469.

Canter, D., & Youngs, D. (2009). *Investigative psychology: Offender profiling and the analysis of criminal action*. Chichester: John Wily & Sons Ltd.

College of Policing. (2013). *Risk*. Available at: https://www.app.college.police.uk/app-content/risk-2/risk/#top. Accessed 16 Jan 2017.

College of Policing. (2016). *National policing vision 2016*. Available at: http://www.college.police.uk/About/Pages/National-policing-vision-2016.aspx. Accessed 14 Nov 2016.

Collins, P. I., Johnson, G. F., Choy, A., Davidson, K. T., & MacKay, R. E. (1998). Advances in violent crime analysis and law enforcement: The Canadian violent crime linkage analysis system. *Journal of Government Information, 25*(3), 277–284. doi:10.1016/S1352-0237(98)00008-2.

Craik, M., & Patrick, A. (1994). Linking serial offences. *Policing, 10*, 181–187.

Davies, K., Tonkin, M., Bull, R., & Bond, J. W. (2012). The course of case linkage never did run smooth: A new investigation to tackle the behavioural changes in serial car theft. *Journal of Investigative Psychology and Offender Profiling, 9*(3), 274–295. doi:10.1002/jip.1369.

Deslauriers-Varin, N., & Beauregard, E. (2013). Investigating offending consistency of geographic and environmental factors among serial sex offenders: A comparison of multiple analytical strategies. *Criminal Justice and Behavior, 40*(2), 156–179.

Deslauriers-Varin, N., & Beauregard, E. (2014). Consistency in crime scene selection: An investigation of crime sites used by serial sex offenders across crime series. *Journal of Criminal Justice, 42*(2), 123–133. doi:10.1016/j.jcrimjus.2013.09.005.

Ellingwood, H., Mugford, R., Bennell, C., Melnyk, T., & Fritzon, K. (2013). Examining the role of similarity coefficients and the value of behavioural themes in attempts to link serial arson offences. *Journal of Investigative Psychology and Offender Profiling, 10*(1), 1–27. doi:10.1002/jip.1364.

Farrington, D. P., & West, D. J. (1993). Criminal, penal and life histories of chronic offenders: Risk and protective factors and early identification. *Criminal Behaviour and Mental Health, 3*(4), 492–523. doi:10.1002/cbm.1993.3.4.492.

Greenfield, L. A. (1997). *Sex offences and offenders: An analysis of data on rape and sexual assault*. Washington, DC: U.S. Department of Justice.

Grubin, D., Kelly, P., & Brunsdon, C. (2001). *Linking serious sexual assaults through behaviour*. Home Office Research Study 215. London: Home Office.

Hanson, R. K., & Morton-Bourgon, K. (2004). *Predictors of sexual recidivism: An updated meta-analysis*. Ottawa: Public Safety and Emergency Preparedness Canada.

Hazelwood, R. R., Reboussin, R., & Warren, J. (1989). Serial rape: Correlates of increased aggression and the relationship of offender pleasure to victim resistance. *Journal of Interpersonal Violence, 4*(1), 65–78.

Her Majesty's Inspectorate of Constabulary. (2014). *Consultation on her majesty's inspectorate of constabulary's programme for regular force inspections: Summary*. London: HMIC.

Her Majesty's Inspectorate of Constabulary & Her Majesty's Inspectorate of the Crown Prosecution Service. (2012). *Forging the links: Rape investigation and prosecution.* Available at: https://www.justiceinspectorates.gov.uk/hmic/media/forging-the-links-rape-investigation-and-prosecution-20120228.pdf. Accessed 14 Nov 2016.

Home Office. (2013). *An overview of sexual offending in England and Wales: Statistics bulletin.* Available at: https://www.gov.uk/government/statistics/an-overview-of-sexual-offending-in-england-andwales. Accessed 14 Nov 2016.

Home Office. (2014). *Criminal casework: Multi agency public protection arrangements (MAPPA).* Available at: https://www.gov.uk/government/uploads/system/uploads/attachment_data/file/488934/MAPPA_v16.0.pdf. Accessed 15 Jan 2017.

Independent Police Complaints Commission. (2010). *Commissioner's report: IPCC independent investigation into the Metropolitan police service's inquiry into allegations against John Worboys.* Available at: https://www.ipcc.gov.uk/sites/default/files/Documents/investigation_commissioner_reports/worboys_commissioners_report.pdf. Accessed 9 Jan 2017.

Innes, M., Fielding, N., & Cope, N. (2005). The appliance of science? The theory and practice of criminal intelligence analysis. *British Journal of Criminology, 45*(1), 39–57. doi:10.1093/bjc/azh053.

Karn, J. (2013). *Policing and crime reduction: The evidence and its implications for practice.* Available at: http://www.police-foundation.org.uk/uploads/catalogerfiles/policing-and-crime-reduction/police-foundation-police-effectiveness-report.pdf. Accessed 14 Nov 2016.

Kelly, L., Lovett, J., & Regan, L. (2005). *A gap or a chasm? Attrition in reported rape cases.* Home Office Research Study 293. London: Home Office.

Kemshall, H. (2001). *Risk assessment and management of known sexual and violent offenders: A review of current issues.* Police Research Series Paper 140. Available at: https://pdfs.semanticscholar.org/9e2c/e6ea526d477ada-6a45897d40b411cb3a50e7.pdf. Accessed 14 Jan 2017.

Lehmann, R. J. B., Goodwill, A. M., Hanson, R. K., & Dahle, K.-P. (2016). Acquaintance rape: Applying crime scene analysis to the prediction of sexual recidivism. *Sexual Abuse: A Journal of Research and Treatment, 28*(7), 679–702.

Lisak, D., & Miller, P. M. (2002). Repeat rape and multiple offending among undetected rapists. *Violence and Victims, 17*(1), 73–84.

Martin, E., & Walsh, C. (2016, October). *Ensuring quality in comparative case analysis.* Presentation at the Using Behavioural Science to Target Prolific Criminals Conference, British Academy, London.

Mclean, F., & Bleak, K. (2012). *Factors associated with serious or persistent violent offending: Findings from a rapid evidence assessment.* Available at: http://whatworks.college.police.uk/Research/Documents/REA_violent_reoffending. pdf. Accessed 14 Jan 2017.

Neyroud, P. (2010). *Cost effectiveness in policing: Lessons from the UK in improving policing through a better workforce, process and technology.* Available at: http://eso.expertgrupp.se/wp-content/uploads/2010/07/2010_3-Neyroud. pdf. Accessed 14 Nov 2016.

Office for National Statistics (2015a). *Crime in England and Wales: Year ending March 2015.* Available at: http://www.ons.gov.uk/ons/rel/crime-stats/crime-statistics/year-ending-march-2015/stbcrime-march-2015.html#tab-Sexual-offences. Accessed 14 Nov 2016.

Office for National Statistics. (2015b). *Crime statistics: Focus on violent crime and sexual offences, 2013/14.* Available at: http://www.ons.gov.uk/ons/rel/crime-stats/crime-statistics/focus-on-violent-crime-andsexual-offences--2013-14/ index.html. Accessed 14 Nov 2016.

Office for National Statistics. (2016a). *Crime in England and Wales: Year ending March 2016.* Available at: http://www.ons.gov.uk/peoplepopulationandcommunity/crimeandjustice/bulletins/crimeinenglandandwales/yearending-mar2016. Accessed 14 Nov 2016.

Office for National Statistics. (2016b). *Focus on violent crime and sexual offences: Year ending March 2015.* Available at: https://www.ons.gov.uk/peoplepopulationandcommunity/crimeandjustice/compendium/focusonviolentcrime-andsexualoffences/yearendingmarch2015. Accessed 14 Nov 2016.

Pakkanen, T., Zappalà, A., Grönroos, C., & Santtila, P. (2012). The effects of coding bias on estimates of behavioural similarity in crime linking research of homicides. *Journal of Investigative Psychology and Offender Profiling, 9*(3), 223–234. doi:10.1002/jip.1366.

Public Administration Select Committee. (2014). *Caught red-handed: Why we can't count on police recorded crime statistics.* Available at: http://www.publications.parliament.uk/pa/cm201314/cmselect/cmpubadm/760/760.pdf. Accessed 14 Nov 2016.

Rainbow, L. (2015). A practitioner's perspective: Theory, research and practice. In J. Woodhams & C. Bennell (Eds.), *Crime linkage: Theory, research and practice* (pp. 173–196). Florida: Taylor & Francis.

Rainbow, L., & Webb, M. (2016, October). *Challenges in providing crime linkage and behavioural investigative advice in practice.* Presentation at the Using Behavioural Science to Target Prolific Criminals Conference, British Academy, London.

Santos, R. B. (2017). *Crime analysis with crime mapping* (4th ed.). Los Angeles: Sage Publications Inc.

Santtila, P., Fritzon, K., & Tamelander, A.-L. (2004a). Linking arson on the basis of crime scene behaviour. *Journal of Police and Criminal Psychology, 19*(1), 1–16. doi:10.1007/BF02802570.

Santtila, P., Korpela, S., & Häkkänen, H. (2004b). Expertise and decision-making in linking car crime series. *Psychology, Crime, & Law, 10*(2), 97–112. doi:10.1080/1068316021000030559.

Santtila, P., Junkkila, J., & Sandnabba, N. K. (2005). Behavioural linking of stranger rapes. *Journal of Investigative Psychology and Offender Profiling, 2*(2), 87–103. doi:10.1002/jip.26.

Santtila, P., Pakkanen, T., Zappalà, A., Bosco, D., Valkama, M., & Mokros, A. (2008). Behavioural crime linking in serial homicide. *Psychology, Crime, & Law, 14*(3), 245–265. doi:10.1080/10683160701739679.

Sherman, L. W. (2013). *The rise of evidence-based policing: Targeting, testing, and tracking.* Available at: http://cebcp.org/wp-content/evidence-based-policing/Sherman-TripleT.pdf. Accessed 9 Jan 2017.

Snelling, M. (2015, February). *From the neighbourhood to Whitehall: Towards a whole system approach to reducing reoffending in London.* Paper presented at the Home Office Integrated Offender Management Conference, Ryton-on-Dunsmore. Available at: https://www.gov.uk/government/uploads/system/uploads/attachment_data/file/414803/2015_03_19_Conference_slides_for_publication__2_.pdf. Accessed 14 Nov 2016.

Snook, B., Luther, K., House, J. C., Bennell, C., & Taylor, P. J. (2012). The violent crime linkage analysis system: A test of interrater reliability. *Criminal Justice and Behavior, 39*(5), 607–619. doi:10.1177/0093854811435208.

Sullivan, T. P., McPartland, T., & Fisher, B. S. (2013). *Guidelines for successful researcher-practitioner partnerships in the criminal justice system: Findings from the researcher-practitioner partnerships study (RPPS).* Available at: https://www.ncjrs.gov/pdffiles1/nij/grants/243918.pdf. Accessed 14 Jan 2017.

Tonkin, M. (2015). Testing the theories underpinning crime linkage. In J. Woodhams & C. Bennell (Eds.), *Crime linkage: Theory, research and practice* (pp. 107–139). Boca Raton: CRC Press.

Tonkin, M., Pakkanen, T., Sirén, J., Bennell, C., Woodhams, J., Burrell, A., Imre, H., Winter, J. M., Lam, E., ten Brinke, G., Webb, M., Labuschagne, G. N., Ashmore-Hills, L., van der Kemp, J. J., Lipponen, S., Rainbow, L., Salfati, C. G., & Santtila, P. (2017). Using offender crime scene behavior to link stranger sexual assaults: A comparison of three statistical approaches. *Journal of Criminal Justice, 50*, 19–28.

Tonkin, M., Santtila, P., & Bull, R. (2012). The linking of burglary crimes using offender behaviour: Testing research cross-nationally and exploring methodology. *Legal and Criminological Psychology, 17*(2), 276–293. doi:10.1111/J.2044-8333.2010.02007.x.

Warren, J., Reboussin, R., Hazelwood, R. R., & Wright, J. (1991). Prediction of rape type and violence from verbal, physical and sexual scales. *Journal of Interpersonal Violence, 6*(1), 55–67.

Warren, J., Reboussin, R., Hazelwood, R. R., Gibbs, N. A., Trumbetta, S. L., & Cummings, A. (1999). Crime scene analysis and the escalation of violence in serial rape. *Forensic Science International, 100*(1-2), 37–56.

Wilson, L., & Bruer, C. (2017). *Violent crime linkage system (ViCLAS)*. Available at: http://www.rcmp-grc.gc.ca/to-ot/cpcmec-ccpede/bs-sc/viclas-salvac-eng.htm#countries. Accessed 30 Nov 2016.

Winter, J., Lemeire, J., Meganck, S., Geboers, J., Rossi, G., & Mokros, A. (2013). Comparing the predictive accuracy of case linkage methods in serious sexual assaults. *Journal of Investigative Psychology and Offender Profiling, 10*(1), 28–56. doi:10.1002/jip.1372.

Woodhams, J. (2008). *Understanding juvenile sexual offending: An investigative perspective* (Unpublished doctoral dissertation). University of Leicester, Leicester.

Woodhams, J., & Bennell, C. (2015a). *Crime linkage: Theory, research and practice*. Boca Raton: CRC Press.

Woodhams, J., & Bennell, C. (2015b). Introduction: Time to consolidate and reflect. In J. Woodhams & C. Bennell (Eds.), *Crime linkage: Theory, research and practice* (pp. 1–9). Boca Raton: CRC Press.

Woodhams, J., & Bennell, C. (2015c). Consistency and distinctiveness of criminal behavior. In J. Woodhams & C. Bennell (Eds.), *Crime linkage: Theory, research and practice* (pp. 11–31). Boca Raton: CRC Press.

Woodhams, J., & Grant, T. (2006). Developing a categorization system for rapists' speech. *Psychology, Crime & Law, 12*(3), 245–260. doi:10.1080/10683160500151134.

Woodhams, J., & Labuschagne, G. (2012a). A test of case linkage principles with solved and unsolved serial rapes. *Journal of Police and Criminal Psychology, 27*(1), 85–98. doi:10.1007/s11896-011-9091-1.

Woodhams, J., & Labuschagne, G. (2012b). South Africa serial rapists: The offenders, their victims, and their offenses. *Sexual Abuse: A Journal of Research and Treatment, 24*(6), 544–574. doi:10.1177/1079063212438921.

Woodhams, J., & Toye, K. (2007). An empirical test of the assumptions of case linkage and offender profiling with serial commercial robberies. *Psychology, Public Policy, and Law, 13*(1), 59–85. doi:10.1037/1076-8971.13.1.59.

Woodhams, J., Bull, R., & Hollin, C. R. (2007a). Case linkage: Identifying crimes committed by the same offender. In R. N. Kocsis (Ed.), *Criminal profiling: International theory, research, and practice* (pp. 117–133). Totowa: Humana Press.

Woodhams, J., Hollin, C. R., & Bull, R. (2007b). The psychology of linking crimes: A review of the evidence. *Legal and Criminological Psychology, 12*(2), 233–249. doi:10.1348/135532506X118631.

Yokota, K., Fujita, G., Watanabe, K., Yoshimoto, K., & Wachi, T. (2007). Application of the behavioral investigative support system for profiling perpetrators of serious sexual assaults. *Behavioral Sciences & the Law, 25*(6), 841–856. doi:10.1002/bsl.793.

2

Assessment of Risk to Sexually Reoffend: What Do We Really Know?

Robin J. Wilson and Jeffrey C. Sandler

Introduction

"Once a sex offender, always a sex offender." In spite of credible evidence to the contrary, this perspective permeates the beliefs and attitudes of many people in the community-at-large, leading to fear and, often, misunderstanding of offenders and the true risks they pose. As a result, the past 30 years have been witness to a flurry of laws and policies enacted to contain the risk posed by sex offenders and to keep the public safe from their deviant intents, as it were. From sex offender registries to residence restrictions and electronic monitoring to lifetime probation, legislators and policymakers have gone to great lengths to keep offenders away from

R.J. Wilson (✉)
Mcmaster University, Hamilton, ON, Canada
Wilson Psychological Services LLC, Sarasota, FL, USA

J.C. Sandler
Private Practice, Albany, NY, USA

© The Author(s) 2017
H. Kemshall, K. McCartan (eds.), *Contemporary Sex Offender Risk Management,*
Volume II, Palgrave Studies in Risk, Crime and Society,
DOI 10.1007/978-3-319-63573-6_2

vulnerable persons upon whom they might prey. Interestingly, many of these measures have been enacted during a time period during which rates of both sexual offending and sexual reoffending have been on a steady decline (Finkelhor and Jones 2006). While some might argue that the declines in offending and reoffending are the result of strict policies, the research literature has not generally found this to be the case (Levenson et al. 2007). Indeed, in some circumstances unintended consequences have resulted, such as homelessness, unemployment, and social isolation.

A perusal of the distribution of risk according to a commonly used actuarial risk assessment instrument (ARAI), the Static-99R (Hanson et al. 2016a; see below), illustrates what is known as a positively skewed distribution. In such distributions, the commonly known "normal" or "bell" curve looks more like a ski slope with the peak well to the left of the center point. Of the many thousands of assessed sex offenders comprising the current standardization sample for the Static-99R, approximately 70% would be characterized as *average* or *below average* risk to sexually reoffend, while less than 10% would be in the highest risk category *well above average* risk to reoffend (see Hanson et al. 2016b). What these numbers mean, essentially, is that the risk posed by the vast majority of sex offenders is probably manageable and that most of those offenders are generally unlikely to reoffend. However, there are surely some sex offenders who pose a significant risk to the community, and there is a need to accurately identify who they are so that appropriate safety measures can be applied.

The history of risk assessment is a long and winding road replete with interesting twists and turns. In this chapter, we will first review some of that history before outlining the current state of the science modern practitioners employ to identify—and eventually manage—those individuals who continue to pose a sexual risk to vulnerable persons in the community. As a prefatory note, we will focus primarily in this chapter on male adult sex offenders, but it is important to note that many of the issues included here may also relate to juveniles, women, or other special groups of persons who have engaged in sexually offensive conduct.

Early Conceptions of Crime and Violence

As has been the case in many aspects of the study of the human condition, researchers have sought to explore the "nature vs. nurture" dilemma. How much of who we are is the product of our genetics? What amount is attributable to our life experiences or environment? Are these exclusive or contributory? The idea that we are the sum of our parts underpins the philosophy of determinism which, in this context, holds that human behavior and actions are determined by causal events and that people act according to their nature. This is to be contrasted with humanism, which asserts that people have free will and that we have the capacity to learn and change according to our wants, wishes, and life experiences.

Early approaches to understanding criminal behavior tended to side with the deterministic perspective. As early as the fourth or fifth century BC, Hippocrates hypothesized that bodily "humors" (and their relative presence or absence) could account for personality and behavior. Much later, the science of phrenology was popular in the nineteenth century. Developed by a German physician named Franz Gall in 1796, phrenology required examination of the contours of the skull; in particular, ascertainment of bumps or indentations would signify particular psychological attributes. Finding a bump in a certain part of the skull would be associated with increased propensity in a certain behavioral vein. For instance, a large bump behind the ear was thought to indicate a tendency toward destructiveness or combativeness. A similar perspective on the nature and origins of human behavior—particularly as it relates to criminal behavior—is found in the notion of atavism, generally associated with the Italian criminologist Cesare Lombroso. Working in the 1870s, Lombroso sought to identify various physical characteristics commonly found in people who engaged in criminal conduct. Lombroso labeled these physical characteristics atavistic or "throwback" traits indicative of primitive, less advanced (and hence more criminally inclined) tendencies. Sloping foreheads with a prominent brow or longer than average arms were seen as evolutionary throwbacks to a time when humanoids were less socialized and more brutish in nature.

Although theories like humors, phrenology, and atavism enjoyed a degree of popularity in their heyday, most serious scientists recognize flaws in the methods used to both establish and underpin such beliefs. Further, the rise of humanistic perspectives suggested other, perhaps more plausible, explanations for engagement in crime and the possibility of desistance. Of particular importance in this regard is the eighteenth-century Italian philosopher and criminologist Cesare Bonesana-Beccaria. Beccaria is widely held as one of the most important figures of the Age of Enlightenment and he is well-regarded for his manuscript *On Crimes and Punishments* (1764), in which he argued against harsh punishments, including the death penalty, which he saw as neither required nor deterrent. Beccaria's views on punishment were largely utilitarian, and he believed that punishment should not be aimed at revenge; rather, it should in some way enhance society through helping those who fell afoul of the law to better understand their condition and the effects of their actions on others. Essentially, given a chance, criminals could be guided and ultimately choose to live offense-free.

Perhaps a natural consequence of the views of Beccaria and his compatriots was the growth of the sociological perspective. Often regarded as the father of sociology, Émile Durkheim (1858–1917) sought to discover the inherent nature of society—the interconnections between individuals and the collective consciousness that allows society to survive and thrive. Regarding crime, Durkheim believed that social integration was threatened by various pathologies such as anomie (a breakdown of the social bonds between individuals and society) and greed (as motivated by power, profit, and a growing divide between haves and have-nots). Durkheim believed that punishment served a positive role in asserting and reinforcing social values, reaffirming the collective consciousness (Burkhardt and Connor 2016).

Notwithstanding the existence of differing perspectives on the origins of criminality and violence potential, the twentieth century was witness to considerable cultural evolution (or, rather, revolution), due in no small part to economic catastrophes (e.g., the Great Depression) and the horrors of war. Advances were made throughout the century in regard to technologies that made life easier, greater consideration of individual rights, and the rise of social services. Greater interest was also developing in the study of human behavior, particularly conduct that violated social convention and was therefore requiring of a social response. In the USA (and to a lesser degree in other countries), the growth of the prison-industrial complex saw an almost exponential rise in the inmate population, to the extent that at its peak, the USA incarcerated more of its citizens on a per capita basis than any other jurisdiction on earth. The pervasive belief amongst non-offending citizens was that criminals were somehow different and that they posed a risk to normal, law abiding people. Prejudices against convicts and ex-convicts persist, with noted difficulties in homelessness, unemployment, social isolation, and other threats to civil liberties. Arguably, these prejudices have been more severely felt by persons convicted of sexual offenses.

Risk Assessment and Management

Mounting a realistic challenge to rising prison populations ultimately required attention to methods of establishing the level of risk someone convicted of a certain crime would pose to re-engage in crime in the future. Theoretically, those individuals at lower risk would not require the same degree of sanction or removal of liberties as someone of comparatively higher risk. The key question was, and often continues to be, how do we divide offenders into different levels of risk so that we might intervene proportionally? And, once the level of risk has been ascertained, what can be done with the offenders at that point?

Nothing Works and the Principles of Effective Correctional Interventions

Debate continues as to the true relative effects of punishment and rehabilitation. Regarding the latter, there appears to be ongoing discussion as to the effectiveness of treatment in reducing reoffending, the idea being that if programming can reduce risk to reoffend, then offenders do not require inordinately long periods of incarceration.

In the mid-1970s, a group of researchers, including Robert Martinson, was interested in finding out whether interventions for offenders were having any measurable effect on outcome. Essentially, did offenders who completed correctional programs reoffend less often than their compatriots who did not complete programming? In 1974, Martinson released his highly influential paper *Nothing Works: Questions and Answers About Prison Reform*, in which he reported no differences in the rates of reoffending between offenders who did or did not attend programming. In the ensuing years, the Nothing Works perspective led to defunding of rehabilitative interventions and a pervasive view among some corrections administrations that such endeavors were an expensive waste of time. Ultimately, Martinson published a retraction (1979) but, as is often the case, nobody remembers the retraction, only the original damning statement(s). As an interesting, on-point aside, Furby et al. (1989) published a similar paper noting a lack of research showing effectiveness of treatment for sexual offenders. However, a key difference in the Furby et al. paper is that they did not contend that treatment did not work; rather, it was their perspective that the state of the research into the effectiveness of sexual offender programming was so poor that no conclusions could be reached.

In direct response to the Nothing Works doctrine, several research groups sought to counter the pessimistic views regarding rehabilitation and criminal behavior. Among those interested were Canadians Donald Andrews, James Bonta, and Paul Gendreau, all leaders in the "What Works?" movement. In the 1980s, Andrews and Bonta began their decades-long inquiry into the nature, manifestations, and consequences of crime. In their seminal tome *The Psychology of Criminal Conduct* (orig. 1994, but now in its sixth edition [2016]), Andrews and Bonta expounded on variables predictive of criminal behavior (leading to the development of the popular Level of Service Inventory-Revised [LSI-R] risk assessment tool) and the social psychological principles associated with effective correctional interventions (known widely as the Risk-Need-Responsivity [RNR] model). Simply put, the RNR model states that correctional interventions are more likely to be successful if the intensity of the intervention matches the level of risk posed by the offender, and if programs specifically target identified criminogenic needs in a manner that accounts for the learning styles, motivation, and individual abilities of the persons being treated. Not following these simple principles risks increasing risk to reoffend, or missing out on opportunities to increase offender reintegration potential (Bonta and Andrews 2016).

Concurrent to, and often in collaboration with, Andrews and Bonta, Paul Gendreau (see Smith et al. 2002) was interested in comparing the relative influences of sanction (punishment) vs. human service (correctional programming) on criminal behavior. Contrary to Martinson's findings, Smith et al. were able to conclusively show an effect of programming on reoffending, declaring that punishment alone will not reduce bad behavior. Taking these findings together with the prescriptions of the RNR model, it would be reasonable to conclude that we now have a workable roadmap for assisting offenders in their efforts at desistance, the first stop on that roadmap being the assessment of risk to reoffend.

Risk Assessment Methods

Some 30 or 40 years ago, the most common way to obtain an evaluation of risk to reoffend was to ask an expert. The scenario might be this: Probation Officer (PO) Smith is concerned about the possibility that Offender Jones might engage in future criminal acts. PO Smith needs a risk assessment in order to determine frequency of contact, and what probation conditions will be most applicable to Offender Jones. Accordingly, PO Smith refers Offender Jones to a local expert, Dr. Wright, who employs certain methods to determine what level of risk Offender Jones likely poses for future criminal behavior. Dr. Wright might also make recommendations regarding programming or restrictions that might assist Offender Jones in remaining offense-free. However, how right was Dr. Wright likely to be in her prognostications?

Unstructured Clinical Judgment and "Experts"

The scenario above describes the earliest form of risk prediction: simple clinical judgment, which is sometimes referred to as the first generation of risk assessment (Bonta 1996). The methods used in such predictions were informal, subjective, difficult to define, and impressionistic (Grove and Meehl 1996). These methods were also unique to the specific clinician making the assessment, being based entirely on the clinician's particular training, experience, and theoretical orientation (Monahan 2008), which made it difficult to replicate the process and prediction, leading to low levels of inter-rater reliability. Indeed, in a landmark study, Monahan (1981) evaluated the risk assessment skills of "experts" by having them provide ratings for a series of case studies for which the outcomes (reoffend or not) were already known. Surprisingly, Monahan found that the risk ratings offered by the experts in his study were no more accurate (and, at times, perhaps less accurate) than what might have been achieved by flipping a coin. Even more surprising, in using the same methodology with otherwise intelligent non-experts, the results were more or less the same. Monahan concluded that the subjective processes used by experts were likely to focus on variables that *seemed* related to risk, but were ultimately not. Having completed similar research, Quinsey (see Quinsey et al. 2006) declared that risk assessment was better accomplished using a completely mechanical process that avoided the influence of clinical judgment of any sort.

Recently, Skeem and Monahan (2011) put forth a continuum of risk assessment approaches distinguished by the presence or absence of elements that compose the risk assessment process. In total, the authors identified four distinct elements to an assessment of risk: "(a) identifying empirically valid risk factors, (b) determining a method for measuring (or 'scoring') these risk factors, (c) establishing a procedure for combining scores on the risk factors, and (d) producing an estimate of violence risk" (p. 39). Unstructured clinical assessment incorporates none of these four elements, making it the bottom of the risk assessment approach continuum. Unstructured clinical assessment is also the approach to risk assessment that has the least empirical research support (Skeem and Monahan 2011).

Mechanical Approaches

Over 60 years ago, Paul Meehl (1954/1996) published a seminal book in the field of psychological risk assessment entitled *Clinical vs. Statistical Prediction: A Theoretical Analysis and a Review of the Evidence*. In it, Meehl reviewed all of the studies conducted up to that time that compared the accuracy of subjective clinical judgments of risk with objective "mechanical" approaches (i.e., approaches that use formal algorithms to evaluate risk in a precisely reproducible manner). The results were striking. In every single comparison, Meehl found that the mechanical approach resulted in accurate predictions as often as, or more often than, the clinical approach. Furthermore, Meehl found that the clinical approach was often less accurate than pure chance (e.g., flipping a coin) and that mechanical approaches performed equal to or better than the clinical approach even when the mechanical approach was developed using suboptimal techniques (e.g., simple counting techniques not statistically derived, or a single variable cut at a specific point).

Grove et al. (2000) later replicated these findings in a meta-analysis[1] of 136 studies that compared the accuracy of clinical and mechanical approaches to prediction. In 64 of the studies (47%) the mechanical approach outperformed the clinical approach, in 64 of the studies (47%) the predictive performance of the two approaches was equal, and in only 8 of the studies (6%) the clinical approach outperformed the mechanical approach. Though some scholars noted the high percentage of studies where the two approaches performed equally and argued that the two approaches are essentially equal in predictive accuracy, Grove and Meehl (1996) noted that the results indicated "many fewer studies favoring the clinician than would be expected by chance…if the two methods were statistically equivalent" (p. 299). Furthermore, mechanical techniques also tended to be considerably more efficient than the clinical approach, in terms of both time and (therefore) cost, which favored using a mechanical approach even in instances where the clinical approach and mechanical approach were equally accurate (Grove et al. 2000).

Grove et al. (2000) noted two other important findings in their study. First, they found that neither greater clinical training nor experience resulted in improved accuracy of the clinical predictions, which casts doubts on the idea of a risk assessment "expert" whose clinical opinion has been honed during years of study and practice. Although it seems counterintuitive that "experienced psychologists frequently show little improvement in the accuracy of their clinical judgments relative to the clinical judgments of psychology graduate students" (p. 25), the authors noted that clinicians often receive no feedback on their predictions. This lack of feedback in turn makes it impossible for clinicians to learn from their mistaken predictions and be reinforced by their accurate predictions. Second, Grove et al. (2000) also found that mechanical approaches derived through statistical techniques (e.g., linear regression weights) outperformed mechanical approaches derived through non-statistical techniques (e.g., simple counting schemes). Both types of mechanical approach, however, outperformed the clinical approach.

Given the totality of the research (which spanned over 60 years' worth of prediction studies), Grove and Meehl (1996) concluded that the evidence clearly showed the superiority of using mechanical approaches to prediction (see also Monahan et al. 2001). Though the research of Meehl and Grove related to prediction in general and did not specifically focus on sex offenders and sexual recidivism, Hanson and Morton-Bourgon (2009) conducted a meta-analysis of 118 sex offender risk assessment studies and also found mechanical risk assessments to significantly outperform clinical judgment.

Meta-Analysis of Risk Prediction Variables

Having gained prominence in the "What Works?" movement within the field of general criminological risk assessment (e.g., Gendreau et al. 1996), the idea of using meta-analysis to statistically combine the results of different studies had a profound impact on the field of sex offender risk assessment. The first meta-analysis to identify a set of valid and reliable risk factors for sexual recidivism risk was by Hanson and Bussière (1998), which combined the results of 61 different sexual recidivism studies with a sample size of 28,972 sex offenders. Until the publication of Hanson and Bussière (1998), much of what was known about sex offender risk assessment came in the form of clinical experience, case studies, and individual research articles (or narrative reviews of those articles), all of which often generated unclear or conflicting results (e.g., Furby et al. 1989; Quinsey et al. 1995). This presented a problem for those tasked with conducting sex offender risk assessments and resulted in little uniformity in criteria and outcomes.

The publication of Hanson and Bussière (1998) clarified much of the confusion surrounding sex offender risk assessments, confirming some beliefs at that time about what factors were important to consider in an assessment and refuting others. For example, the findings of Hanson and Bussière (1998) supported the contention of Quinsey et al. (1995) that both general criminality factors (e.g., antisocial personality disorder, prior non-sexual offenses) and sexual deviance factors (e.g., phallometrically-assessed attraction to children) were significant predictors of sexual recidivism. Hanson and Bussière (1998) also identified a group of factors that were associated with a reduced likelihood of sexual recidivism, such as an offender being older, having prosocial supports (e.g., marriage), and having only offended against a related female child victim. Such factors whose presence reduces the likelihood of sexual recidivism are referred to as protective factors, and researchers have created an instrument called the Structured Assessment of Protective Factors for violence risk or SAPROF (de Vogel et al. 2009, 2012) to assess them.

Some of the most important findings from Hanson and Bussière (1998), however, were factors that the authors found did not predict sexual recidivism. For example, Hanson and Bussière (1998) found victim empathy, denial of index sexual offense, an offender having suffered sexual abuse as a child, and degree of force used/injury to victim during the commission of the index sexual offense, all to be unrelated to sexual recidivism risk. Though these findings were controversial at the time and continue to be debated today, they were supported years later by the findings of Hanson and Morton-Bourgon (2005), a second meta-analysis examining predictors of sexual recidivism (see Hanson and Morton-Bourgon [2004] for a full research report).

The findings of Hanson and Morton-Bourgon (2005) also reiterated the importance of considering both general criminality factors and sexual deviance factors when conducting a sex offender risk assessment, while identifying intimacy deficits as a possible third (and weaker in terms of predictive power) risk domain. Of the two major domains of sex offender risk assessment, however, the consideration of deviant sexual interests presented a problem for many risk evaluators. That is, though many general criminality factors can be easily found by examining an offender's criminal history file (e.g., parole/probation violations, instances of non-sexual violence), how can evaluators quickly and easily get measures of sexual deviance when phallometric or viewing time test results are not available? In response to this problem, several researchers have developed short scales designed to measure sexual deviance attributes that can be scored entirely from an offender's file, such as the revised Screening Scale for Pedophilic Interests or SSPI-2 (Seto et al. in press) and the Severe Sexual Sadism Scale or SSSS (Nitschke et al. 2009).

The Rise of ARAIs

The Hanson and Bussière (1998) meta-analysis also had another important influence on sex offender risk assessment: it helped to establish which variables held the greatest predictive validity, which led to the development of ARAIs. Hanson's first attempt at comprising a scale resulted in the four-item Rapid Risk Assessment of Sex Offender Risk or RRASOR (Hanson 1997):

1. Prior sex offenses (not including index offenses)
2. Age at release (current age)
3. Victim gender
4. Relationship to victim

This short scale proved to be moderately accurate in identifying offenders more likely to reoffend, and represented a big step forward in comparison to the poor results obtained via unstructured clinical judgment. Concurrently, David Thornton of Her Majesty's Prison Service in the UK was also working on an ARAI for sexual offense risk, named the Structured Anchored Clinical Judgment – Minimum or SACJ-Min (see Grubin 1998). In 1999, Hanson and Thornton combined their two scales to comprise the Static-99 (Hanson and Thornton 2000), which has since become the most widely used ARAI in the world for sexual violence risk potential. The resultant scale is comprised of 10 items:

1. Age at release
2. Ever lived with a lover for at least two years?
3. Index non-sexual violence convictions
4. Prior non-sexual violence convictions
5. Prior sexual offenses (excluding index)
6. Prior sentencing dates (excluding index)
7. Any convictions for non-contact sexual offenses?
8. Any unrelated victims?
9. Any stranger victims?
10. Any male victims?

Since its initial release in 1999, the Static-99 has undergone major revisions in 2009 regarding scoring of the age item and interpretation of the total score, as well as in 2016 with respect to updated coding rules and a different framework for reporting risk levels (see Phenix et al. 2016). Several replications of the Static-99R have been published, with predictive accuracy typically being reported as moderate (i.e., d = .70). Additionally, other authors have contributed analogous scales to the literature (e.g., Risk Matrix-2000, Vermont Assessment of Sex Offender Risk or VASOR, and Violence Risk Scale: Sexual Offender version or VRS:SO, the last of which also includes dynamic predictor variables; see below). Generally speaking, the introduction of the Static-999R and similar instruments to the assessment of sex offender risk was a monumental leap forward in increasing accuracy; however, it would be inappropriate to suggest that the Static-99R or any single scale could stand on its own as a comprehensive evaluation of risk to sexually reoffend.

Controversies Surrounding Use of ARAIs

Despite the widespread use of ARAIs (McGrath et al. 2010), several criticisms and controversies surround their use. For example, several critics have argued that the consistent ability to sort low- and high-risk offenders, and to do so at levels significantly better than either chance or unguided clinical opinion, mask problems in applying the recidivism estimates from an instrument's normative samples to samples not included in the normative research (Mossman 2006). The base rates of recidivating (i.e., the rates of recidivism within any given sample) can vary significantly from sample to sample, which makes it inappropriate to apply the recidivism estimates from the normative actuarial tables to new groups of offenders. This has led many evaluators to report the results of their ARAI scoring in terms of relative risk ratios, instead of absolute recidivism estimates.

Other critics have claimed that the actuarial tables from instruments such as the Static-99 do not accurately account for the reduction in recidivism risk that naturally comes with aging (Wollert et al. 2010). They suggested that any items relating to age should be removed from ARAIs, and that separate actuarial recidivism tables should be constructed for separate age groups. Wollert et al. (2010) proposed doing this to the Static-99 and creating the multisample age-stratified table of sexual recidivism rates (MATS-1). As noted earlier, however, the age item of the Static-99 was revised to more accurately capture the effects of aging, resulting in the Static-99R (Helmus et al. 2012). Research on the psychometric properties of the MATS-1 has found it to have significantly lower predictive accuracy than the Static-99R, and that the method used to develop the MATS-1 resulted in it having unstable properties across samples (Helmus and Thornton 2016).

Other critics of ARAIs have argued that since actuarial recidivism risk estimates are derived from large groups of offenders, the estimates cannot be applied to any specific individual (Cooke and Michie 2010; Hart et al. 2007), and that doing so results in margins for error so large that they make it impossible for any evaluator to make any predictions about the behavior of a single individual with any degree of confidence. Hanson and Howard (2010) argued that these large margins for error result from the dichotomous nature of the outcome variable in any prediction (e.g., either someone commits another act of violence [100% recidivism] or they do not [0% recidivism]), but they do not preclude estimates derived from group data from informing the likelihood of an individual event.

For example, some people who smoke get lung cancer and some do not, but doctors still counsel individuals to stop smoking based on group-level data that show smoking to significantly increase the chance of someone getting lung cancer. (Grove and Meehl [1996] preferred a similarly morbid example using a game of Russian roulette.)

Not all criticisms of ARAIs are directed at the applicability of their actuarial tables. Some critics have argued that, despite having operational definitions, enough subjectivity remains in the items of ARAIs for there to be substantial disagreement among raters. For example, Boccaccini et al. (2012) found high levels of inter-rater reliability for the Static-99 in field studies, but still found the total scores assigned by separate raters to differ in approximately 45% of the cases, with the score differences being two or more points in roughly 12% of the cases. Critics argue that a difference of two points can have substantial impacts on custodial and treatment decisions, and that such scoring discrepancies can be exacerbated in adversarial contexts. That is, that any subjectivity in the scoring of an instrument could lead experts hired by opposing sides in a legal action to adjust their scoring of the instrument (even subconsciously) to favor the side that hired them, a phenomenon known as allegiance effects (Murrie et al. 2013). Murrie et al. (2013) found evidence of such allegiance effects in an experiment they conducted, in which forensic experts were randomly assigned to do evaluations for the either the prosecution or the defense in a trial. The more structured nature of the Static-99R made it significantly less susceptible to allegiance effects than the PCL-R, but there was evidence of allegiance effects in the scoring of both instruments. This is more an issue relating to the use of ARAIs than a criticism of the instruments themselves, but is something evaluators should keep in mind when doing an assessment.

Comprehensive Evaluations

As noted above, it would be foolish to suggest that the Static-99R or any other single ARAI could stand as a comprehensive risk assessment on its own. The variables included in most scales of this sort are historical in nature or are not subject to intervention. In essence, the Static-99R is a measure establishing level of risk based on what someone has done in the past, in keeping with the old adage, "the best predictor of future behavior is past behavior." Although we know this to be generally true, it is not 100% true and we know that there are likely to be other variables that would serve to either mitigate or aggravate risk to reoffend. Dynamic risk variables (e.g., see Hanson et al. 2007) are also included in what we might term psychologically meaningful risk factors (see Mann et al. 2010). Whereas static variables speak to history, dynamic variables give us some sense of how the offender's current circumstances might either alleviate or inflame risk.

One of the more common scales used to assess dynamic risk potential is the Stable-2007 (Hanson et al. 2007), which is a natural counterpart to the Static-99R. This scale is comprised of 13 items in five sections (Significant Social Influences, Intimacy Deficits, General Self-regulation, Sexual Self-regulation, and Cooperation with Supervision). Theoretically, how someone scores on a measure of dynamic risk might be informative regarding their static risk presentation. For instance, someone with a relatively low static risk score but whose life is in shambles might be viewed as higher risk overall because of their unstable current circumstances. On the contrary, someone with a relatively high static score might be viewed more favorably if he has stable accommodation, employment, and a prosocial network of community supports.

In seeking to provide a comprehensive evaluation of risk to reoffend, we would suggest that the following components and processes are likely to result in better outcomes:

- Review of relevant file materials (e.g., prior psychological reports, police records, victim reports, corrections records)
- Clinical interview with the offender
- Contacts with collateral sources (e.g., family members, spouse/partner, friends)
- Psychometrics (e.g., personality, mood/affect, entrenched antisociality, inventories of sexuality)
- ARAIs (e.g., Static-99R, Static-2002R, VRS:SO, RM-2000, MnSOST-3, VASOR; some of these are specific to certain jurisdictions)

- Depending on client presentation, use of other measures might also be worthwhile (e.g., LSI-R for general reoffense risk, and BARR-2002R or VRAG-R for violence risk)
- Dynamic risk scales (e.g., Stable-2007, Acute-2007, VRS:SO, SRA-FV, SOTIPS)
- Where possible and feasible, it may be useful to employ either the penile plethysmograph or a viewing time measure (see Wilson 2016; Wilson and Miner 2016)
- Diagnostic considerations (e.g., DSM-5), especially regarding sexual deviance

Ultimately, the evaluator is responsible for accumulating and making sense of all of the assessment data, coming to a conclusion about not only what level of risk the offender may pose for future sexually offensive behavior, but also what risks may exist in other domains, and finally, what should be done about them. Regarding the latter aspect, it is incumbent upon the evaluator to give recommendations as to what risk factors are likely to cause concerns, under what circumstances, and what (if any) interventions might be appropriate. And all of this must be offered in keeping with the RNR principles noted earlier in this chapter.

Sexual Deviance

In both Hanson meta-analyses (Hanson and Bussière 1998; Hanson and Morton-Bourgon 2005), possession of sexually deviant interests was the single best predictor of sexual reoffending in a known sexual offender. Identifying sexually deviant interests or preferences with any certainty is a contentious issue in sex offender risk assessment, to say the least. On the one hand, some practitioners question whether paraphilic (sexually deviant) interests are a matter of clinical concern at all, whereas others contend that having a strong and persistent sexual interest in children, sexualized violence, or other sexually anomalous targets or behaviors is critically important to consider when attempting to evaluate risk to the community.

The most common framework used to describe sexually deviant interests and preferences is found in the Diagnostic and Statistical Manual of Mental Disorders or DSM-5 (American Psychiatric Association 2013). The general description of a paraphilia is as follows:

> ...any intense and persistent sexual interest other than sexual interest in genital stimulation or preparatory fondling with phenotypically normal, physically mature, consenting human partners ... (or *alternatively*) sexual interests greater than or equal to normophilic sexual interests.

The DSM-5 lists and provides criterion sets for eight paraphilias: Exhibitionism, Frotteurism, Voyeurism, Fetishism, Pedophilia, Sexual Masochism, Sexual Sadism, and Transvestic Fetishism. There are also two catch-all diagnostic frameworks for paraphilias other than the named eight: Other Specified Paraphilic Disorder (in which the clinician would add a specifier, such as Gerontophilia or Urophilia) and Unspecified Paraphilic Disorder (in which the clinician believes the condition meets the general definition of a paraphilia, but there is no literature or previously existing information to assist in providing a specifier).

Sexual psychodiagnostics can be a particularly controversial enterprise, especially in the context of sex offender civil commitment in the USA (see Brandt et al. 2015), where possession of a "mental abnormality" (i.e., paraphilic disorder) may result in indefinite, involuntary civil placement in a high security treatment center. Indeed, in the run-up to the publication of the DSM-5 in 2013, controversies raged as to whether new paraphilias should be added to the existing roster (i.e., Paraphilic Coercive Disorder, Pedohebephilic Disorder, Hypersexual Disorder). While all three of these disorders were ultimately not included in the text of the DSM-5, research and debate continues as to their viability and utility in sex offender risk assessment and risk management. Additionally, some jurisdictions have explored the utility of these diagnoses in certain legal proceedings by holding evidentiary hearings (e.g., Frye or Daubert hearings); however, there has been a general lack of consistency, with some courts accepting the diagnoses while others have not.

A further source of controversy in sexual psychodiagnostics regards the use of specialized testing methods, such as penile plethysmography (PPG, also referred to as phallometry) or viewing time (VT) measures (see reviews in Wilson 2016; Wilson and Miner 2016). The PPG is a psycho-physiological test of sexual arousal which measures changes in penile circumference or volume during presentation of a variety of sexually explicit media, the idea being that you are attempting to ascertain what arouses the client most, something appropriate (e.g., adults) or something inappropriate (e.g., children, non-consenting scenarios). Viewing time procedures focus more on sexual interests, and clients are seated in front of a computer and are instructed to press buttons, either to switch the image to the next slide or to signify some element of the picture on the screen. Although both methodologies are not without their drawbacks or critics, both PPG and VT are commonly used to aid in either the diagnosis of paraphilia or the identification of problematic sexual interests.

Public Policy

In recent years, sex offender risk assessment has played an increasingly prominent role in public policy, particularly US public policy. This increase has resulted from the spread of public policies designed to manage sex offenders in the community following the end of their criminal justice sanction, policies such as sex offender registration and notification (SORN) and sex offender civil commitment (Brandt et al. 2015; Mossman 2006). Under US SORN laws, offenders must register their personal information with law enforcement at the end of their criminal justice sanction, then verify their information every few months afterward. The regularity of verification (e.g., every three months, every six months) as well as how that information is made available to the public (e.g., passively posted on a website, actively mailed to neighbors) is determined by risk (Freeman and Sandler 2010). Those offenders deemed to be the highest risk are subject to the most frequent verification requirements, and their information is more actively and broadly made available to the public. To date, the vast majority of research on these policies has failed to find that they increase public safety (Sandler et al. 2008; Zgoba et al. 2010), with a common criticism of the laws being that the risk assessments done by various states and the federal government are not accurately sorting offenders by risk. For example, under the Adam Walsh Child Protection and Safety Act (2006), the US federal government uses as its sole risk classification factor the severity of an offender's index sexual offense, which research has failed to find is at all related to sexual recidivism risk (Freeman and Sandler 2010; Zgoba et al. 2016).

Risk assessment plays a much larger and more visible role in sex offender civil commitment. Under civil commitment laws, governments can civilly commit a sex offender they find to have a mental abnormality that reduces the offender's ability to desist from sexual offending, thereby making the offender particularly high risk for sexual recidivism (James et al. 2007). Central to the idea of civil commitment, therefore, is the ability to accurately assess the risk an offender poses to sexually recidivate. Recent court rulings on the constitutionality of the civil commitment programs in Minnesota (see *Karsjens v. Jesson* 2015) and Missouri (see *Van Orden v. Schafer* 2015) have stressed the importance of accurate risk assessment to the process, stating that civil commitment programs are only constitutional when they are as narrowly-tailored as possible. This means not only accurately evaluating the risk of offenders to place in civil commitment, but also regularly and accurately reevaluating the risk of offenders who have been placed in civil commitment so that they can be released when their risk level drops. From a public safety standpoint, civil commitment (as well as all other public policies designed to manage sex offenders following the end of their criminal justice sanction) are only likely to increase public safety if they are directed at the offenders who are most likely to sexually recidivate (Sandler and Freeman in press).

Evaluating Clients with Special Needs

In conducting any psychological evaluation, it is always important to use methods and tools that are appropriate to the clientele you are assessing. This actually applies to all of what we have written about in this chapter, but it is especially important to consider when the client you are evaluating belongs to a minority group within the greater population of sex offenders. One particular group that requires some special consideration are those offenders we might deem "special needs" (see Wilson et al.

2014), which can include persons with intellectual disabilities, brain injuries, severe mental health conditions, fetal alcohol difficulties, and other presentations that would serve to limit cognitive abilities.

Generally, the most important consideration here surrounds the use of tools and procedures that are appropriate to persons with compromised cognitive presentations. With respect to the Static-99R and other ARAIs, it is critical to assess the degree to which the standardization sample of the instrument includes sufficient numbers of persons like your client, in order for the tool to be applicable. The Static-99R sample includes sufficient numbers of persons with cognitive limitations, to the extent that the test's authors cite no major concerns in the applicability of the instrument (see Hanson et al. 2013). However, there may be concerns in attempting to modify or adapt dynamic risk assessment schemes (e.g., Stable-2007) to use with special needs offenders, especially those with intellectual disabilities. Overall, it is important to be cognizant of the effects on the evaluative process that certain cognitive limitations will pose, in addition to considering that many persons with such disabilities are found in care facilities (group homes, hospitals, habilitative settings, and similar environments). This latter element requires evaluators to consider the environment in which clients are likely to be found, or the degree to which the environment may mitigate or inflame risk.

For evaluation of dynamic risk potential, the *Assessment of Risk and Manageability for Individuals Who Offend Sexually* or ARMIDILO-S (see Boer et al. 2012) is a particularly useful tool. Specifically, it is a Stable-2007 analog and many or most of the items are quite similar, but it also allows for a reframing of all risk items as potential protective factors. Additionally, over and above measuring risk in the client-stable and client-acute domains, the ARMIDILO-S also allows for consideration of stable and acute risk factors dependent on the environment in which the client is most likely to be found, or in relation to the quality of care and guidance they receive from agency or facility staff. The ARMIDILO-S has been shown to have moderate predictive accuracy (Blacker et al. 2011; Lofthouse et al. 2013), and both research groups suggest that it may outperform commonly used ARAIs.

Female Sex Offender Risk Assessment

As noted earlier, all of the risk assessment research discussed to this point pertains only to male sex offenders. Very little research has been done on female sex offenders and their risk to sexually recidivate, and research is lacking in this area for several reasons, most notably sample size. That is, although a meta-analysis of self-reported victimization surveys found females to have committed 11.6% of all sexual offenses (Cortoni et al. 2017), females make up only about 2% of all offenders arrested and con-victed for sexual offenses (Cortoni et al. 2017; Freeman and Sandler 2008). Additionally, female sex offenders have been found to have five-year sexual recidivism rates of less than 2% (Cortoni et al. 2010; Sandler and Freeman 2009; Wijkman and Bijleveld 2015). This combination of (a) low numbers of females convicted for sexual offenses and (b) low rates of sexual recidivism among convicted female sex offenders makes it dif-ficult to generate large enough samples of female sex offenders with enough sexual recidivists to analyze quantitatively. For example, Wijkman and Bijleveld (2015) analyzed the recidivism of 261 female offenders convicted of hands-on sexual offenses in the Netherlands, and so few females sexually recidivated (1.1%) that the authors were unable to iden-tify any significant sexual risk factors.

Because of these issues, Sandler and Freeman (2009) is the only study to date that has been able to quantitatively identify significant risk factors for purely sexual recidivism among female sex offenders, and that required a sample of 1466 offenders (every female convicted of a sexual offense in New York State over a 21-year period). The results of this analysis showed that once the sample was limited to offenders with hands-on sexual or child pornography offenses, three criminal history factors indicated increased risk for sexual recidivism: (a) prior child victim offenses, (b) at least one prior felony offense, and (c) at least one prior drug offense. More recently, Cortoni et al. (2015) matched 13 female sexual recidivists to 13 female non-recidivists and compared them to find any indicators of increased sexual recidivism risk. Although the small sample for the analy-sis means the findings can only be thought of as preliminary, results indi-cated that the sexual recidivists tended to be younger, to have offended against a single male victim (generally a pubescent or post-pubescent male victim), and to have committed a hands-on sexual offense.

Given the difficulties in simply identifying sexual recidivism risk factors for female sex offenders, no validated sexual risk assessment instrument has been developed to date specifically for female sex offenders (Cortoni et al. 2015). Although some of the risk factors and possible risk factors for female sex offenders appear to overlap with male sex offenders (e.g., male victims, prior non-sexual felonies, being younger), female sex offenders have been found to differ from male sex offenders in terms of their pathways to offending (Gannon et al. 2008) and rates of recidivism (Cortoni et al. 2010). As such, risk instruments developed for, and designed to be used with, male sex offenders should not be used with female sex offenders; gender-specific measures and risk markers are needed (Van Voorhis et al. 2010).

Summary & Conclusions

We began this chapter by stating that a lot has changed in how we conduct risk assessments of sexual offenders over the last 30 or so years. What once may have seemed to be a process using veritable stone knives and bearskins has become a much more scientifically informed and rigorous process. It would be foolish to suggest that we get it right all the time; however, there are clearly technologies that exist in the present that have increased our ability to get it right more often. The Hanson and Bussière meta-analysis (1998) of the predictors of sexual reoffending clearly represented a watershed moment in the development of greater understanding of our sex offender clientele. The subsequent development of ARAIs and dynamic risk assessment tools led to increased precision and decreased reliance on subjective decision making processes. All of this has been good for both community safety and offender reintegration potential, but we are mindful that there is still a lot of work to be done. As we have noted at various junctures in this chapter, a lot of controversy remains regarding various perspectives and procedures in sexual violence prevention.

The other major influence on practice in working with offenders, including sex offenders, has been the work of Andrews, Bonta, and their group. At this point, the majority of work done in Western corrections relies heavily on the RNR model. This model represents a framework in which good assessment and treatment can occur, but it is important to note that it is not a treatment model, *per se*. The important take-away message we wish to leave you with is that assessments have to use empirically validated tools and procedures, and that subsequent interventions must focus on those risk factors related to the offender's propensity to re-engage in criminal behavior (see Wilson et al. 2009). Last, all interventions—whether they be evaluation or treatment oriented—must take the client and his/her individual characteristics into consideration. Although it may be fine to tell an offender that he/she poses a high degree of risk to reoffend and that treatment will therefore focus on aspects A, B, and C, the ultimate key factor in ensuring desistance will be the degree to which the offender buys-in to the need to manage his risk, and build a balanced and self-determined lifestyle free of future inappropriate conduct.

Notes

1. A meta-analysis is essentially a study of studies. Researchers pull together all the individual studies on a particular subject and then, to the extent that all studies are reasonably conducted and focus on similar issues, those studies form a much larger study with a more representative sample size. Meta-analyses are commonly used to establish the validity of certain procedures, such as risk assessment or treatment effectiveness.

References

Adam Walsh Child Protection and Safety Act. (2006). 42 U.S. C. § 16911.
American Psychiatric Association. (2013). *Diagnostic and statistical manual of mental disorders* (5th ed.). Washington, DC: Author.
Andrews, D. A., & Bonta, J. (1994). *The psychology of criminal conduct* (1st ed.). Cincinnati: Anderson.

Blacker, J., Beech, A. R., Wilcox, D. T., & Boer, D. P. (2011). The assessment of dynamic risk and recidivism in a sample of special needs sex offenders. *Psychology, Crime & Law, 17*, 75–92.

Boccaccini, M. T., Murrie, D. C., Mercado, C., Quesada, S., Hawes, S., Rice, A. K., & Jeglic, E. L. (2012). Implications of the Static-99 field reliability findings for score use and reporting. *Criminal Justice and Behavior, 39*, 42–58.

Boer, D. P., Haaven, J. L., Lambick, F., Lindsay, W. R., McVilly, K., Sakdalan, J., & Frize, M. (2012). *ARMIDILO-S manual: Web version 1.0.* Available at www.armidilo.net

Bonta, J. (1996). Risk-needs assessment and treatment. In A. T. Harland (Ed.), *Choosing correctional options that work: Defining the demand and evaluating the supply* (pp. 18–32). Thousand Oaks: Sage.

Bonta, J., & Andrews, D. A. (2016). *The psychology of criminal conduct* (6th ed.). Cincinnati: Anderson.

Brandt, J., Wilson, R. J., & Prescott, D. S. (2015). Doubts about SVP programs: A critical review of sexual offender civil commitment in the US. In B. Schwartz (Ed.), *The sex offender* (Vol. 8). Kingston: Civic Research Institute.

Burkhardt, B. C., & Connor, B. T. (2016). Durkheim, punishment, and prison privatization. *Social Currents, 3*, 84–99.

Cooke, D., & Michie, C. (2010). Limitations of diagnostic precision and predictive utility in the individual case: A challenge for forensic practice. *Law and Human Behavior, 34*, 259–274.

Cortoni, F., Babchishin, K. M., & Rat, C. (2017). The proportion of sexual offenders who are female is higher than thought: A meta-analysis. *Criminal Justice and Behavior, 44*, 145–162.

Cortoni, F., Hanson, R. K., & Coache, M. E. (2010). The recidivism rates of female sexual offenders are low: A meta-analysis. *Sexual Abuse: A Journal of Research and Treatment, 22*, 387–401.

Cortoni, F., Sandler, J. C., Freeman, N. J., & Kozlowski, K. (2015). *Factors related to sexual recidivism among women.* Paper presented at the Annual conference of the Association for the Treatment of Sexual Abusers, Orlando.

de Vogel, V., de Ruiter, C., Bouman, Y., & de Vries Robbe, M. (2009). *SAPROF. Guidelines for the assessment of protective factors for violence risk.* Utrecht: Forum Educatief.

de Vogel, V., de Ruiter, C., Bouman, Y., & de Vries Robbe, M. (2012). *SAPROF. Guidelines for the assessment of protective factors for violence risk* (2nd ed.). Utrecht: Forum Educatief.

Finkelhor, D., & Jones, L. M. (2006). Why have child maltreatment and child victimization declined? *Journal of Social Issues, 62*, 685–716.

Freeman, N. J., & Sandler, J. C. (2008). Female and male sex offenders: A comparison of recidivism patterns and risk factors. *Journal of Interpersonal Violence, 23*, 1394–1413.

Freeman, N. J., & Sandler, J. C. (2010). The Adam Walsh Act: A false sense of security or an effective public policy initiative? *Criminal Justice Policy Review, 21*, 31–49.

Furby, L., Weinrott, M. R., & Blackshaw, L. (1989). Sex offender recidivism: A review. *Psychological Bulletin, 105*, 3–30.

Gannon, T. A., Rose, M. R., & Ward, T. (2008). A descriptive model of the offense process for female sexual offenders. *Sexual Abuse: A Journal of Research & Treatment, 20*, 352–374.

Gendreau, P., Little, T., & Goggin, C. (1996). A meta-analysis of the predictors of adult offender recidivism: What works! *Criminology, 34*, 575–607.

Grove, W., & Meehl, P. (1996). Comparative efficiency of informal (subjective, impressionistic) and formal (mechanical, algorithmic) prediction procedures: The clinical-statistical controversy. *Psychology, Public Policy, and Law, 2*, 293–323.

Grove, W. M., Zald, D. H., Lebow, B. S., Snits, B. E., & Nelson, C. E. (2000). Clinical vs. mechanical prediction: A meta-analysis. *Psychological Assessment, 12*, 19–30.

Grubin, D. (1998). *Sex offending against children: Understanding the risk*. Police Research Series Paper 99. London: Home office.

Hanson, R. K. (1997). *The development of a brief actuarial risk scale for sexual offense recidivism* (User Report 1997-04). Ottawa: Department of the Solicitor General of Canada.

Hanson, R. K., & Bussière, M. T. (1998). Predicting relapse: A meta-analysis of sexual offender recidivism studies. *Journal of Consulting and Clinical Psychology, 66*, 348–362.

Hanson, R. K., & Howard, P. (2010). Individual confidence intervals do not inform decision-makers about the accuracy of risk assessment evaluations. *Law and Human Behavior, 34*, 275–281.

Hanson, R. K., & Morton-Bourgon, K. E. (2004). *Predictors of sexual recidivism: An updated meta-analysis* (Research Rep. No. 2004–02). Ottawa: Public Safety and Emergency Preparedness Canada.

Hanson, R. K., & Morton-Bourgon, K. E. (2005). The characteristics of persistent sexual offenders: A meta-analysis of recidivism studies. *Journal of Consulting and Clinical Psychology, 73*, 1154–1163.

Hanson, R. K., & Morton-Bourgon, K. E. (2009). The accuracy of recidivism risk assessments for sexual offenders: A meta-analysis of 118 prediction studies. *Psychological Assessment, 21*, 1–21.

Hanson, R. K., & Thornton, D. (2000). Improving risk assessments for sex offenders: A comparison of three actuarial scales. *Law and Human Behavior, 24*, 119–136.

Hanson, R. K., Harris, A. J. R., Scott, T. L., & Helmus, L. (2007). *Assessing the risk of sexual offenders on community supervision: The Dynamic Supervision Project* (User Report 2007-05). Ottawa: Public Safety Canada.

Hanson, R. K., Sheahan, C. L., & VanZuylen, H. (2013). Static-99 and RRASOR predict recidivism among developmentally delayed sexual offenders: A cumulative meta-analysis. *Sexual Offender Treatment, 8*, 1–14.

Hanson, R. K., Babchishin, K. M., Helmus, L. M., Thornton, D., & Phenix, A. (2016a). Communicating the results of criterion-referenced prediction measures: Risk categories for the Static-99R and Static-2002R sexual offender risk assessment tools. *Psychological Assessment*. Advance online publication.

Hanson, R. K., Thornton, D., Helmus, L., & Babchishin, K. M. (2016b). What sexual recidivism rates are associated with Static-99R and Static-2002R scores? *Sexual Abuse: A Journal of Research and Treatment, 28*, 218–252.

Hart, S. D., Michie, C., & Cooke, D. J. (2007). Precision of actuarial risk assessment instruments: Evaluating the 'margins of error' of group versus individual predictions of violence. *British Journal of Psychiatry, 190*(Suppl), 60–65.

Helmus, L., & Thornton, D. (2016). The MATS-1 risk assessment scale: Summary of methodological concerns and an empirical validation. *Sexual Abuse: A Journal of Research and Treatment, 28*, 160–186.

Helmus, L., Thornton, D., Hanson, R. K., & Babchishin, K. M. (2012). Improving the predictive accuracy of Static-99 and Static-2002 with older sex offenders: Revised age weights. *Sexual Abuse: A Journal of Research and Treatment, 24*, 64–101.

James, N., Thomas, K. R., & Foley, C. (2007). *CRS report for Congress: Civil commitment of sexually dangerous persons*. Washington, DC: Congressional Research Services.

Karsjens et al. v. Jesson et al. (2015). 11-3659.

Levenson, J. S., D'Amora, D. A., & Hern, A. (2007). Megan's law and its impact on community re-entry for sex offenders. *Behavioral Sciences & the Law, 25*, 587–602.

Lofthouse, R. E., Lindsay, W. R., Totsika, V., Hastings, R. P., Boer, D. P., & Haaven, J. L. (2013). Prospective dynamic assessment of risk of sexual reoffending in individuals with an intellectual disability and a history of sexual offending behaviour. *Journal of Applied Research in Intellectual Disabilities, 26*, 394–403.

Mann, R. E., Hanson, R. K., & Thornton, D. (2010). Assessing risk for sexual recidivism: Some proposals on the nature of psychologically meaningful risk factors. *Sexual Abuse: A Journal of Research and Treatment, 22*, 191–217.

Martinson, R. (1974). Nothing works: Questions and answers about prison reform. *The Public Interest, 35*, 22–54.

Martinson, R. (1979). New findings, new views: A note of caution regarding sentencing reform. *Hofstra Law Review, 7*, 242–258.

McGrath, R. J., Cumming, G. F., Burchard, B. L., Zeoli, S., & Ellerby, L. (2010). *Current practices and emerging trends in sexual abuser management: The Safer Society 2009 North American survey.* Brandon: Safer Society Press.

Meehl, P. E. (1954/1996). Clinical vs. statistical prediction: A theoretical analysis and a review of the evidence. Minneapolis: University of Minnesota Press.

Monahan, J. (1981). *The clinical prediction of violent behavior.* Originally published by National Institute of Mental Health. Reprinted as *Predicting violent behavior: An assessment of clinical techniques* by Sage Publications, also 1981.

Monahan, J. (2008). Structured risk assessment of violence. In R. Simon & K. Tardiff (Eds.), *Textbook of violence assessment and management* (pp. 17–34). Washington, DC: American Psychiatric Publishing.

Monahan, J., Steadman, H., Silver, E., Appelbaum, P. S., Robbins, P. C., Mulvey, E. P., Roth, L. H., Grisso, T., & Banks, S. (2001). *Rethinking risk assessment: The MacArthur study of mental disorder and violence.* New York: Oxford University Press.

Mossman, D. (2006). Another look at interpreting risk categories. *Sexual Abuse: A Journal of Research and Treatment, 18*, 41–63.

Murrie, D. C., Boccaccini, M. T., Guarnera, L. A., & Rufino, K. A. (2013). Are forensic experts biased by the side that retained them? *Psychological Science, 24*, 1889–1897.

Nitschke, J., Osterheider, M., & Mokros, A. (2009). A cumulative scale of severe sexual sadism. *Sexual Abuse: A Journal of Research and Treatment, 21*, 262–278.

Phenix, A., Fernandez, Y., Harris, A. J. R., Helmus, M., Hanson, R. K., & Thornton, D. (2016). *Static-99R coding rules, revised 2016.* Ottawa: Public Safety Canada.

Quinsey, V. L., Lalumiere, M. L., Rice, M. E., & Harris, G. T. (1995). Predicting sexual offenses. In J. C. Campbell (Ed.), *Assessing dangerousness: Violence by sexual offenders, batterers, and child abusers* (pp. 114–137). Thousand Oaks: Sage.

Quinsey, V. L., Harris, G. T., Rice, M. E., & Cormier, C. A. (2006). *Violent offenders: Appraising and managing risk* (3rd ed.). Washington, DC: American Psychological Association.

Sandler, J. C., & Freeman, N. J. (2009). Female sex offender recidivism: A large-scale empirical analysis. *Sexual Abuse: A Journal of Research and Treatment, 21*, 455–473.

Sandler, J. C., & Freeman, N. J. (in press). Evaluation of New York State's sex offender civil management assessment process: Recidivism outcomes. *Criminology & Public Policy.*

Sandler, J. C., Freeman, N. J., & Socia, K. M. (2008). Does a watched pot boil: A time-series analysis of New York State's sex offender registration and notification law. *Psychology, Public Policy, and Law, 14*, 284–302.

Seto, M. C., Stephens, S., Lalumiere, M. L., & Cantor, J. M. (in press). The revised Screening Scale for Pedophilic Interests (SSPI-2): Development and criterion-related validation. *Sexual Abuse: A Journal of Research and Treatment.*

Skeem, J. L., & Monahan, J. (2011). Current directions in violence risk assessment. *Current Directions in Psychological Science, 20*, 38–42.

Smith, P., Goggin, C., & Gendreau, P. (2002). *The effects of prison sentences and intermediate sanctions on recidivism: General effects and individual differences* (Research Report 2002-01). Ottawa: Solicitor General Canada.

Van Orden et al. v. Schafer et al. (2015). 4:09CV00971 AGF.

Van Voorhis, P., Wright, E. M., Salisbury, E., & Bauman, A. (2010). Women's risk factors and their contributions to existing risk/needs assessment: The current status of a gender-responsive supplement. *Criminal Justice and Behavior, 37*, 261–288.

Wijkman, M., & Bijleveld, C. (2015). Criminal career features of female sexual offenders. In A. J. Blokland & P. Lussier (Eds.), *Sex offenders: A criminal career approach.* Chichester: Wiley.

Wilson, R. J. (2016). The use of phallometric testing in the diagnosis, treatment, and risk management of male adults who have sexually offended. In L. Craig & M. Rettenberger (Eds.), *The Wiley handbook on the theories, assessment & treatment of sexual offending: Volume 2* (pp. 823–849). Chichester: Wiley-Blackwell.

Wilson, R. J., & Miner, M. H. (2016). Measurement of male sexual arousal and interest using penile plethysmography and viewing time. In D. R. Laws & W. T. O'Donohue (Eds.), *Treatment of sex offenders: Strengths and weaknesses in assessment and intervention*. New York: Springer.

Wilson, R. J., Cortoni, F., Picheca, J. E., Stirpe, T. S., & Nunes, K. (2009). *Community-based sexual offender maintenance treatment programming: An evaluation* (Research Report R-188). Ottawa: Correctional Service of Canada.

Wilson, R. J., Prescott, D. S., & Burns, M. (2014). People with special needs and sexual behaviour problems: Balancing community and client interests while ensuring effective risk management. In K. McCartan & H. Kemshall (Eds., Special issue), Sex offender (re)integration into the community: Realities and challenges. *Journal of Sexual Aggression, 21*, 86–99.

Wollert, R., Cramer, E., Waggoner, J., Skelton, A., & Vess, J. (2010). Recent research ($N = 9,305$) underscores the importance of using age-stratified actuarial tables in sex offender risk assessments. *Sexual Abuse: A Journal of Research and Treatment, 22*, 471–490.

Zgoba, K., Veysey, B. M., & Dalessandro, M. (2010). An analysis of the effectiveness of community notification and registration: Do the best intentions predict the best practices? *Justice Quarterly, 27*, 667–691.

Zgoba, K., Miner, M., Letourneau, E., Levenson, J., Knight, R., & Thornton, D. (2016). A multi-state recidivism study using Static-99 and Static-2002 risk scores and tier guidelines from the Adam Walsh Act. *Sexual Abuse: A Journal of Research and Treatment, 28*, 722–740.

3

Critical Reflections on the Risk-Based Prevention of Sexual Offending by Young People

Stephen Case

Introduction

Contemporary understandings of youth offending and consequent youth justice practices in the Anglophone world have been driven by a specific risk discourse focused on the identification, measurement and prevention of 'risk'—the risk of (re)offending and the risk of committing serious harm to others. The concept of 'risk' has been framed, assessed and understood as a series of statistical, quantifiable 'factors' amenable to targeted intervention. However, limited cogent evidence is available regarding the risk predictors for sexual offending by young people in this field. Knowledge in this area is nascent and under-developed (YJB 2008), with available evidence largely limited to the North American context (Zimring 2004). Taken together, these limitations raise concerns over the validity of employing risk-based assessment and intervention models with young people who sexually offend.

S. Case (✉)
Loughborough University, Loughborough, UK

© The Author(s) 2017
H. Kemshall, K. McCartan (eds.), *Contemporary Sex Offender Risk Management,*
Volume II, Palgrave Studies in Risk, Crime and Society,
DOI 10.1007/978-3-319-63573-6_3

This chapter will critically evaluate the discourse of risk within youth justice practice, particularly its animation through the 'Risk Factor Prevention Paradigm' (RFPP), exploring its (questionable) relevance to and appropriateness for assessment and intervention practice with young people who commit sexual offences. Discussion will take the form of a five-stage journey, tracing the evolution of a risk assessment and intervention framework (henceforth known as 'risk assessment-intervention') in the Youth Justice System (YJS) of England and Wales since the Crime and Disorder Act 1998. The journey begins by outlining the birth of risk assessment-intervention in the 1990s, linking this development to the emergence of risk management approaches in criminal justice in the 'risk society' and their increasing application through techniques of actuarial justice and through the RFPP. The second stage charts the growth of risk assessment-intervention following its formalisation in the Crime and Disorder Act 1998. The Act required multi-agency youth offending teams (YOTs) to conduct 'Asset' risk assessments with all young people who came to their attention and to link subsequent interventions to the risk of (general) reoffending assessed through Asset, which included a 'Risk of Serious Harm' component to assess the risk of future serious (sexual or violent) offending. Stage three explores the prime of risk assessment-intervention in the YJS, manifested in the Scaled Approach, which explicitly weighted (scaled) the frequency of intervention to the young person's assessed risk category (high, medium, low). Next comes an examination of the decline of risk assessment-intervention due to long-standing criticisms of the invalidating reductionism of both its evidence base and practice processes. The chapter concludes with a more optimistic outline of the rebirth of assessment-intervention in the YJS through the new 'AssetPlus' framework, which moves both assessment and intervention away from their previous emphasis on risk and towards a more meaningful integration of practitioner discretion and the strengths, positive foundations for change, and qualitative perspectives of young people, including those who sexually offend. At each stage, there will be consideration of the relatively under-developed and inconsistent evidence base for the RFPP in relation to assessment and intervention practice with young people who offend, particularly in the form of specific, validated assessment tools for this cohort.

The Birth of Risk Assessment-Intervention in the Youth Justice System: Enter Risk Management

It is a well known, largely accepted in critical academic discourse, that the history of youth justice approaches has been characterised by a tension between the relative merits of prioritising a young person's welfare compared to responding to the offence of the primary concern—the so-called 'welfare versus justice' debate (Smith 2005). However, in the 1990s an alternative model of youth justice began to gain momentum in the industrialised Western world, a model far more concerned with pragmatism than academic or philosophical debates over the relative merits of welfare or justice. The risk management approach emphasised the identification (through assessment) and targeting (through intervention) of those 'risk factors' in the lives of young people that allegedly placed them at increased risk of offending in later life. Risk management had its origins in at least three areas: the growing acknowledgment of a 'risk society', the popularity of actuarial justice techniques and the burgeoning evidence base from developmental risk factor research.

The risk society thesis of the 1990s (the 'risk' element of risk management) suggested that the Western world was becoming beset with increasing socio-economic, political and physical risks and insecurities, many of which were the result of the dynamic and sweeping social, political and technological changes brought about by globalisation (Beck 1992). In this context, 'risk' signified danger, threat, uncertainty and anxiety that needed to be managed by politicians, with help from practitioners, academics, the media and the general public. Concurrently, the extent and nature of the risk society was being exacerbated by governmental perceptions of a crisis in youth justice across Western systems, 'evidenced' by the perception of an increasing 'problem' of youth offending and the urgent requirement for more effective, efficient and economical responses to this behaviour that simultaneously protected the public from young people (Kemshall, in Blyth et al. 2007). The response to the perceived failures of previous welfare and justice approaches was to introduce an enhanced focus on more tightly managing youth justice systems and processes ('managerialism'; see Muncie 2008). This focus was logically pursued through a 'new penology' animated by actuarial justice and its 'new technologies to identify and classify risk' (Feeley and Simon 1992: 454–55) using risk assessment/prediction tools and advanced statistical testing. Actuarial justice constituted the statistical identification of low/high risk groups in order to plan interventions and inform criminal sanctions (cf. Feeley and Simon 1992). The introduction of actuarial risk assessment instruments into the youth justice arena has been rationalised by at least three pragmatic arguments. First, the claim is that actuarial techniques increase the accuracy and consistency of organisational and practitioner decision-making. Second, actuarialism is seen to offer a standardised, practical alternative to clinical and subjective practitioner judgments and the potential for indeterminate intervention. Third, advocates argue that actuarial methods underpin assessments and decisions with a much-needed empirical evidence base for predicting youth offending (Case and Haines 2009; Grove and Meehl 1996). The risk assessment-intervention processes that constitute risk management in the youth justice systems of the industrialised Western world (especially in England and Wales, Australasia and North America) are underpinned by evidence largely drawn from developmental risk factor research. This rapidly expanding research movement has provided an enormous, replicable evidence base that exposure to 'psychosocial' risk factors (in the domains of the personal, family, school, neighbourhood) in early life (e.g. childhood, early adolescence) can statistically predict general offending behaviour in later life (e.g. late adolescence, adulthood), although the evidence base for the prediction of specific forms of youth offending lags far behind to this day. This risk management-based model for understanding and responding to youth crime has become dominant across the westernised youth justice systems, prompting Laub and Sampson (2003: 289) to assert that:

> the risk-factor and prediction paradigms have taken hold of criminology, especially for those interested in crime prevention and crime control policies

It must be stressed, however, that only a particular form of risk factor research became popular in the 1990s onwards, so popular that it has arguably achieved explanatory hegemony in contemporary understandings of youth offending. The evidence base for risk management has privileged what Kemshall (2008) dubbed 'artefactual' risk factor research, which employs positivist research methods and converts psychosocial risks into quantitative, numerical 'factors' or 'artefacts' that can be readily measured and plugged into statistical tests. This understanding of risk contrasts with 'constructivist' risk factor research (Case and Haines 2009), which measures experiences and perceptions of risk in more personalised, qualitative terms. The quantitative, predictive 'risk factors' consistently identified in artefactual risk factor research were used to populate risk assessment instruments and to shape a risk assessment-intervention model known as the 'Risk Factor Prevention Paradigm' or RFPP (Hawkins and Catalano 1992). This paradigm had been imported into the field of criminal justice from the medical/public health domain, where it had been validated as a method for identifying/assessing risk factors for heart disease (e.g. lack of exercise, obesity, high cholesterol) and for informing preventative interventions (e.g. exercise programmes, health education) targeted on groups identified as 'high-risk' of developing health problems. Transfer of the RFPP to the youth justice arena has provided a readily applicable and practical assessment-intervention model with a clear rationale:

> Identify the key risk factors for offending and implement prevention methods designed to counteract them. There is often a related attempt to identify key protective factors against offending and to implement prevention methods designed to enhance them. (Farrington 2007: 606)

In the 1990s risk society, the evidence-based, quantitative nature of the RFPP was hugely appealing to politicians, policymakers and practitioners seeking more effective, efficient and economical methods of responding to youth offending and managing the YJS in an increasingly risk-averse society. The RFPP afforded a method of controlling and managing insecurities and anxieties around risk and meeting governmental desires for policy and practice to be explicitly 'evidence-based' (Mason and Prior 2008; Prior and Paris 2005). In addition, the paradigm provided a rationale for distancing youth justice policy and practice from its previous obsession with causality and treatment; it offered a 'third way' alternative to welfare and justice approaches and a mechanism for managing the so-called youth 'problem' (France 2008: 3). Therefore, arguments for the evidence-based management of the risk presented by young people in the YJS were pervasive and persuasive (Case and Haines 2016). The application of the RFPP offered an:

> ostensibly neat and coherent approach to the messy and ill-defined complexities of practice ... a consistent risk management methodology resting on a platform of knowledge ... a cautious and defensive response to the challenges of modern society. (Stephenson et al. 2007: 3–4)

In England and Wales, the RFPP became the guiding framework for youth justice practice following the Crime and Disorder Act 1998, a root and branch reform of the YJS that had been shaped by a thorough review of the YJS entitled 'Misspent Youth' (Audit Commission 1996). The new primary aim of the YJS became the *prevention* of offending and this objective was to be pursued through risk management—specifically risk-focused early intervention informed by structured risk assessment.

The Growth of Risk Assessment-Intervention in the Youth Justice System: Asset et al.

For the radically reorientated YJS that emerged from the Crime and Disorder Act 1998, RFPP was an idea whose time had come. The emphasis on early intervention(ism) and prevention through effectively managed and evidenced practice was ideally suited to a risk-led approach. The Labour government committed fully to this managerialist form of 'new youth justice' (Goldson 2000). In 2000, the Youth Justice Board for England and Wales (YJB) introduced 'Asset', a structured, standardised risk assessment instrument to be administered by YOT staff to all young people who entered the YJS (YJB 2000). The purpose of Asset was to enable YOT practitioners to assess a young person's risk of reoffending (in general, not specific forms of offending) in order to target resources and plan preventative interventions more effectively, efficiently and economically. The Asset form consisted of a series of risk-related questions in 12 domains of psychosocial risk: living arrangements, family/personal relationships, education/training/employment, neighbourhood, lifestyle, substance use, physical health, emotional/mental health, perception of self/others, thinking/behaviour, attitudes to offending/motivation to change. In each domain, practitioners were instructed to rate whether specific risks were present in the young person's life currently or recently, based on a yes or no response to risk-based statements. They then had to provide a summative assessment of the extent of association between the risks in each domain and the 'likelihood of further offending' on a scale of from 0 to 5: 0 = no association, 1 = slight or limited indirect association, 2 = moderate direct or indirect association, 3 = quite strong association, normally direct, 4 = very strong, clear and direct association. This summative, quantitative assessment of risk of reoffending in each domain was supplemented in a small evidence box with narrative, qualitative explanations of the nature of the perceived association. The psychosocial risk domains were complemented by six additional sections:

- Demographic information (not assessed/scored)
- Offence details and offending history (not assessed/scored)
- Protective factors
- Indicators of vulnerability
- Indicators of risk of serious harm to others (the most relevant section for the assessment of young people who sexually offend)
- 'What do you think?' self-assessment

The quantitative ratings were then totalled to provide a 'risk of reoffending' score from 0 to 64 (16 assessed domains, each scored 0–4). From the YJB's perspective, Asset was the essential component of the 'Assessment, Planning Interventions and Supervision' (APIS) framework (YJB 2003). In the growing performance management culture of the YJS, APIS constituted one of the central 'Key Elements of Effective Practice' (KEEP), a set of practice principles and guidance documents produced by the YJB to inform the work of YOT staff based on evidence of 'what works' in preventing youth offending, typically through risk-focused interventions. APIS guided practitioners to link their assessments to intervention using risk-based understandings of youth offending drawn from developmental/life course theories and related research, particularly the criminal careers model (Farrington 1996) that had inspired the content of Asset. In this way, APIS formalised risk assessment-intervention practice with all young people who entered the YJS. This practice was to underpin all other KEEP guidance and was to drive forwards the work of YOTs in pursuit of a host of other performance management measures such as National Standards, Case Management Guidance and Key Performance Indicators (e.g. reducing first-time entrants into the YJS, reducing reoffending, reducing custody).

At this stage, however, it is crucial to emphasise the generic nature of the Asset risk assessment tool. The instrument assesses the risk of general reoffending as a means of informing preventative intervention, rather than focusing on predicting and responding to specific types of offending behaviour by young people, such as sexual recidivism. Indeed, there has been an alarming paucity of risk assessment instruments developed specifically to assess young people who sexually offend. Those instruments that do exist have largely adapted adult-based prediction tools (cf. Caldwell 2002; Worling), despite the predictors of youthful sexual recidivism being different than those for adults (Miner 2002). The associated evidence base for risk assessment with young people who sexually offend is extremely limited, inconsistent and inconclusive (cf. Campbell et al. 2016; Hempel et al. 2013; YJB 2008; Worling 2004; Righthand et al. 2005). For example, in their review of risk assessment instruments applied to young people who sexually offend, Hempel et al. (2013) identified widespread inconsistencies in the predictive accuracy of different instruments, citing a particular lack of accuracy amongst generic assessment tools when applied to sexual offending. The lack of bespoke risk assessment tools for young people who sexually offend, the uncritical application of adult-based tools and the widespread lack of cogent evidence of predictive accuracy, all raise serious questions regarding the validity of an 'evidence-based' approach to working with sexual offenders that understands and responds to their behaviour in terms of risk—in other words, through the application of generic youth justice risk assessment-intervention. These questions are certainly not ameliorated by the use of

Asset, which incorporates only a single, small section that can be applied to sexual offending: the Risk of Serious Harm (ROSH) category.

In Focus: Risk of Serious Harm (ROSH)

Although neither a bespoke assessment of sexual offending nor an adaptation of any specific (risk) assessment of sexual offending, the ROSH assessment allegedly enables a more detailed examination of any factors that practitioners identify as increasing the young person's risk of causing serious harm to others, such as a history of sexual or violent behaviour (YJB 2008). This three-part Asset section assesses:

1. **Evidence of harm-related behaviour**: assessment of current and previous harm-related behaviour, including unusual behavioural features (e.g. sophisticated methods, recklessness, ritual or bizarre elements), type of victim and context/circumstances of the behaviour (e.g. prior experiences of abuse, emotional instability, certain triggers);
2. **Current risk indicators**: identification of current attitudes, interests and circumstances that may indicate risk of causing harm to others. This section may build on existing findings from the first section, but may also identify new issues concerning attitudes to previous harm-related behaviour (e.g. denials, attitudes to victims), other relevant attitudes (e.g. regarding the acceptability or otherwise of sexual or violent behaviour), current behaviour (e.g. elements from the 'life-style' or 'thinking/behaviour' sections of the core profile that may cause concern) and current circumstances (e.g. access to potential victims, association with peers demonstrating harmful behaviour);
3. **Future harmful behaviour**: practitioners are required to make a judgment regarding the type of harmful behaviour that the young person may commit in the future. This can include deliberate/intentional behaviour (e.g. to inflict harm, to fulfil sexual fantasies) and unplanned/unintentional behaviour (e.g. response to provocation, reckless activity). It is also necessary to flag up any indicators of potential serious harm in the future (e.g. previous patterns of harmful behaviour, current attitudes and interests, forthcoming circumstances, intentions and plans), predicted nature of this harmful behaviour (e.g. sexual offending, violence) and of the potential victim (e.g. younger children, peers, vulnerable adults).

YOT practitioners are required to summarise their ROSH assessment by categorising the young person as low, medium, high or very high risk of causing serious harm to others in the future. This risk rating is then linked to a requirement for additional supervision and monitoring by multiple agencies within the YJS.

Notwithstanding the generic nature of Asset and its questionable (peripheral at best) applicability to the prediction of sexual offending by young people, the government of England and Wales (advised by its semi-independent expert body partner organisation, the YJB) fully committed to risk assessment-intervention in the early 21st century. This position was strengthened by exponential increases in the (generic) evidence bases for developmental risk factor research and 'what works' interventions (Case and Haines 2009), complemented by ostensibly successful evaluations of the predictive validity of Asset (Baker et al. 2002, 2005). So strong was the official support for risk-based youth justice policy and practice (shaped by the RFPP) that a new tool was introduced in 2003 to enable risk assessment-intervention with young people on the cusp of the YJS, but who had yet to become convicted of an offence. The 'Onset' risk assessment instrument was essentially a smaller, abridged version of Asset for use with young people aged 8–13 years who are identified as 'at risk' of offending due to their behaviour and their assessed exposure to a host of psychosocial risk factors. Those young people considered at risk of (first time) offending were then referred to bespoke pre-offending, early intervention schemes offering individualised support packages and situated outside of the formal YJS: Youth Inclusion and Support Panels and Youth Inclusion Programmes' (McCarthy et al. 2004). Consequently, the introduction of Onset demonstrated governmental faith in risk assessment-intervention and illustrated two significant (risk-led) features of the 'new youth justice' that emerged from the Crime and Disorder Act 1998:

1. *Net-widening*: broadening the remit of the YJS and the scope of its influence to incorporate increasing numbers of children and young people (in this case, including children below the age of criminal responsibility, which was set at 10 years) for an increasing range of criminal behaviours (e.g. sexual offending) and non-criminal behaviours (e.g. certain forms of antisocial behaviour), justified by a risk-focused early intervention model. Such net-widening is particularly inappropriate and unnecessary for encompassing young people who sexually offend, as this is a relatively small group of offenders committing a behaviour that is arguably unsuited to and largely unexplored by risk assessment-intervention research and practice;

2. *Interventionism*: employing the risk assessment-intervention rationale to underpin increasing levels of adult-led systemic intervention in order to support, monitor and control young people on the basis of the exposure to risk factors can exert a deterministic influence on later offending unless practitioners intervene. However, research evidence regarding youth offending, including sexual offending, indicates that the majority of young people grow out of crime (the 'maturation hypothesis'), and thus intervention could be largely unnecessary, disproportionate and even criminogenic in many instances (see Case 2017; McAra and McVie 2007).

The Prime of Risk Assessment-Intervention in the Youth Justice System: The Scaled Approach

The risk assessment-intervention project in the YJS of England and Wales reached its peak in November 2009 with the introduction of a new framework known as the 'Scaled Approach' (YJB 2009), which necessitated 'tailoring the intensity of intervention to the assessment' (YJB 2007: 4). The YJB formalised the Scaled Approach for two key practical purposes: to guide the intervention planning of YOT staff administering the new Youth Rehabilitation Order and to encourage more explicit links between risk assessment through Asset and the extent and nature of intervention that resulted. Associated guidance from the YJB instructed practitioners to weight/scale the frequency, nature and intensity of intervention with young people based on their Asset risk score (from 0 to 64), which was to be categorised into three risk groups: low/standard (Asset score 0–14), medium/enhanced (15–32) and high/intensive (33+). Therefore, the Scaled Approach represented 'the zenith of the UK Government commitment to risk-based youth justice (and the RFPP) in policy and practice terms' (Case and Haines 2009: 66).

The Scaled Approach essentially formalised risk assessment-intervention as the explanatory and practice model delivering youth justice in England and Wales. The purported 'evidence base' beyond the developmental risk factor research movement—which has actually generated only limited cogent evidence for the effectiveness of risk-focused intervention (Case and Haines 2009)—was a 'successful' pilot exercise prior to its national roll-out. The new Scaled Approach assessment and intervention framework was piloted in four YOTs across England and Wales. The evaluators claimed to have identified 'broad and clearly defined consensus among the practitioners in the four pilot YOTs that the risk-based approach results in better outcomes for young people' (YJB 2010: 23). However, this further ostensible support for risk assessment-intervention could be seen as premature and somewhat misleading by a critic, even to the point of illustrating a government predilection for 'policy-based evidence'— manipulating evidence to support preformed policy trajectories (Hughes et al. 2002). Criticism is possible on at least four fronts:

1. *Exaggeration:* the evaluation was not conducted over a long enough period to incorporate an analysis of reconviction rates in the pilot areas, so the claim of 'better outcomes' cannot be fully supported;
2. *Uncertainty:* there was a 'lack of information' regarding exactly what practices and interventions (risk-based or otherwise) produced what types of outcomes, which was acknowledged as 'a constraint in making objective assessments of the variety practices that were adopted' (YJB 2010: 14);
3. *Inconsistency:* the information that was available illustrated 'variations in implementation and the different elements of risk-based approaches' (YJB 2010: 23), indicating that the so-called standardised framework was applied inconsistently, making its effectiveness extremely difficult to assess (cf. Sutherland 2009);
4. *Ineffectiveness:* the pilot area considered to have most assiduously implemented the Scaled Approach in line with YJB guidance evidenced a 64% increase in reoffending over the pilot period, indicative of an alarming lack of effectiveness (see Haines and Case 2012).

Notwithstanding the obvious limitations and weaknesses of the pilot exercise, the Scaled Approach framework was rolled out across England and Wales, exemplifying the continued dominance of the RFPP throughout the first decade of the 21st century.

Towards the end of the 2000s, the need for a revised assessment-intervention framework emerged, in part a response to long-standing dissatisfaction with the existing approach from practitioners and critical academics and in part motivated by a change in government (in 2010), which raised concerns over the continued efficacy of the YJB and the nature of the youth justice that it promoted. AssetPlus, a new assessment-intervention framework was formulated to update and progress youth justice assessment-intervention (see stage five) by addressing many of the key, long-standing criticisms of risk assessment-intervention. It is to these criticisms that we now turn.

In Focus: Is the Scaled Approach firt for purpose with young people who sexually offend?

The 'Young People Who Sexually Abuse' KEEP guidance (YJB 2008) advises practitioners that Asset should be the primary assessment tool for use with young people who commit sex offences, with particular attention paid to the Core Record sections covering 'Emotional and Mental Health' and 'Thinking and Behaviour' and the ROSH section). YOT staff are advised that:

> The purpose of assessment is to ensure that accurate decisions have been made in relation to the needs of young people who sexually abuse, and to inform the planning of interventions and supervision to address these needs. (YJB 2008: 10)

Assessment is presented as a cyclical process with five objectives (see Hackett 2004): problem explanation (understanding the behaviour as linked to psychosexual, emotional and social functioning), risk formulation (ROSH assessment), risk management (ROSH management), intervention planning (to prevent sexual offending) and evaluation (measurement of change). Therefore, there is a notable lack of focus on 'risk' factors across the cyclical assessment process, which raises doubts as to the validity and utility of using Asset as the central means of collecting evidence to address each of the stated YJB objectives and of using a scaled risk-led approach as the basis for intervention.

The guidance specifies, however, that Asset risk assessment must not be conducted in isolation, but rather should be integrated with a common assessment model for young people who sexually offend in order to maximise the validity of assessment and subsequent intervention, thus backing away from full commitment to the Scaled Approach framework for use with sexual offenders. An example common assessment model is provided in the form of 'AIM' (Assessment, Intervention and Moving on), which assesses sexual behaviour, development, parents/carers and the environment for 'indicators of concern' and 'strengths' with which to inform intervention. The AIM assessment model sets out 'to obtain the maximum amount of valid information that, when synthesised, can help to shape an informed and graduated inter-agency response' (YJB 2008: 13). The intention is to employ a clinical judgment framework with a simple scoring system that rates static and dynamic factors (like Asset) that are linked explicitly to Asset assessments and are also focused on protecting victims (unlike Asset). Practitioners are instructed to prioritise certain high risk groups, particularly those who have experienced sexual, physical or emotional abuse in the past, young people demonstrating poor social competence of high impulsivity, those with disrupted family backgrounds and young people with educational or learning difficulties. Recommended elements of effective interventions include: emotional competence skills; changing cognitive distortions about sex; prosocial, emotional, cognitive and behaviour skills; risk assessment; sex education; family work; and empathy development (YJB 2008). It could be argued here, however, that the AIM tool contains very little emphasis on 'risk' (only one of multiple components, framed as 'concerns') as its guide to assessment-intervention. It is possible, therefore, to view the Scaled Approach (including Asset) as superfluous (rather than complementary) to the AIM assessment process and to the requirements of practitioners when conducting assessment and intervention with young people who sexually offend.

The Decline of Risk Assessment-Intervention in the Youth Justice System: Reductionist Dichotomies

It is possible to characterise the animation of the RFPP through risk assessment-intervention in the YJS as a series of dichotomies linked to different elements of reductionist practice. These dichotomies cohere around a central debate regarding whether the RFPP facilitated a practical or invalid model of youth justice, particularly for use with young people who sexually offend. In this section, there will be a critical discussion around five key reductionist dichotomies:

1. *Simplification:* practical or invalid?
2. *Determinism:* developmentalism or predictive guesswork?
3. *Individualisation:* appropriate or biased?

4. *Standardisation:* guidance or prescription?
5. *Interventionism:* necessary or disproportionate?

Simplification: Practical or Invalid?

The simplification of the concept of 'risk' by converting it to a quantifiable factor has been intended to reduce complexity, to facilitate replicable research findings and to enable practical, standardised assessment with young people. For example, the quantification and aggregation of risk renders it more amenable to being rated, measured and entered into statistical models that produce clear and consistent conclusions regarding predictive relationships between risk factors and offending. The relationships can then be used as evidence to inform resource allocation and intervention planning. However, critics have asserted that the 'factorisation' of risk actually over-simplifies the area by reducing its potentially complex, multi-faceted and dynamic nature and associated processes to blunt, static numbers solely to facilitate easier measurement and analysis (Case and Haines 2009). These crude factors, it is argued, can dumb down and wash away the inherent complexities of young people's lives, most importantly the ways in which they experience, perceive and construct risks (France 2008). Consequently, the artefactual results of reductionist risk assessment-intervention are unlikely to represent the lived realities of young people who offend in any meaningful or valid ways (see Kemshall 2011; France et al. 2010). Furthermore, far from providing a 'comprehensive profile of the young person's risks and needs that includes both sexual and non-sexual offending' (YJB 2008: 12), neither the predictive accuracy nor validity of Asset (or any equivalent generic/specific risk assessment instrument) has been evidenced sufficiently to date (Campbell et al. 2016; Hempel et al. 2013). The reductionist dichotomy, therefore, is whether the simplification of 'risk' through factorisation is a process that enhances practicality or invalidity.

Determinism: Developmentalism or Predictive Guesswork?

The RFPP and its animation through risk assessment-intervention is founded on academic and political confidence that risk factors exert a developmental and predictive influence on offending. The developmental evidence base indicates that early exposure to risk factors is deterministic of later offending in the absence of risk-focused, preventative intervention. This overriding confidence in the deterministic nature of risk factors has underpinned the evolution of the RFPP in the YJS, most notably through the inception of the Scaled Approach. However, doubts have been raised over the validity of these deterministic claims, especially as they relate to the prediction of reoffending by young people who sexually offend (cf. YJB 2008). Most notably, there has been an insidiously indefinite element to much artefactual, developmental risk factor research relating to the relationship between risk factors and offending. First, the precise nature of a 'risk factor' has not been convincingly concluded across this body of research, with studies variously claiming risk factors as determinants, causes, predictors and indicators of offending. Others identify them as correlates with and symptoms of offending—neither of which would justify the label of 'risk factor', as they are not predicting an outcome. Second, the precise nature of the 'offending' outcome has not been consistent across a risk factor evidence base that has variously linked risk factors to offending at different stages of the criminal career (e.g. first-time offending, reoffending, reconviction), different forms of offending (e.g. serious, violent, persistent, sexual) and different measures of offending (e.g. self-reported, official, recent, lifetime). Third, with regard to sexual offending specifically, there are clear differences between typologies of sexual offending, alongside a very limited knowledge base as to their shared (risk) factors and etiological pathways (Hempel et al. 2013; Hendriks 2006). Consequently, the risk factor research that shapes the evidence base for risk assessment-intervention has been unable to determine and agree upon definitions of risk factors and offending, nor can it determine and agree upon the nature of the relationship between the two—despite an espoused confidence that risk factors determine and predict offending. The reductionist dichotomy, therefore, relates to whether the determinist influence of the risk factors targeted through intervention is justified by the developmental evidence-base or whether it is actually a product of the predictive guesswork required to make sense of an inconsistent and conflicting evidence base.

Individualisation: Appropriate or Biased?

Processes of risk assessment and intervention in the YJS have been individualised in the sense that they tend to target the individual, rather than targeting high risk groups (more typical of pre-offending prevention schemes such as Youth Inclusion Programmes) or offering universal (non-targeted) intervention to all young people in a particular group or area. Risk assessment-intervention has also been individualised in terms of the location of the risk factors being assessed and targeted, prioritising psychosocial risk domains that address risk factors within the individual (e.g. psychological, emotional, attitudinal) or within their immediate social environment (e.g. family, school, neighbourhood). This individualisation has been driven by a developmental evidence-based approach that has consistently identified, replicated and validated a small group of psychosocial risk factors that can be easily measured by practitioners' standardised assessment and that offer straightforward, common-sense targets for intervention. However, a by-product (some critics would argue a specific objective) of the individualisation of risk assessment-intervention has been a psychosocial bias that inadvertently or deliberately neglects to fully consider the potential influence of risk factors in broader socio-structural and contextual domains such as the criminogenic roles of 'socio-economic status, local area...cultural, political or historical context' (Case 2007: 93), not to mention poverty, unemployment, neighbourhood disorganisation and the damaging outcomes of interactions with youth justice agencies. It may well be that such influences have been relatively neglected In both research and policy because many are considered beyond the capability of practitioners seeking to exert a preventative influence on young people. That being said, neglect of such issues and their potential influence on both offending and on psychosocial risk factors for offending (perhaps most notably the notion of criminogenic interactions with the YJS) could be seen as artificially restricting and biasing the evidence base and the explanations and interventions that are privileged by practitioners. The explanations resulting from the RFPP are further biased and restricted by their prioritisation of (preventing/reducing) negative behaviours and outcomes (e.g. reoffending, exposure to risk) to the almost total exclusion of pursuing positive behaviours and outcomes (e.g. educational achievement, access to rights, citizenship); the result is a deficit-based approach that marginalises the potentialities, strengths and capacities of young people that may promote positive outcomes and actually reduce negative outcomes (cf. Case and Haines 2015). In contrast, however, the (non-risk focused) AIM assessment model for sexual offenders prioritises individual strengths as a means of informing future interventions (Griffin and Beech 2004). The reductionist dichotomy, therefore, relates to whether the individualisation of risk factors and risk-focused intervention is an appropriate and valid process based on the guiding evidence-base or whether it biases, restricts and ultimately invalidates assessment and intervention in the YJS.

Standardisation: Guidance or Prescription?

Asset was introduced as a structured risk assessment tool to encourage standardised practice (in conjunction with National Standards and Case Management Guidance) in a YJS where (the government perception was that) there had been too much inconsistency and excessive practitioner discretion in the past, resulting in indeterminate, ineffective and expensive responses to youth offending. The KEEP guidance that accompanied APIS and the Scaled Approach guidance documents sought to standardise and modernise youth justice practice by grounding it in a contemporary evidence base and providing YOT staff with clear information as to how assessment and intervention should be implemented. However, some critics argued that in the pursuit of standardised, 'evidence-based' and 'effective' practice, performance management guidance went too far. In order to both support practitioners in delivering the 'new youth justice' and to avoid allowing excessive practitioner discretion to distort practice, guidelines became prescriptions, becoming too inflexible and restrictive, thus depriving practitioners of the ability to fully utilise their professional expertise, judgment and discretion. An obvious example of such prescription is the Scaled Approach assessment and intervention process, wherein YOT staff are compelled to measure only certain types of risk (psychosocial factors) in certain ways (quantified on a ratings scale), leading to certain explanations of their influence (based on the criminal careers model) that must be responded to with only certain types of intervention (taking from the 'what works' literature that informs the KEEP manuals). This led John Pitts (2001) to describe 21st century youth justice practice as 'korrectional karaoke', characterised by overly technical, routine, mechanical instructions rather than guidance, all of which contributed to the 'zombification of youth justice' (see also Souhami 2007).

Interventionism: Necessary or Disproportionate?

The government's strong belief in risk assessment-intervention culminated in the Scaled Approach framework, which was introduced for the practical purpose of formalising and standardising the relationship between assessment and intervention outcomes. The developmental evidence base and the RFPP suggested that were predictive of later offending and so should be targeted through increasing amounts of intervention (the concept of 'interventionism'), particularly as young people were passive recipients of risk exposure and were helpless to resist or negotiate this exposure without adult support—'crash test dummies' inevitably damaged by risks that they cannot control (Case and Haines 2009). However, the alleged appropriateness of risk-focused intervention is a problematic claim, both evidentially and in practice. In evidential terms, there is a wealth of evidence (albeit problematic in itself) that identified risk factors statistically predict offending, yet there is nothing like the same level of evidence that intervention targeting these risk factors can prevent or reduce offending (Goldson 2005). Indeed, many of the risk factor research studies that form the evidence base for the Scaled Approach (e.g. the Cambridge Study in Delinquent Development, West and Farrington 1973) did not include an intervention element. The most well-known and significant risk factor studies that have included an intervention element (e.g. the Cambridge Somerville Youth Study, McCord 1978; the Seattle Social Development Project, Hawkins et al. 2003) have tended to find no convincing impact on offending or even damaging effects (e.g. labelling, criminalisation) on the young person. Therefore, confidence in the utility of risk-focused intervention is arguably disproportionate to the extent and nature of the supporting evidence for this approach. On a practical level, there is further danger of disproportionality. Scaling level of intervention to assess the risk of what a young person might do in the future (rather than what they have actually done) has the potential to encourage excessive or insufficient intervention if risk level is misjudged and the potential for maturation/growing out of crime is ignored. For example, a young person assessed as high risk of reoffending, but who ultimately does/would not reoffend (a 'false positive'), could receive an unjustified, excessive level of intervention, whereas a 'low risk' young person who ultimately does/would reoffend (a 'false negative') may receive insufficient support to address their needs and to prevent them experiencing further problems. The predictive validity of Asset attests to this potential danger. Following evaluation, Asset was found to correctly predict outcomes (reoffending or not) in 69% of cases after one year (Baker et al. 2002) and 67% after two years (Baker et al. 2005). This level of predictive accuracy may outperform equipment adult assessment tools, but it still incorrectly predicts outcomes for one in three young people, with the potential false positives and negatives receiving disproportionate intervention. The reductionist dichotomy, therefore, regards whether interventionism is a necessary response to an evidence base that views risk-focused intervention as an effective method of supporting young people exposed to psychosocial risk factors that they cannot resist, or whether such intervention is disproportionate based on the lack of cogent evidence of effectiveness, low levels of predictive validity and inconsistent to non-existent predictive validity when assessing young people who sexually offend.

It is clear the risk assessment-intervention in the YJS can be evaluated against a series of dichotomies that focus on the reductionist methods and explanations that underpin the approach, most notably whether this reductionism is justified as a practical tool compared to whether the processes actually invalidate the results of research and recommendations for practice. Arguments that risk assessment-intervention is unrepresentative of the real lives of young people have been consolidated by further criticisms that assessment methods marginalise and neglect the voices, experiences and expertise of key stakeholders, most notably the young people who have offended and the practitioners assessing the reasons for this behaviour and planning appropriate responses to it (Case 2006, 2007). Perhaps the real 'risk' in the youth justice assessment-intervention process is the risk of producing invalid explanations and responses to youth offending due to insufficient integration on the experiences and perspectives of the two main parties in the process, in favour of pursuing an inflexible, restricted explanatory and practice model (the RFPP) produced by academics and validated based on its political expedience.

The Rebirth of Assessment Intervention in the Youth Justice System: AssetPlus

The growing body of critique aimed at (Scaled Approach) risk assessment-intervention in the YJS, along with an emerging sense that the paradigm was becoming outdated, encouraged the YJB to consult widely with practitioners, policymakers and academics in an attempt to identify a more effective assessment-intervention model. Following a protracted and politically complex process of consultation and development, a revised assessment and intervention framework known as 'AssetPlus' (YJB 2013, 2014; see also Haines and Case 2015) was rolled out across England and Wales in 2015. This new and improved framework committed to addressing the perceived limitations and weaknesses of the previous Scaled Approach model by providing practitioners with a more holistic, contextualised and dynamic assessment-intervention framework that was no longer wedded to risk, nor the inherently reductionist processes and explanations associated with it. AssetPlus was promoted as a modernised, sensitive and reflective assessment-intervention process that placed more emphasis on elements much neglected by the more technical Scaled Approach, such as on the perspectives of young people, the discretion and expertise of practitioners, and young people's needs, strengths and aspirations to change and to desist from offending (YJB 2013, 2014). The Asset risk assessment instrument was abandoned and replaced by a tripartite, iterative 'Core Record' process consisting of information gathering and description, explanations and conclusions, pathways and planning.

Information Gathering and Description

The opening section of the Core Record is the initial assessment portion of AssetPlus (essentially replacing Asset) with four quadrants of assessment. The first quadrant, 'personal family and social factors', measures young people's exposure to problems in their current life relating to family and environment, parenting, care and supervision and personal development. Although situated in psychosocial domains (equivalent to Asset), these 'problems' are to be identified as needs to be addressed rather than risks to be prevented and were not quantified/factorised, thereby signifying an explicit move away from artefactual risk assessment. The second quadrant measures 'offending/antisocial behaviour' (equipment to Asset), supplementing previous measures with a more detailed focus on patterns of offending over time. The third 'foundations for change' quadrant is new, exploring factors that can promote/prevent behavioural change in the young person (e.g. resilience to risk, desistance), including change that leads to positive outcomes. The final quadrant is a self-assessment section completed by young people and their parents/carers. This renewed emphasis on self-assessment (a reboot of the poorly completed 'What do you think?' section of Asset) is intended to facilitate the integration of young people's perspectives on their own needs and the type of intervention that will promote desistance and positive outcomes.

Explanations and Conclusions

Data from the Information Gathering and Description section is extrapolated in the second assessment element of AssetPlus, entitled 'Explanations and Conclusions', which constitutes a larger, consolidated version of the previous narrative evidence boxes in Asset and subsumes the previous ROSH assessment section. The emphasis here is on enhanced use of practitioner discretion to produce more holistic, comprehensive explanations of the influences on young people's offending behaviour.

These explanations are intended to be more dynamic, less reductionist and deterministic than those promulgated through Asset, with more contextual and temporal sensitivity to interactions between a broad range of influences (including psychosocial factors and life events) in the young person's past and present life (Haines and Case 2015; YJB 2013, 2014). Once again, there is a move away from quantified ratings. However, the insidious reliance on risk-based perspectives seems to re-emerge by stealth in the required summative ratings of 'likelihood of reoffending' ('indicative' and 'final') as high, medium or low (YJB 2013) and ROSH rated as very high, high, medium or low—clear throwbacks to the categorisation of the Scaled Approach.

Pathways and Planning

The final, intervention-focused section of AssetPlus is called 'Pathways and Planning'. This section is intended to animate foregoing assessment sections by assisting YOT staff to design appropriate, meaningful and responsive interventions that address the influences on offending behaviour and promote positive outcomes around well-being, safety, engagement, participation, desistance, change and strengths. The nature of the interventions implicated in this final section signifies a further move away from risk-focused prevention/intervention responses and towards interventions that are more relevant and valid to the young person's assessed circumstances, experiences and perceptions (YJB 2013; see also Case and Haines 2015). It is important to note at this stage, however, that the implementation of AssetPlus (which was never formally piloted or evaluated in the public domain) remains in its infancy. Lessons have let yet to be learned regarding its practicality, effectiveness, efficiency, economy or appropriateness from the perspectives of key stakeholders in the process: the YJB, practitioners, victims, communities, parents/carers and young people who come into contact with the YJS. It is also notable that there is no specific guidance relating to (or even mention of) the assessment and intervention of sexual offending (only guidance relating to young people who have experienced sexual abuse), so the ongoing applicability of this less risk-focused framework remains unexplored and unsupported.

Conclusion: Risk Assessment-Intervention with Young People Who Sexually Offend

This chapter has charted the trajectory of risk assessment-intervention in the YJS of England and Wales, evaluating its appropriateness as a framework for responding to young offenders in general and those who sexually offend specifically. The trajectory of risk assessment-intervention has been represented as a five-stage journey (a 'life course') beginning with its birth in the YJS in the 1990s as a response to the pressures of the risk society and the popularity of actuarial justice and the RFPP. The growth of the risk assessment-intervention model in the YJS was perpetuated by the Crime and Disorder Act 1998 and the formalisation of the Asset tool (along with its Onset baby brother) as a structured, standardised (psychosocial) risk assessment instrument that was considered appropriate for use with young people who sexually offend. Risk-based assessment and intervention peaked in the YJS with the inception of the Scaled Approach framework in 2009. This framework consolidated and extended the government's commitment to the RFPP as the central tool for understanding youth offending by explicitly linking evidence of assessed risk with intervention outcomes, including its continued application to sexual offenders, regardless of the absence of detailed or supportive evidence of validity in this area. Stage four (2010 onwards) represented a crisis in confidence for risk assessment-intervention, prompted by long-standing academic criticisms and a change in government rendering the future of the YJB insecure. Academic critique of the widespread reductionism of the RFPP and its related risk factor research cohered around five clear dichotomies concerned with: simplification (practical-invalid), determinism (developmentalism-predictive guesswork), individualisation (appropriate-biased), standardisation (guidance-prescription) and interventionism (necessary-disproportionate). The final stage of (d)evolution risk assessment-intervention in the YJS was the loss of faith in the Scaled Approach and its replacement with a revised assessment-intervention framework called AssetPlus, which (largely) marked a move away from a risk focus and towards more valid, meaningful and holistic assessment-intervention that incorporates a broader range of (qualitative) measures, enhanced practitioner discretion and more emphasis on young people's perspectives. However, AssetPlus remains wedded to risk to some degree. Furthermore, the risk prediction project remains flawed and uncertain in its generic form, particularly in relation to young people who sexually offend. The evidence base relating to the predictive validity of risk assessment-intervention for young people who sexually offend and its contribution to understanding their etiological influences, typologies and pathways, remains inconsistent and insufficient, to the extent that the validity of shaping interventions based on these assessments must be seriously questioned (see Campbell et al. 2016; Hempel et al. 2013; YJB 2008; Hendriks 2006; Worling 2001). Such invalidity and uncertainty has encouraged the YJB to pursue a more 'comprehensive assessment framework' by complementing Asset data with data from the specific AIM instrument. In their guide to effective practice with young people who sexually offend, the YJB (2008) concedes that more research is required on assessment and outcome in order to better understand how Asset and AIM are related to one another and enhance the management of risk. However, now that Asset and the Scaled Approach have been abandoned and replaced, this recommendation appears obsolete.

This chapter demonstrates that the use of risk assessment with young people who sexually offend has, to date, been underpinned by three uncritical and ultimately invalid assumptions: that adult-focused assessments of sexual offending are readily transferable/applicable to young people, that risk assessment tools have an appropriate level of predictive validity to guide intervention, and that risk is a useful concept to enhance understandings of sexual offending by young people. The inevitable conclusion is that the practical validity of risk assessment-intervention/the RFPP for use with young people who sexually offend remains questionable/uncertain at best and at worst inappropriate and unhelpful.

References

Audit Commission. (1996). *Misspent youth*. London: Audit Commission.

Baker, K., Jones, S., Roberts, C., & Merrington, S. (2002). *Validity and reliability of asset*. London: YJB.

Baker, K., Jones, S., Roberts, C., & Merrington, S. (2005). *Further development of asset*. London: Youth Justice Board.

Beck, U. (1992). *Risk society: Towards a new modernity*. London: Sage.

Blyth, M., Solomon, E., & Baker, K. (2007). *Young people and risk*. Bristol: Policy Press.

Caldwell, M. F. (2002). What we do not know about juvenile sexual reoffense risk. *Child Maltreatment, 7*, 291–302.

Campbell, F., Booth, A., Stepanova, E., Hackett, S., Sutton, A., Hynes, K., Sanderson, J., & Rogstad, K. (2016). *Harmful sexual behaviour in children*. https://www.nice.org.uk/guidance/NG55/documents/evidence-review-2. Accessed Jan 2017.

Case, S. P. (2006). Young people 'at risk' of what? Challenging risk-focused early intervention as crime prevention. *Youth Justice, 6*(3), 171–179. doi:10.1177/1473225406069491.

Case, S. P. (2007). Questioning the 'evidence' of risk that underpins evidence-led youth justice interventions. *Youth Justice, 7*(2), 91–106. doi:10.1177/1473225407078771.

Case, S. P. (2017). *Contemporary youth justice*. London: Routledge.

Case, S. P., & Haines, K. R. (2009). *Understanding youth offending: Risk factor research, policy and practice*. Cullompton: Willan.

Case, S. P., & Haines, K. R. (2015). Risk management and early intervention. In B. Goldson & J. Muncie (Eds.), *Youth, crime and justice*. London: Sage.

Case, S. P., & Haines, K. R. (2016). Taking the risk out of youth justice. In C. Trotter, G. McIvor, & F. McNeill (Eds.), *Beyond the risk paradigm in criminal justice*. London: Palgrave.

Farrington, D. P. (1996). *Understanding and preventing youth crime*. York: Joseph Rowntree Foundation.

Farrington, D. (2007). Childhood risk factors and risk-focused prevention. In M. Maguire, R. Morgan, & R. Reiner (Eds.), *The Oxford handbook of criminology*. Oxford: Oxford University Press.

Feeley, M. M., & Simon, J. (1992). The new penology: Notes on the emerging strategy of corrections and its implications. *Criminology, 30*, 449–474. Available at: http://scholarship.law.berkeley.edu/facpubs/718

France, A. (2008). Risk factor analysis and the youth question. *Journal of Youth Studies, 11*(1), 1–15. doi:10.1080/13676260701690410.

France, A., Freiberg, K., & Homel, R. (2010). Beyond risk factors: Towards a holistic prevention paradigm for children and young people. *British Journal of Social Work, 40*(4), 1192–1210. doi:10.1093/bjsw/bcq010.

Goldson, B. (2000). *The new youth justice*. Lyme Regis: Russell House.

Goldson, B. (2005). Taking liberties: Policy and the punitive turn. In H. Hendrick (Ed.), *Child welfare and social policy*. Bristol: Policy Press.

Griffin, H., & Beech, A. (2004). *Evaluation of the AIM framework for the assessment of adolescents who display harmful sexual behaviour*. London: YJB.

Grove, W. M., & Meehl, P. E. (1996). Comparative efficiency of informal (subjective, impressionistic) and formal (mechanical, algorithmic) prediction. *Psychology, Public Policy and Law, 2*, 293–323. http://citeseerx.ist.psu.edu/viewdoc/download?doi=10.1.1.514.1187&rep=rep1&type=pdf. Accessed 10 Apr 2017.

Hackett, S. (2004). *What works for children and young people with harmful sexual behaviours*. Essex: Barnardo's.

Haines, K. R., & Case, S. P. (2012). Is the scaled approach a failed approach? *Youth Justice, 12*(3), 212–228. doi:10.1177/1473225412461212.

Haines, K. R., & Case, S. P. (2015). *Positive youth justice: Children first, offenders second*. Bristol: Policy Press.

Hawkins, J. D., & Catalano, R. F. (1992). *Communities that care*. San Francisco: Jossey-Bass.

Hawkins, J. D., Smith, B. H., Hill, K. G., Kosterman, R., Catalano, R. F., & Abbott, R. D. (2003). Understanding and preventing crime and violence. Findings from the Seattle social development project. In T. P. Thornberry & M. D. Krohn (Eds.), *Taking stock of delinquency: An overview of findings from contemporary longitudinal studies*. New York: Kluwer.

Hempel, I., Buck, N., Cima, M., & van Marle, H. (2013). Review of risk assessment instruments for Juvenile sex offenders. What is next? *International Journal of Offender Therapy and Comparative Criminology, 57*(2), 208–228. doi:10.1177/0306624X11428315.

Hendriks, J. (2006). *Jeugdige zedendelinquenten: Een studie naar subtypen en recidive* [Juvenile sexual offenders: A study of subtypes and recidivism]. Utrecht: Forum Educatief.

Hughes, G., Muncie, J., & McLaughlin, E. (2002). *Crime prevention and community safety. New directions*. London: Sage.

Kemshall, H. (2008). Risk, rights and justice: Understanding and responding to youth risk. *Youth Justice, 8*(1), 21–38. doi:10.1177/1473225407087040.

Kemshall, H. (2011). Crime and risk: Contested territory for risk theorising. *International Journal of Law, Crime and Justice, 39*(4), 218–229. doi:10.1016/j.ijlcj.2011.05.009.

Laub, J., & Sampson, R. (2003). *Shared beginnings, delinquent lives. Delinquent boys to age 70*. London: Harvard University Press.

Mason, P., & Prior, D. (2008). The children's fund and the prevention of crime and anti-social behaviour. *Criminology and Criminal Justice, 8*(3), 279–296. doi:10.1177/1748895808092430.

McAra, L., & McVie, S. (2007). Youth justice? The impact of system contact on patterns of desistance from offending. *European Journal of Criminology, 4*(3), 315–345.

McCarthy, P., Laing, K., & Walker, J. (2004). *Offenders of the future: Assessing the risk of children and young people becoming involved in criminal or antisocial behaviour.* London: Department for Education and Skills. http://217.35.77.12/research/england/welfare/RR545.pdf. Accessed 10 Apr 2017.

McCord, J. (1978, March). A thirty year follow-up of treatment effects. *American Psychologist, 33,* 284–289.

Miner, M. (2002). Factors associated with recidivism in juveniles: An analysis of serious juvenile sex offenders. *Journal of Research in Crime and Delinquency, 39,* 421–436. doi:10.1177/002242702237287.

Muncie, J. (2008). Managerialism. In B. Goldson (Ed.), *The dictionary of youth justice.* Cullompton: Willan.

Pitts, J. (2001). Korrectional karaoke: New labour and the zombification of youth justice. *Youth Justice, 1*(2), 3–16.

Prior, D., & Paris, A. (2005). *Preventing children's involvement in crime and antisocial behaviour: A literature review.* Birmingham: DfES.

Righthand, S., Prentky, R., Knight, R., Carpenter, E., Hecker, J. E., & Nangle, D. (2005). Factor structure and validation of the juvenile sex offender assessment protocol (J-SOAP). *Sexual Abuse: Journal of Research and Treatment, 17,* 13–30. doi:10.1007/s11194-005-1207-7.

Smith, R. (2005). Welfare versus justice – Again! *Youth Justice, 5*(1), 3–16. doi:10.1177/147322540500500102.

Souhami, A. (2007). *Transforming youth justice. Occupational identity and cultural change.* Cullompton: Willan.

Stephenson, M., Giller, H., & Brown, S. (2007). *Effective practice in youth justice.* Cullompton: Willan.

Sutherland, A. (2009). The 'scaled approach' in youth justice. Fools rush in…. *Youth Justice, 9*(1), 44–60. doi:10.1177/1473225408101431.

West, D. J., & Farrington, D. P. (1973). *Who becomes delinquent?* London: Heinemann.

Worling, J. R. (2001). Personality-based typology of adolescent male sexual offenders: Differences in recidivism rates, victim-selection characteristics, and personal victimization histories. *Sexual Abuse: A Journal of Research and Treatment, 13,* 149–166. doi:10.1177/107906320101300301.

Worling, J. R. (2004). The estimate of risk of adolescent sexual offence recidivism (ERASOR): Preliminary psychometric data. *Sexual Abuse, 16,* 235–254. doi:10.1177/107906320401600305.

Youth Justice Board. (2000). *ASSET*. London: YJB.
Youth Justice Board. (2003). *Assessment, planning interventions and supervision. Source Document*. London: YJB.
Youth Justice Board. (2007). *The scaled approach*. London: YJB.
Youth Justice Board. (2008). *Young people who sexually abuse*. London: YJB.
Youth Justice Board. (2009). *Youth justice: The scaled approach. A framework for assessment and interventions. Post-consultation version two*. London: YJB.
Youth Justice Board. (2010). *Process evaluation of the pilot of a risk-based approach to interventions*. London: YJB.
Youth Justice Board. (2013). *Assessment and planning interventions framework – AssetPlus. Model Document*. London: YJB.
Youth Justice Board. (2014). *AssetPlus*. London: YJB.
Zimring, F. E. (2004). *An American travesty: Legal responses to adolescent sexual offending*. Chicago: University of Chicago Press.

4

Managing Sexual and Violent Offenders Across EU Borders

Sarah Hilder

Introduction and Context

This chapter discusses the challenges presented by the increased ease of opportunity for transient serious violent or sexual offenders to move across European Union (EU) borders. The Serious Offending by Mobile European Criminals (SOMEC) project was commissioned by the European Commission Directorate-General for Home Affairs, running from 2013 to 2015.[1] It brought together a range of EU law enforcement and probation personnel to investigate the use of existing mechanisms for information exchange available to EU Member States, to assist in the monitoring and management of serious violent or sexual offenders who are mobile across the EU community. The discussion here focuses on key themes mirrored elsewhere in this volume and highlights issues pertaining to varied understandings and commitments to concepts of risk, multi-agency working, and privacy and data protection. A number of EU

S. Hilder (✉)
Nottingham Trent University, Nottingham, UK

© The Author(s) 2017
H. Kemshall, K. McCartan (eds.), *Contemporary Sex Offender Risk Management,*
Volume II, Palgrave Studies in Risk, Crime and Society,
DOI 10.1007/978-3-319-63573-6_4

legislative frameworks support a proactive engagement in shared cross-border understandings of who is high risk and outline when it is legitimately viable to disclose such information, how such information should be exchanged, and with whom (ICMPD 2010). However, establishing an EU-wide commitment to such practices remains in its infancy. The chapter explores the challenges of pursing this endeavour, together with the implications of not doing so. It also reflects on the UK's future withdrawal from the EU community and assumptions that 'closed borders' are a quick fix solution.

Cross-Border Criminality and Cooperation

The recognition of crimes which transcend national borders and which require international police, judicial, and penal policy cooperation is well established across the EU community (Thomas 2011). The rise in transnational crime over recent years is broadly attributed to the opportunities presented by the internet, an increase in the ease and costs of international travel, and globalisation[2] (Messenger 2012). The 'open space' of the Schengen area and the freedom of movement provided by membership of the EU has also been characterised as a 'security risk' and a 'potential crime space' (Jacobs and Blitsa 2008; Parkin 2011), requiring strengthened police cooperation. The tension between addressing commonly identified, mobile threats (such as terrorism and organised crime) and the benefits of open borders has been frequently debated (Bigo 1998, 2008; Hobbing 2011; Nanz 1996; Stelfox 2003; Zaiotti 2007), and is largely managed by cross-border information exchange and joint investigation teams facilitated by Europol. Whilst cross-border issues pertaining to terrorism and other forms of serious organised crime have tended to dominate EU law enforcement collaborations, the cross-border movement of serious violent or sexual offenders has also been evident[3] (May-Chahal and Herczog 2003). In 2010, the UK Child Exploitation and Online Protection Service (CEOP 2010) found that some 70% of high and very high risk sexual offenders had travelled abroad to offend against children, whilst others may move in order to avoid detection and supervisory conditions (Lammers and Bernasco 2013, Thomas 2011,

2013). However, due to the under-reporting of such offences and variable detection, prosecution, and recording practices across EU jurisdictions, obtaining reliable data on the prevalence of serious violent and sexual crimes, including those committed by individuals from other EU Member States, presents some profound challenges (Davies 2013, p. 6). Until the launch of the European Criminal Information System (ECRIS) in 2012,[4] there were no shared definitions of such offences across the EU, and currently any estimate of the number of serious violent and sexual offenders who travel across borders to offend should be treated with some scepticism. Nevertheless, the seriousness of the issue has been recognised (De Pourbaix-Lundin 2010), with a number of high profile cases illustrating the tragic consequences of failing to manage the mobility and risk posed by what is likely, in reality, to be 'a critical few'.[5]

The impact of organised crime and terrorism[6] and issues such as football hooliganism have been met with a coordinated European response and the development of an overarching EU framework which enables the exchange of information for the prevention of serious crime to occur. Whilst this facility has been utilised to provide effective exchanges of information on known high risk perpetrators, such as those who are travelling to sporting events with the primary purpose of engaging in violence (Frosdick and Marsh 2005), the risk and modus operandi of the single transient violent or sexual offender has received far less attention. This enables the perpetrator to enter another EU Member State unmonitored and unchecked, with the receiving Member State only becoming aware of the risk of harm posed following the commission of further serious offences. Such insights and concerns have prompted developments such as the issue of Directive 2011/36/EU of the European Parliament and of the Council of 5 April 2011 on preventing and combating trafficking in human beings and protecting its victims and Directive 2011/93/EU of the European Parliament and of the Council of 13 December 2011 on combating the sexual abuse and sexual exploitation of children and child pornography. Although still limited to organised crime and child sexual offending, this interest from the EU and Europol has focused more directly on the mobility of sexual offenders. Attempts to develop an EU-wide sex offender register have also been pursued, although ultimately thwarted, by the lack of any identification of such offenders by some EU Member States at a national level and differences in approaches to offender supervision, legislative systems, and data protection mandates (De Pourbaix-Lundin 2010; Hilder and Kemshall 2014).

Existing Frameworks and Mechanisms for Information Exchange

The EU Swedish Framework Decision 2006/960/JHA principle of availability[7] established a permissive framework for law enforcement information exchange and cooperation across EU borders. Several mechanisms for the actual transfer of different types of criminality information then exist, which include ECRIS, Interpol disseminations, communication via Central Bureau and Embassy staff and Europol National Units, with facilities for more general alerts possible via the second generation of the Schengen Information System (SIS II) and Interpol Notices. Communication between prisons and probation across the EU primarily occurs in relation to the transfer of custodial (Framework Decision 2008/909/JHA) and community sentences (Framework Decision 2008/947/JHA (FD947)).[8] Some mechanisms have a particular function, whereas others provide flexibility to support a range of different communications. The ECRIS system, for example, exchanges conviction data in order to retain a central record of a home national's offending in other EU Member States. However, it can also be utilised to facilitate requests to obtain information on an EU foreign national appearing in other European Courts, to assist in a comprehensive assessment of the individual's past pattern of offending and current level of risk, although it is less well utilised in this respect. Other systems may be used to disseminate information to find missing children, track down known offenders who have evaded investigative and prosecution proceedings, to detect or prevent crime, or to disrupt organised crime or other serious criminal activities. Criminal intelligence data as well as convictions may be exchanged and circulated (for a fuller discussion see Hilder and Kemshall 2014).

Earlier research studies have highlighted a number of significant barriers to the operational use of exchange mechanisms (EC 2010), including a level of reluctance to do so from some EU Member States. The provision of opportunities for these various types of exchange can therefore be very different from an effective implementation of such measures (EC 2010; ICMPD 2010; Walsh 2006). Practical difficulties arise, such as lack of resources to manage both incoming and outgoing communications. National legal restrictions and varying ethical views of the right to make such disclosures also exacerbate inconsistencies in the approach taken to managing criminality information exchanges across the EU (Hilder and Kemshall 2016). Magee (2008) highlights that whilst the principles of law enforcement cooperation and information exchange may be generally supported, in practice this requires some level of uniformity which may be challenging to achieve. Such observations were also reflected in the SOMEC data, and whilst a pragmatic approach might be taken to address inconsistencies in the process and quality of information exchanges between EU Member States, other barriers are more heavily steeped in historically embedded ideologies which may prove more challenging to resolve. The discussion of the SOMEC research which follows therefore focuses particularly on these latter issues and pertains to data findings on risk assessment, multi-agency working, and privacy and data protection.

The SOMEC Project

Methodology Overview

The SOMEC project ran from 2013 to 2015. The research team, led by De Montfort University and including a leading police expert and probation specialists, sought to fulfil two specific project aims:

- To identify the methods and effectiveness of information exchange mechanisms used by EU Member States in the management of serious violent or sexual offenders travelling across borders.

- To explore critical success factors and provide recommendations to facilitate the improved exchange of information for the prevention of crime.

These aims were achieved via the mapping of existing criminality information exchange mechanisms and their relevance to the single, transient, serious violent or sexual offender (see Hilder and Kemshall 2014). A field study was then undertaken focusing on the understanding and use of such mechanisms by relevant operational law enforcement and probation staff (see Kemshall et al. 2015). In brief, the methodology comprised 37 structured interviews with law enforcement personnel from 23 Member States using an interview schedule of predetermined questions,[9] and 28 structured interviews with probation personnel from 20 Member States. Structured interviews with experts were also conducted on key EU-wide information exchange systems such as ECRIS, Europol, and SIS II, involving law enforcement officers in the Supplementary Information Request at National Entry (SIRENE) Bureau and embassy liaison officers, with specialist law enforcement officers responsible for combating serious sexual and violent offending. The interview schedules were developed following initial background interviews with subject experts, a literature review, and test interviews with project partners from four different Member States. Initial findings and draft recommendations were disseminated via three task groups held in the UK, Latvia, and the Netherlands, attended by 37 law enforcement and probation participants from 17 EU Member States. These task groups largely comprised of personnel who had previously participated in the structured interviews, and enabled a limited participant check and validation of findings.

Whilst the study targeted lead law enforcement and offender management staff in all 28 EU Member States, the difference in national structures and local organisation meant that a range of personnel with varying policy and operational responsibilities participated. The position was also complicated by the range of information exchange mechanisms currently available, managed by various arrangements of specialist staff across the

EU with differing national structures for cross-border information exchange and offender supervision. Other factors that may have influenced the information that respondents disclosed included the potential gap between management and frontline staff perspectives, with a degree of probability that some responses reflected a particular role and responsibility in the relevant agency. On occasion, the depth of the interview may also have been influenced by the researcher's background knowledge of the Member States, their working processes, and the limited availability of interpretation services, resulting in the majority of the interviews being conducted in English. Where possible, case studies were also sought to gain a more comprehensive picture of information exchange and the management of serious violent or sexual offenders. A full evaluation of participant recruitment, the development of research tools, limitations to the data, and the iterative process of comparative analysis which was applied are detailed in the full report (Kemshall et al. 2015).

Commonalities with previous studies were identified, and whilst there was an overall willingness from respondents to improve the quality and effectiveness of cross-border information exchanges more generally, there was a clear disparity of views on the legality and necessity to do so in the case of the individual serious violent or sexual offender. Some of the more practical issues raised—which are not covered in detail in this chapter but are addressed in the original research report (Kemshall et al. 2015)—included: variations in the use of conditional release from custody; a lack of knowledge of the permissive EU framework which enables cross-border information exchanges to occur; a lack of centralised management of exchange mechanisms at a national level; poor targeting and quality of information in the exchanges being made; and the limited capacity of some receiving Member States to respond proactively. Perhaps more poignant, however, were issues which reflected more fundamental contrasts in penal approaches and the perception and prioritisation of concepts of risk assessment, collaborative working, and privacy and individual rights (McAlinden 2012; Ruggiero 2013). It is to a discussion of these particular challenges that this chapter now turns.

The Assessment of Serious Violent or Sexual Offenders

A selected list of offence codes from ECRIS was used as a starting point to examine how serious violent or sexual offenders were identified at the national level (see Kemshall et al. 2015, pp. 30–35). Whilst there was a general consensus that these categories reflected serious violent or sexual offending, issues of interpretation and transferability to national legal frameworks were recognised. Probation personnel were more likely to see the index offence as only one strategy by which a serious violent or sexual offender could be identified, and argued for further contextual information in order to establish whether the potential harm was still apparent or had changed in any way. However, probation respondents from only six Member States stated that structured assessment processes were utilised at a national level to ascertain the level of harm posed by a serious violent or sexual offender. For three of these Member States this included the use of an appropriately validated structured risk assessment tool. A further two Member States reported using structured assessment processes, but without the use of a formalised assessment tool or checklist. Another two Member States described comprehensive assessment systems based within the prison system, in one instance linked to a strong focus on rehabilitative programmes undertaken during the custodial period, with the other example being used to inform community supervision.

Five Member States identified serious violent or sexual offenders as a distinct category subject to special measures and/or formal assessment; in other jurisdictions they were not distinguished from other offender types in any way. Where identification and assessments did occur, they were undertaken by a range of personnel at various stages of the criminal justice process. These differing views of, and varied levels of engagement in, the identification and assessment of serious violent or sexual offenders also reflected the diverse forms and functions of the probation service across the EU. Those Member States who might be considered Anglophone jurisdictions[10] tended to have a greater focus on public protection and risk assessment (Kemshall 2008), with other jurisdictions more centred on welfare, and on rehabilitation and reintegration models (van Kalmthout and Durnescu 2008). These variations have significant implications for effective cross-border information exchange, as risk and protective factors may be weighted differently by assessors as a result of the underpinning focus and philosophy of the approach taken, and in some instances assessment will not focus on risk concerns at all. An expectation that a final assessment will occur at the end of any supervisory period of contact with an offender either in custody or the community is also not universal. Whilst approaches to managing the risk of sexual and violent offenders varied in this manner, concerns were raised by respondents themselves that inaccurate assessments were highly problematic in any process of cross-border information exchange. Probation personnel, in particular, were concerned that a subjective approach may prevail, resulting in significant infringements on an individual's human rights. There were tendencies, however, to see this as a rationale for not exchanging information with other Member States rather than seeking to address the approach to assessment which occurred at a national level. It was emphasised during task group discussions that any assessment which leads to a specific categorisation as a serious violent or sexual offender needs to be subject to routine opportunities for review and de-categorisation.

Joined Up, Collaborative Working Across Agencies

In addition to the varied understandings of, and approaches taken to, the assessment of a serious violent or sexual offender across EU Member States, the research highlighted that the identification and assessment of serious violent and sexual offenders is also rarely carried out in partnership. Again, whilst task group activities and focus groups highlighted that the value of effective joint working between law enforcement and probation personnel in the assessment and management of serious violent or sexual offenders was broadly recognised, for the majority of EU Member States this was not a reality. Information exchange between agencies at a national level was often impeded, for example, by a lack of protocols, formal systems, legal frameworks, and simply a lack of trust between different criminal justice partners. The varying profile, professional status, and primary function of probation services across the EU is likely to influence their standing with other agencies. However, there were also examples of disconnections internally across the law enforcement sector where, in particular, federal, regional, and local divisions were not always fully apprised of the various possibilities for cross-border information exchange that could occur, with knowledge of such systems often limited to those responsible for them operationally. Similarly, probation staff were often unaware of the sources of information available to them, such as ECRIS. This could result in court assessment reports lacking appropriate conviction details, and sentences being made in the absence of full conviction histories.

Three interview respondents from the same Member State provided details of formal multi-agency arrangements for the identification and assessment of serious violent or sexual offenders. A single point of contact (SPOC) in every Member State was promoted as an effective method of managing both the collection of nationally held data on a high risk individual and any subsequent cross-border information exchanges required. It was acknowledged that the development of SPOCs in every EU Member State was being pursued, housing all of the existing facilities utilised, such as Interpol, SIS II, and Europol National Units. At the time of the study, SPOCs were primarily operated by law enforcement personnel, although the SOMEC project findings indicate that this should be extended to include probation personnel to further assist appropriate assessments, transmissions, and responses to information on transient serious violent or sexual offenders.

Probation personnel participating in the research tasks groups also emphasised that offender movement across borders can serve a very positive rehabilitative function which should not be over looked in the pursuit of public protection and prevention priorities. Offenders may cross a border for a short period of time for work, family commitments, or holidays, or routinely cross a border for employment, then returning home again.[11] In these situations, a number of Member States faced an operational need to exchange information, resulting in the development of bilateral agreements and a memorandum of understanding, although this predominantly facilitates information sharing between law enforcement rather than probation services. However, where multi-agency arrangements have been developed at a national level, probation is also often integral to such cross-border strategies.[12] These agreements have been driven by an operational need and are effective for Member States with shared borders, but they are not necessarily transferable on a wider scale across the EU as a solution. These arrangements can often require a common language, and justice systems which share strongly compatible approaches to offence definitions and to judicial and penal responses, which is not commonplace across the wider EU community.

Ethical Issues and the Right to Make Disclosures

Concerns were raised by research participants regarding the safeguards which were needed to ensure that rights to privacy and data protection were observed in any process of cross-border information exchange. Respondents from seven Member States highlighted the different legal parameters and national restrictions on making such disclosures as barriers to effective cross-border communications. Probation personnel also highlighted ethical and philosophical objections to the specific categorisation, surveillance, and ongoing monitoring of serious violent or sexual offenders. Respondents from five Member States thought this was particularly problematic once a formal sanction had come to an end and where the offender's full rights of citizenship, data protection, and privacy were often seen to be fully restored. Changes to this situation would require some Member States to make adjustments to their penal code, but political and policymaker appetite to do so varied. Concepts of privacy are embedded within varied historical contexts across the EU, and a number of Member States strongly prioritise the privacy and rights of the individual above disclosures for crime prevention. Therefore, tensions between risks, rights, and freedom of movement have evolved differently (Hilder and Kemshall 2016). Actions which some probation staff viewed as preventative public protection measures (e.g. the UK), were viewed by others as a potential violation of an individual's basic human rights. Again, the varying nature and status of probation work across EU jurisdictions provides an indication of the broader ideologies underpinning the various national penal systems and the differing relationships between citizenship, exclusion, and the State (Burke and Collett 2015). Whilst the majority of organisations engaged in what may be classified as 'probation work' across the EU have their origins in philosophies of social inclusion, the rehabilitation and welfare of offenders, and the possibility of change, there has been a significant shift for many towards more neoliberal trends with increasing rates of imprisonment, centralised management, and public protection agendas (Kemshall 2003, 2008). EU criminal justice and social policies and recent legal initiatives have also established that the commission of serious violent or sexual offences is itself an infringement of the human rights of victims. This has been particularly apparent in the combat of sexual tourism, sexual exploitation, and violence against women and girls.[13] This shift is likely to result in a broader EU focus on victim issues and protection in the supervision of offenders, particularly serious violent or sexual offenders. Therefore the requirement for probation services to address such issues more explicitly is likely to become more widespread, balancing the rights of offenders to privacy and movement with those of victim safety.

Restricting Movement, a Retreat to National Borders

The challenges of acquiring accurate information on the mobility of serious violent and sexual offenders and/or seeking to restrict travel were also highlighted in the research data. Although six Member States had some form of capacity to formally restrict foreign travel, this tended to apply only to sex offenders, and the practicalities and efficacy of foreign travel bans were questioned. In some Member States such restrictions could only be applied at the point of sentence at court but not retrospectively, and they mainly operated as a condition attached to community supervision or conditional release from the custodial component of a sanction. Significantly, however, there were no indications from the research respondents that imposing more general restrictions on the movement of EU citizens would address such challenges. In the UK, for example, 50 Foreign Travel Orders (FTOs) were made between 2005 and the first four months of 2012, lower numbers than those expected relative to offenders with a qualifying conviction (The Davies Review 2013, p. 15), although

3000 foreign travel bans were made on football hooligans in 2008 alone (http://news.bbc.co.uk/1/hi/uk_politics/7571451.stm). Underused FTOs were replaced in the UK in 2015 by the Sexual Risk Order and the Sexual Harm Prevention Order (Thomas 2016, pp. 66–67).

Nevertheless, given the current political climate, with heightened concerns regarding broader patterns of EU migration, counter-arguments are apparent, contending that a retreat back to a state of national sovereignty with a more rigorous monitoring of national borders would negate the need for such extensive EU-wide law enforcement and judicial cooperation. A number of security professionals still consider that a government should have control of its own specific territory to ensure the protection of its citizens, and should make its own decisions regarding the exchange of information with others (Bigo 2008, p. 92). However, closing or restricting access across borders to manage threats to public security, real or perceived, is not a new idea, and Hobbing (2011) suggests that such developments are often not cost-effective, demonstrating a lack of efficiency and disproportionality. He describes them as:

> a rather blunt weapon in the fight against crime, whereas cross-border and EU-wide police cooperation promise far better results. Illicit traffic tends to follow the path of least resistance, so if official border crossings are (more intensely) controlled, traffic routes switch to the open green and blue borders. If fences or other obstacles are erected, criminal organisations will find a way around or across them. (Hobbing 2011, p. 6).

Ruggiero (2013) has also highlighted that the exclusionary treatment of migrants, ethnic minorities, and non-nationals, with trends of harsher sentencing for these groups, have been apparent across EU Member States for many years. To this extent there is a risk that a violation of offender rights is seen as inevitable in the pursuit of public safety, and even countries with a strong traditional use of offender rehabilitation have seen a growth in their prison population as a result of the perceived threat of external communities' security concerns (Ruggiero 2013). These are important cautionary notes for the SOMEC project, which must ensure that the assessments of serious violent or sexual offenders crossing EU borders are robust and that cross-border information exchange only occurs where it is legitimate and justified. An exacerbation of a misguided perception that non-nationals and incoming EU citizens have an inherent elevated level of risk must be avoided.

Conclusion

Across the EU, law enforcement, judicial, and probation service collaboration and the exchange of information remains largely bound by the diverse and varied justice procedures and different constitutional balances of liberty and security specific to each individual EU Member State system. Whilst some areas of agreement exist—for example, on the need to address issues of terrorism, child sexual abuse, exploitation and trafficking—a consensus has yet to be reached about the full range of criminal activity that should be subject to such concern. EU-wide shared understandings of punishment and its purpose are still far from being realised (Ryan 2013). The SOMEC findings indicate that some very real tensions and challenges remain.

There is, however, some apparent desire for change. There are 17 SOMEC project recommendations (Kemshall et al. 2015) which might reasonably be presented as the initial first steps towards improving the management of serious violent or sexual offenders who move across EU borders. They address issues of identification and assessment, knowledge and awareness of the EU legislative framework which enables information exchange to occur, an emphasis on joint working at national and international levels, and a centralised, coordinated response at a national level to the generation and receipt of information. Any further developments, however, which assumes that policies and working practices can simply be imported and transposed across the EU community are likely to fail, and it is vital that the varying ideologies and concerns of EU Member States highlighted here are not dismissed.

From a UK perspective, the landscape is clearly changing following the referendum and Brexit decision of 23 June 2016. Whilst UK law enforcement agencies have promoted the value of being able to utilise the information exchange processes highlighted in this discussion (House of Lords 2016), their immediate access to systems such as ECRIS, Prüm, and the opt-in to SIS II is not guaranteed in the longer term. Concerns are that following the UK's departure from the EU, vital information, which currently takes a matter of hours to obtain, may take much longer to secure. The direct access that the UK currently enjoys to systems such as European Information System (EIS) may no longer be available, and individual requests may need to be made to Europol and Eurojust for the transfer of relevant data. As a way forward from this position, a bilateral treaty arrangement with the whole of the EU has been advocated, rather than a series of individual agreements with all other 27 EU Member States (House of Lords 2016), and comparisons have been made with the positions of Switzerland and Norway. However, such an approach leads to a country being bound by a treaty to certain EU arrangements without having any influence on the further development of policy frameworks (Deutscher Bundestag 2016). Whilst a more bespoke arrangement may be pursued, there is currently no precedent set for non-EU membership of SIS II and ECRIS, and negotiating access with a presumption of an active involvement and continuing input in the shaping of EU frameworks appears incredibly ambitious and overly optimistic. The length of time required to establish and implement such agreements is also a cause for concern.

Acknowledgements Acknowledgement and thanks to the research team of Hazel Kemshall, Michael Scott, Tony Grapes, Gill Kelly, Bernadette Wilkinson, and Jo Chilvers; and thanks to the EU for the research grant for the Serious Offending by Mobile European Criminals project and for the EU Action Grant for the Prevention of and Fight Against Crime programme, ISEC, 2011/ AG/4000002521. The views expressed here are the author's.

Notes

1. Serious Offending by Mobile European Criminals (SOMEC), EU Action Grant, 'Prevention of and Fight Against Crime', ISEC, 2011/ AG/4000002521. Available at: www.svdv.org.uk/somec-project/ Accessed on 15 January 2017.
2. The term 'globalisation' is a contested term, often generally applied and open to differing definitions (Hirst and Thompson 2000; Kirby and Penna 2011). However, it is accepted by most commentators that increased levels of global connectedness, through both travel and media and technology, has resulted in increased levels of transnational crime and a permeability of national borders to criminality.

3. As defined by the SOMEC project from the shared EU European Criminal Record Information System (ECRIS) codes, serious violent offences are: intentional killing, aggravated case of intentional killing, unintentional killing, violence causing death, causing grievous bodily injury, disfigurement or permanent disability, and torture; and sexual offences are: rape, aggravated rape other than a minor, sexual assault, rape of a minor, and sexual assault of a minor.

4. For further information on ECRIS, see http://ec.europa.eu/justice/criminal/european-e-justice/ecris/index_en.htm

5. One such example is the case of Robert Mikelson. Originally from Latvia, Mikelson left his home Member State to live and work in Germany, where he served a prison sentence in 2003 for distributing child pornography. On his release from custody, he moved to the Netherlands. The authorities there were not aware of his offending history and he secured employment in day care centres, child care facilities, and as a private baby sitter. Child protection employment checks were not made by the manager of the main centre where he worked, but even if this had occurred, it is not clear that the information pertaining to the previous convictions in Germany would have been available. Robert Mikelson went on to sexually assault many of children in his care from 2007 to 2010. He was charged with 67 counts of raping a minor and sentenced in April 2013 to 18 years' imprisonment.

6. See EU Counter Terrorism Strategy 2005 14469/4/05 REV4.

7. The principle of availability under the Swedish Framework Decision 2006/960/JHA sets timescales for information exchanges across EU borders and advises that communication should not hampered by formal procedures, administrative structures, and legal obstacles.

8. For an over view of all existing information exchange mechanisms, see Hilder, S. and Kemshall, H. (2014) European Union Information Exchange Mechanisms A Mapping Report of existing frameworks, available at: www.svdv.org.uk/somec-project/ Accessed on 15 January 2017.

9. Interview schedules are available in Kemshall, Hilder, Kelly and Wilkinson et al. (2015) Information Exchanges, Monitoring and Management – A Field Work Study of Current Responses by Member States. Available at: http://www.svdv.org.uk/somec-project/ Accessed on 15 January 2017.

10. These are jurisdictions within the English-speaking world (notably Australia, Canada, New Zealand, the UK, and the USA). They derive

much of their approach to criminal justice, and particularly to violent and sexual offenders, from the USA and the UK.

11. For example, in the case of Northern Ireland and the Republic of Ireland, Gibraltar and Spain, Spain and Portugal, and the Nordic States.

12. For example, the Memorandum of Understanding between Northern Ireland and the Republic of Ireland allowing for cross-border information exchange between police and probation services on those sex offenders who move across their shared land border. This has extended to regular information exchange on cases of concern, and has involved joint training on, and joint adoption of, risk assessment methods. For a discussion on how this agreement works, see Thomas, T. (2010) European developments in sex offender registration and monitoring in *European Journal of Crime, Criminal Law and Criminal Justice* 18.

13. See the Council of Europe (2011) *Council of Europe Convention on Preventing and Combating Violence Against Women and Domestic Violence*, Strasbourg: Council of Europe.

References

Bigo, D. (1998). Frontiers and security in the European Union: The illusion of migration control. In M. Anderson & E. Bort (Eds.), *The frontiers of Europe*. London/Washington, DC: Pinter.

Bigo, D. (2008). EU police cooperation: National sovereignty framed by European security? In E. Guild & F. Geyer (Eds.), *Security versus justice. Police and judicial cooperation in the European Union* (pp. 91–108). Hampshire: Ashgate.

Burke, L., & Collett, S. (2015). *Delivering rehabilitation. The politics, governance and control of probation*. London: Routledge.

Child Exploitation and Online Protection (CEOP). (2010). *Strategic overview 2009–2010*. Available at: http://www.ceop.police.uk/Documents/Strategic_Overview_2009- 10.(Unclassified).pdf. Accessed 17 Jan 2017.

Council Framework Decision 2008/909/JHA on the application of the principle of mutual recognition to judgments in criminal matters imposing custodial sentences or measures involving deprivation of liberty for the purpose of their enforcement in the European Union.

Council Framework Decision 2008/947/JHA on the application of the principle of mutual recognition to judgments and probation decisions with a view to the supervision of probation measures and alternative sanctions.

Davies, H. (2013). *Civil prevention orders. Review*. London: Association of Chief Police Officers (ACPO).

De Pourbaix-Lundin, M. (2010). *Reinforcing measures against sex offenders.* Report to the Committee on Legal Affairs and Human Rights Doc 12243, Council of Europe Parliamentary Assembly.

Deutscher Bundestag. (2016). *Consequences of Brexit for the realm of justice and home affairs. Scope for future EU cooperation with the United Kingdom.* Deutscher Bunderstag: Research Section for European Affairs. PE 6-3000.

EU Directive 2011/93/EU of the European Parliament and of the Council of 13 December 2011 on combating the sexual abuse and sexual exploitation of children and child pornography. Available at: http://europa.eu/legislation_summaries/justice_freedom_security/fight_against_trafficking_in_human_beings/jl0064_en.htm. Accessed 17 Jan 2017.

European Commission (EC). (2010). *Study on the status of information exchange amongst law enforcement authorities in the context of existing EU instruments.* International Centre for Migration Policy Development JLS/2009/ISEC/PR/001-F3.

Frosdick, S., & Marsh, P. (2005). *Football hooliganism.* Cullompton: Willan.

Hilder, S., & Kemshall, H. (2014). *Serious offending by mobile european criminals (SOMEC).* Mapping Report on Existing EU Information Exchange Systems. https://www.svdv.org.uk/somec-project/. Accessed 6 Feb 2017.

Hilder, S., & Kemshall, H. (2016). Serious violent or sexual offenders travelling across European Union Borders: Ideological and ethical challenges of information exchange. *European Probation Journal, 8*(3), 128–145. doi:10.1177/2066220316678749.

Hirst, P., & Thompson, G. (2000). *Globalization in question: The international economy and the possibility of governance* (2nd ed.). Cambridge: Polity Press.

Hobbing, P. (2011, November). A farewell to open borders? The Danish approach. *Centre for European Policy Studies (CEPS).* Paper in Liberty and Security in Europe Series.

House of Lords. (2016). *Brexit: Future UK-EU security and police cooperation. House of Lords European Union Committee.* 7th Report of Session 2016–17. London: Published by the Authority of the House of Lords. HL Paper 77.

International Centre for Migration Policy Development (ICMPD). (2010). *Study on the status of information exchange amongst law enforcement authorities in the context of existing EU instruments.* Available at: http://ec.europa.eu/dgs/home-affairs/doc_centre/ police/docs/icmpd_study_lea_infoex.pdf. Accessed 17 Jan 2017.

Jacobs, J. B., & Blitsa, D. (2008). Sharing criminal records: The United States, the European Union and Interpol Compared. *International and Comparative Law Review, 30*(125), 125–210.

Kemshall, H. (2003). *Understanding risk in criminal justice*. Maidenhead: McGraw-Hill/OUP.

Kemshall, H. (2008). *Understanding the community management of high risk offenders*. Maidenhead: Open University Press.

Kemshall, H., Hilder, S., Kelly, G., & Wilkinson, B. (2015). *Information exchanges, monitoring and management – A field work study of current responses by member states* (Report 2, part 2). https://www.svdv.org.uk/somec-project/. Accessed 6 Feb 2017.

Kirby, S., & Penna, S. (2011). Policing mobile criminality: Implications for police forces in the UK. *Policing: An International Journal of Police Strategies and Management, 34*(2), 182–197. doi:10.1108/13639511111131030.

Lammers, M., & Bernasco, W. (2013). Are mobile offenders less likely to be caught? The influence of the geographical dispersion of serial offenders' crime locations on their probability of arrest. *European Journal of Criminology 10*(2), 168–186. Euc.sagepub.com: SAGE.doi:10.1177/1477370812464533.

Magee, I. S. (2008). *The review of criminality information*. London: ROCI.

May-Chahal, C., & Herczog, M. (2003). *Child sexual abuse in Europe*. Strasbourg: Council of Europe.

McAlinden, A. M. (2012). The governance of sexual offending across Europe: Penal policies, political economies and the institutionalization of risk. *Punishment and Society, 14*(2), 166–192. doi:10.1177/1462474511435573.

Messenger, I. (2012). *An examination of the dynamics of multi-agency arrangements in different cultural contexts: The case of the Child Exploitation and Online Protection Centre and the International Child Protection Network.* Professional Doctorate, Criminal Justice Studies, University of Portsmouth.

Nanz, K.-P. (1996). Free movement of persons according to the Schengen Convention and in the framework of the European Union. In A. Pauly (Ed.), *De Schengen à Maastricht: voie royale et course d'obstacles* (pp. 61–79). Maastricht: European Institute of Public Administration.

Parkin, J. (2011). *The difficult road to the schengen information system II. The legacy of laboratories and the cost for fundamental rights and rule of law.* CEPS paper, April 2011, www.ceps.eu. Accessed 6 Jan 2017.

Ruggiero, V. (2013). Conclusion. In V. Ruggiero & M. Ryan (Eds.), *Punishment in Europe. A critical anatomy of penal systems*. Basingstoke: Palgrave Macmillan.

Ryan, M. (2013). Introduction. In V. Ruggiero & M. Ryan (Eds.), *Punishment in Europe. A critical anatomy of penal systems*. Basingstoke: Palgrave Macmillan.

Stelfox, P. (2003). Transnational organised crime: A police perspective. In A. Edwards & P. Gill (Eds.), *Transnational organised crime: Perspectives on global security* (pp. 114–126). London: Routledge.

Thomas, T. (2011). *The registration and monitoring of sex offenders*. London: Routledge.

Thomas, T. (2013). The travelling sex offender. Monitoring movements across international borders. In K. Harrison & B. Rainey (Eds.), *Handbook of legal and ethical aspects of sex offender treatment and management*. Chichester: Wiley.

Thomas, T. (2016). *Policing sexual offences and sex offenders*. London: Palgrave.

van Kalmthout, A. M., & Durnescu, I. (Eds.). (2008). *Probation in Europe*. Nijmegen: Wolf Legal Publishers (WLP).

Walsh, J. I. (2006). Intelligence sharing in the EU: Institutions are not enough. *Journal Common Market Studies, 44*, 625, 629. Available at: http://jamesigoewalsh.com/jcms.pdf. Accessed 7 Apr 2017.

Zaiotti, R. (2007). Revisiting Schengen: Europe and the emergence of a new culture of border control. *Perspectives on European Politics and Society, 8*(1), 31–54. doi:10.1080/15705850701204087.

5

Online Sex Offending and Risk Management

M. Brennan, H. L. Merdian, and D. Perkins

Introduction

The impetus for improved management of online sex offending has come into sharp focus over the last two decades with the ascent of the Internet, Information, and Communications Technologies (ICT) and an attendant increase in online sexual offences against children. Put most simply, online child sex offending involves the sexual abuse and exploitation of children, mediated through the Internet and online ICT. This form of offending has traditionally manifested in the production, exchange, viewing, and sale of Child Sexual Exploitation Material (CSEM), or the

M. Brennan (✉)
University College Cork, Cork, Ireland

H.L. Merdian
University of Lincoln, Lincoln, UK

D. Perkins
Royal Holloway, University of London, London, UK

© The Author(s) 2017
H. Kemshall, K. McCartan (eds.), *Contemporary Sex Offender Risk Management,
Volume II*, Palgrave Studies in Risk, Crime and Society,
DOI 10.1007/978-3-319-63573-6_5

solicitation of children and young people to engage in sexual acts via online ICT (Quayle 2008). Moreover, online sex offending behaviour frequently involves other activities and media which accompany or facilitate the commission of abuse. For example, in describing the functions of ICT for the online child sex offender, Durkin (1997) and Gillespie (2012) outlined several such additional practices, for example engaging with other like-minded individuals, in sub-criminal, sexualised communication with children, or accessing textual or audio depictions of sexual activities involving children.

In spite of protective legislation and policy in many state parties to the 1989 United Nations Convention on the Rights of the Child, together with increased intervention on the part of the public, private, and third sectors, children and young people continue to be sexually abused and exploited with the support of technology. Increased use of mobile devices, social media, online gaming, cloud computing, live streaming, and encryption technologies have made it easier for offenders to create and access CSEM for private use, exchange, or commercial gain. Furthermore, these advances have provided unprecedented opportunities for children and young people to engage with online media. These offer powerful and unbounded interactive spaces for communication, in which some children become vulnerable to online sexual abuse and exploitation, and others become involved in the abuse or exploitation of their peers.

The effect of this situation is that increasing numbers of sexually abused and exploited children are being visually recorded, and these records are being distributed worldwide. Within the last decade, there have been significant increases in the numbers of arrests and convictions for CSEM-related offences, both in the UK and internationally (e.g. Crown Prosecution Service 2014; Hamilton 2011). Various reasons have been proposed for these increases, including increased Internet penetration, which can facilitate anonymised access to CSEM by networks of individuals with a sexual interest in children (Seto 2013), increased availability of CSEM online (Akdeniz 2016), and an increasing concentration of law enforcement effort in the detection of these offences (Eke et al. 2011). These increases have presented challenges of caseload, and case complexity to professionals in policing, the judiciary, probation, prisons, and elsewhere, particularly in relation to the assessment and management of those implicated in these offences (Hernandez 2000; Kimball 2011; Netclean 2015).

At the time of writing, many countries maintain proscriptive legislation in relation to visual depictions of child sexual abuse and exploitation, or online grooming and solicitation offences, yet many other manifestations of the problem of online sex offending are not accommodated in international legislatures. Nevertheless, there is an emerging international consensus that other activities and materials associated with online sexual abuse are inherently harmful to children, by, for example, exposing them to exploitation and abuse, and therefore merit inclusion in our working definitions of Child Sexual Exploitation Material (e.g. Interagency Working Group on Sexual Exploitation of Children [IWGSEC] 2016). Indeed, several countries have extended their statutory definitions to criminalise practices such as engagement with non-visual (e.g. written and audio) depictions of child sexual abuse—these have been included in recent legal definitions of 'child pornography' (e.g. Canada and Ireland) and 'child exploitation material' (Australia).

Regardless of their eligibility for legal proscription, these additional activities and materials may maintain psychological significance for the offender or for victims and can provide important, corollary information for risk assessment and management. Therefore, in this chapter, we use the term 'Child Sexual Exploitation Material' as a referent for any type of material depicting the sexual exploitation of children, including material covered in legal terminology such as *indecent photographs of children* (UK) or *child pornography* (USA), but also depictions of sexual activity involving children not consistently included in the relevant legislature, such as written narratives and audio representations of abuse, and sexualised chat room conversations with young people.

The gravity of the challenge of online child sex offending has led to a significant concentration of effort in the development of empirical research on the characteristics, risks, and management needs of this population. Notwithstanding this effort, this body of research remains equivocal and sometimes contradictory. More generally, the heterogeneous psychological and behavioural profiles of online sex offenders identified in the psychological literature have translated to a notable absence of professional consensus around a theoretical or empirical framework to support effective assessment and management of this cohort.

Therefore, this chapter will explore the current situation regarding the assessment and management of those who have engaged in CSEM and related forms of online sexual offending activity. We wish to provide professionals with insight into current legal, contextual, and psychological issues in the assessment and management of online sex offending, including the evidence concerning the link between CSEM use and contact sexual offences against children, and on the function and significance of contextualised assessment of this offending behaviour.

Current Challenges in Online Child Sex Offending Behaviour

The archetype of online child sex offending behaviour has been evolving over several decades. This has resulted in a changing understanding of the kinds of sexual abuse and exploitation that may be considered eligible as CSEM, the forms of offending which support the manifestation of online child sexual abuse, and attendant criminogenic needs that may be salient to the assessment and management of online sexual offending populations.

Much of the empirical research in this domain has focused on CSEM-related offences, variously involving acts of viewing, possession, distribution, or production (Gillespie 2012). Whilst significant legal and media attention has been concentrated on adults who use technology to engage children in sexual contact through processes of sexual grooming and solicitation, comparatively little empirical attention has been given to advancing their risk assessment and management (Seto et al. 2012). Similarly, little empirical focus has been given to more recent, related concerns around children and young people's own sexualised use of technology that could inform the development of apposite management interventions (Phippen 2017). The evidence suggests that the incidence of these latter offences is increasing (Phippen and Brennan 2016; Virtual Global Taskforce 2015) and lack of empirical attention will become an increasing challenge to management and prevention of this offence type.

CSEM is perhaps the most pervasive and notorious manifestation of online child sexual offending behaviour, and one which is a necessary feature of almost every form of online offending, with the possible exception of online grooming and solicitation. While CSEM has persisted as a feature of adult sexual interest in children over many thousands of years (Gillespie 2012) and has proliferated with advances in online ICT, conceptualisations of CSEM have developed in a disjointed manner, largely advanced from a legal perspective. Notwithstanding recent attempts to achieve consensus in relation to the scope of this material, there is, as yet, no universally accepted definition of CSEM and consequently inter-jurisdictional differences in the nature of proscribed materials arise (e.g. Frangez et al. 2015). Legal definitions of materials within this category have grown in scope in an effort to address and manage underlying sexually abusive practices. These definitions have been subject to on-going revision in light of technological developments that have changed the nature of online child sexual offending and attendant manifestations of CSEM, as well as attitudes towards children's rights and sexually abusive practices (Gillespie 2010). One case in point was the recent move to criminalise possession of *prohibited images* of children in the UK, thereby encompassing non-photographic depictions of child sexual abuse; these materials largely comprise computer-generated images, cartoons, and manga images, although some such materials may be physically indistinguishable from real images (e.g. Antoniou 2013). Similarly, Section 69 of the UK's Serious Crime Act 2015 created the offence of possession of paedophile manuals, that is, any item that contains advice or guidance about abusing children sexually. While the scope of relevant legislation has adapted in line with changing forms of online CSEM, it has long since been suggested that these revisions have done little to manage the underlying problems of CSEM-related offending behaviour (e.g. Nair 2010).

Notwithstanding this slowly evolving legal conceptualisation of CSEM, a number of recent manifestations of online sex offending behaviour are worthy of consideration at this juncture. While a full review of recent developments is beyond the scope of this chapter, two key challenges are considered here, namely those of live online child sexual abuse and children's own involvement in the production and exchange of Self-generated Sexual Exploitation Material (SGSEM; Virtual Global

Taskforce 2015). These challenges are significant for the assessment and management of online offenders for several reasons: (1) they blur the conceptual distinction traditionally drawn between CSEM-only and contact sexual offending; (2) they significantly advance adult opportunities to access, sexually abuse, and exploit children; and (3) they create unprecedented opportunities for peer-on-peer abuse in young people who become engaged with the production and exchange of SGSEM.

Live Online Child Sexual Abuse

Recently, the attention of international public protection professionals has been concentrated on a rise in the phenomenon of live online child sexual abuse. This practice involves sexual activity with a child that is transmitted live through online ICT such as Voice Over IP and Skype services, and is viewed by others from a remote location. Commonly, those viewing the live stream have commissioned the sexual abuse, dictating how the acts should be carried out, and sometimes paying for the abuse to take place. Thus, this activity involves manifold forms of child sexual exploitation, through prostitution, sexual performances, and the production of CSEM (IWGSEC 2016, p. 46).

Live online child sexual abuse has attracted substantial international concern for several reasons, notably because of the financial exploitation arising from offender-victim interactions spanning developed and developing countries (Virtual Global Taskforce 2015). Significantly, from a management and prevention perspective, live streaming leaves no obvious trace on the offenders' devices, because no visual depiction of the abuse is downloaded: unless an offender records the live stream, the abuse and associated CSEM disappear when the streaming is stopped. This increases the perceived anonymity and impunity of the offender, and creates challenges for intervention, particularly the recovery of evidence and effective identification and management of offenders and their victims. While the exploitative use of children in broadcast sexual activity has been proscribed for decades (see, e.g. Article 34 of the UNCRC or Article 2(e) of EU Directive 2011/93), what is new in this context is the fact that contact sexual abuse can now be carried out remotely (IWGSEC 2016), with perpetrators engaging in highly interactive, personalised forms of abuse that are often produced to order. Finally, the psychological and criminological significance of this abuse for offenders and victims merits some concern in the context of risk assessment and management efforts. This form of online offending closely resembles a contact sexual offence; while the offender in question may not physically touch the child, the streamed contact sexual abuse occurs at the direction of the offender, often for their own personal gratification, thereby blurring the distinction that could traditionally be drawn between contact sexual offence and CSEM offence types. This situation raises fundamental questions for accurate classification, assessment, and management of those who engage in such activities, both in the context of empirical research and public protection efforts.

Children, Young People, and Self-generated Sexual Exploitation Material

There is increasing concern about the abusive and exploitative experiences of children who become engaged with the production and exchange of self-generated sexual material (e.g. Powell 2010), particularly in view of some recent empirical studies suggesting that sexual materials produced by children themselves have become a substantive component of the larger corpus of CSEM in circulation (Internet Watch Foundation 2015).

Sexting is the exchange of sexually explicit material via communication technologies (Yeung et al. 2014). These sexual communications are largely graphic, encompassing picture, video, and textual content. In recent literature and practice, focus has been given to more explicit, legally problematic materials produced in the context of young people's sexting activities. These materials have been described, inter alia, as SGSEM (Virtual Global Taskforce 2015) or Youth-produced Sexual Images, defined as 'pictures created by minors (age 17 or younger) that depict minors and that are or could be child pornography under applicable criminal statutes' (Wolak and Finkelhor 2011, p. 2). While most research in this space has addressed the problematic aspects of children's sexting behaviours, it should be remembered that young people's experiences of electronic sexual expression can be positive, comprising yet another facet of contemporary sexual development. For many, sexting behaviour can serve as a form of flirting and adolescent experimentation, or a way of enhancing a sexual relationship (Cooper et al. 2016). However, while a peer-to-peer exchange might be consensual, other factors, such as exploitation, coercion, or deception can also prompt young people's sexting behaviour. Therefore, the central challenge that presents is to reliably distinguish sexting and SGSEM-related behaviours where some form of identifiable harm is apparent and where there is a public interest in sanctioning and managing the perpetrator.

While the prevalence of SGSEM-related sexting activities is difficult to measure (Phippen 2017), professionals working at grassroots level with children across educational, health, and social care settings increasingly encounter cohorts of whose formative sexual experiences are based upon self-generated sexual imagery, and who, problematically, perceive little wrong with the redistribution of sexually explicit images of their peers (Phippen and Brennan 2016). The longer-term implications of these kinds of SGSEM-related activities for children are uncertain. Notably, however, a recent Freedom of Information request to the UK's Ministry of Justice by Phippen and Brennan (2016) has demonstrated a recent year-on-year increase in the number of prosecutions of offenders aged 18–24 years for crimes under section 1 of the Protection of Children Act 1978 (see Fig. 5.1). This data indicates an increasing number of young adult CSEM users coming into contact with the criminal justice system in need of effective assessment and management regimes.

While causation may not be directly inferred from such data, these findings point to an upcoming cohort of young people who develop or maintain an interest in CSEM upon reaching adulthood. They also speak to the potential of earlier intervention with adolescent populations before their activities reach criminal thresholds, and to the value of exploring changing attitudes to CSEM in youth populations.

Sexting-related cases that come to the attention of public protection services are highly varied in presentation and comprise a cross-section of cases, ranging from those which feature comparatively innocent activities (e.g. where SGSEM is produced in the context of a romantic adolescent

The number of persons (aged 18–24) proceeded against at
magistrates' courts under section 1 of the Protection of
Children Act 1978, England and Wales, 2010–2015

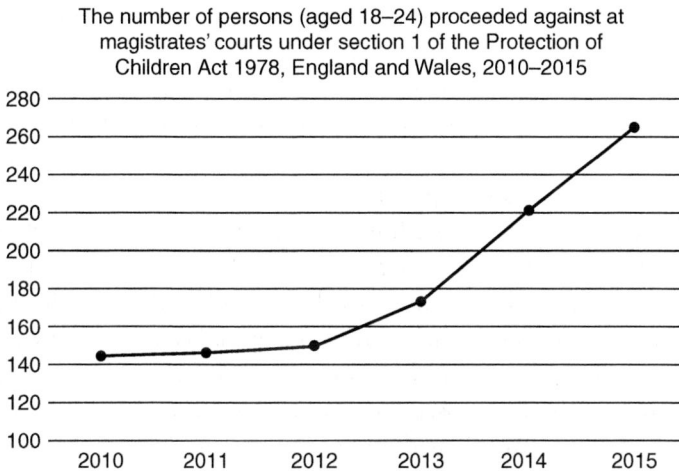

Fig. 5.1   Excerpted from Phippen and Brennan (2016) (Reprinted with permission of the authors)

relationship), to cases where explicit criminal harm features (e.g. where a child is coerced into producing the SGSEM). Quite apart from the clearer case of illegal adult involvement, there is a public interest in criminal sanction in a proportion of peer-perpetrated sexting cases, for example where the case features extortion, coercion, or the exploitation of prepubertal children. Whether peer or adult-perpetrated, the online sexual extortion of children has emerged as a particular recent challenge for police services. This crime involves the targeting and commoditisation of the child and/or their sexual image for the procurement of sexual gains, such as sexually explicit images of that child and/or sexual activity with the child, or for financial gain. This process is supported by a range of manipulative strategies, typically involving the use of coercion, through threats and intimidation, but also the use of deceptive strategies such as impersonation, hacking, or the theft of the child's image. Online sexual extortion activities targeting children occur at the intersection of a number of criminal behaviours, including adult sexual extortion, sexual grooming, and online solicitation, and variously bear the hallmarks of these offences. This apparent overlap can give rise to conceptual confusion regarding the nature of online child sexual extortion, the criminal offences that may be implicated in these activities, and appropriate avenues for assessment and management.

Given the variable presentation of sexting and SGSEM-related behaviours, reliably distinguishing cases where some form of criminal harm is apparent can be challenging, particularly where the victim has been threatened or deceived into producing SGSEM. Notwithstanding, some efforts have been made in the literature to provide a framework for the identification of cases which merit intervention, and to guide intervention planning (e.g. Wolak and Finkelhor 2011), while in the UK the Crown Prosecution Service has introduced guidance to assist law enforcement and other relevant authorities in establishing the threshold for criminal harm where a prosecution should proceed. Moreover, the UK Policing College has also issued guidance that case officers should distinguish between incidents of SGSEM redistribution *without malicious intent* and redistribution *with malicious intent with evidence of grooming or coercion*. However, this guidance is limited in the sense that the defining features of the offence such as malicious intent or coercion are poorly specified; these determinations must ultimately be made at the discretion of the investigating officer (Phippen and Brennan 2017).

In the context of risk assessment and management, it is still unclear whether, like adult CSEM users, populations of children and young people who engage in criminal SGSEM-related activity resolve into *contact-motivated* and *fantasy motivated* groups (e.g. Merdian et al. 2013), and whether standardised risk assessments used with young people who sexually harm such as the Structured Assessment of Violence Risk in Youth (SAVRY) are appropriate for youth SGSEM offender populations.

CSEM Use, Contact Sex Offending, and the Risk of Crossover

One of the most important and frequently posed questions for those involved in the risk assessment and management of online sex offending populations relates to an individual's risk of crossover from a CSEM offender to a contact sex offender (CSO; Eke et al. 2011). Those involved in the risk assessment and management of online offenders may wish to assess the risk an individual may present for contact sexual offences against children, including their own (Merdian et al. 2017), or to identify and manage future risk of escalation in those who present with identifiable contact-offence-related propensities. Similarly, law enforcement may wish to identify CSEM offenders at risk of contact offending as a basis for case prioritisation, in the interests of child protection and rationalising the allocation of limited police resources (Brennan and Hammond 2017).

The empirical data drawn from official, prosecuted offender samples show very little crossover between CSEM and contact sex offending. A large-scale meta-analysis (Seto et al. 2011) identified 12.2% of CSEM users with historical contact sex offences (17.3% when additional self-report data was considered) but did not differentiate by victim type (e.g. adult vs child victims). Predictably, the empirical research on this topic reflects a discrepancy between crossover rates reported in official and self-reported data, one which has also become apparent in studies on undetected CSEM users (see Neutze et al. 2011) or studies involving CSEM users' polygraph assessments as a form of information validation (Buschman et al. 2010).

In terms of reconviction rates, progression from CSEM viewing to CSO appears to be rare. In their meta-analysis, Seto et al. (2011) found that less than 5% of online offenders (n = 2,630) reoffended with any sex offence within the follow-up period of six years; 2% reoffended with a CSO. Faust et al. (2014) provided reoffending rates for online sex offenders in the US (n = 638) over a nine-year follow-up, reporting a 3% recidivism rate for CSO and 1.6% CSEM offending. The significance of these findings is that such low base rates of (detected) CSO within the CSEM population limit the utility of probabilistic risk predictions. Thus, existing risk assessment tools for contact sex offenders (Risk Matrix 2000) not only require validation regarding the offending base rates of CSEM users but are unlikely to make reliable and accurate risk predictions when applied to this population (Osborn et al. 2010).

In an effort to support the development of risk assessment and management strategies with online offenders, some work has been undertaken to identify a series of predictive factors that can help isolate CSEM users at risk of contact sexual offending. While this work has identified a series of prospective risk factors for contact sexual offending, the available evidence is far from conclusive. One factor that has attracted significant attention in relation to indecent image offenders is sexual deviance; there is a substantial corpus of evidence to indicate that CSEM offenders are aroused by sexual images of children. This suggestion has been evidenced through self-reports as well as phallometric assessments (Seto et al. 2006; Surjadi et al. 2010), leading some to propose that arousal to CSEM may be a valid diagnostic indicator of paedophilia (Seto 2010).

However, some challenges to this contention have been identified. For example, while arousal to CSEM may be a good indicator of sexual interest it does not necessarily predict whether that arousal might be acted upon. For example, Goode (2009) reported on men who acknowledged sexual responsiveness to children but who did not condone, or apparently act upon, these interests. In two recent meta-analyses, Seto et al. (2011) examined the contact sexual offense histories of online offenders, and in the second, the recidivism rates from follow-up studies of online offenders. The authors concluded that there is likely a distinct subgroup of online only offenders who pose a relatively low risk of committing contact sexual offenses over time.

Existing risk appraisal is largely based on studies of risk factors in offline sex offender populations and these may have relevance for online sex offenders. An important series of studies (Eke et al. 2011; Seto and Eke 2005) examined how traditional risk factors might apply to CSEM offenders. From their full data set it appeared that offenders with either prior or concurrent violent offences, including sexual offences, were significantly more likely to be charged with a contact sexual recidivism compared to other offenders. There was a negative relationship between offenders who had solely CSEM offenses in their criminal records and recidivism outcomes. Contact sexual recidivism was therefore predicted by criminal history (particularly violent offence history), age at the time of the first detected criminal offence (24 years and younger), and failure upon conditional release. More recent work by Eke and Seto (2012) extended these empirically identified risk factors to include low education, substance abuse problems, 'single' relationship status and a sexual interest in children. Similar efforts to predict contact sexual offending traits in a sample of online-accessed CSEM possessors determined that mixed offenders (i.e. those who both accessed CSEM and who had committed a contact offence) could be distinguished from contact and CSEM-only offenders on the basis of their antisocial behaviour and Internet preoccupation profiles. CSEM offenders scored high on measures of Internet preoccupation and low on antisocial behaviour, while conversely, CSOs measured low on Internet preoccupation and high on antisocial behaviour scales. Mixed offenders, perhaps predictably, scored high on both measures of antisocial behaviour and Internet preoccupation (Lee et al. 2012).

However, the persistence of general criminality factors in predicting both crossover and recidivistic CSEM offending was borne out in a later meta-analysis by Babchishin et al. (2014). Based on their meta-analysis comparing CSEM users (n = 2,284) and offenders with convictions for both CSEM and CSO (n = 1,086), CSEM offenders most at risk of crossover to CSO can be distinguished by *sexual interest in children* (measured through self-report or implicit assessment), *access to children, few psychological barriers* to acting on their impulses, and *comparatively high levels of antisociality* (measured through psychometric assessments and behavioural indicators, e.g. prior offending, supervision failures, employment problems/unemployment, and substance use). Moreover, these authors added that propensities for rule violation appeared to predict crossover offence behaviours, but the importance of opportunity was also apparent, with paedophilic (motivated) offenders more likely to crossover to contact sexual offending where access to a child was consistently available, whereas similarly motivated offenders with frequent computer access tended to reoffend through repeated CSEM engagement.

These factors, predictive of crossover between CSEM and contact-offending activities provide a useful starting point in the assessment of CSEM users but are far from a comprehensive solution. Similarly, group-based typologies of CSEM offending have been developed, which propose that different types of CSEM users can be identified, who present different risks and needs. These typal distinctions (Beech et al. 2008; Merdian et al. 2013) are useful in the sense that they are accessible to mainstream assessment and management frameworks such the Risks Needs Responsivity Model, but none are empirically validated at present, and thus cannot be reliably employed in individualised assessments with CSEM offenders.

In summary, what has been established thus far is that whilst some individuals use CSEM in conjunction with contact offences against children (*contact-driven offenders*), there appears to be a distinct group motivated to use CSEM without intent to commit a contact offence (*fantasy-driven offenders*; Merdian et al. 2013), whose use of CSEM is dependent upon the function they place on it (e.g. for sexual arousal or fostering non-offence-related social contacts; Gillespie 2012). CSEM users in general, but fantasy-driven users in particular, display characteristics distinguishing them from contact sex offenders (Babchishin et al. 2014), indicating that they require distinct assessment and management strategies (Seto et al. 2010).

The empirical literature on the risk assessment and management needs of online solicitation offenders is yet more scarce than that concerning broader CSEM user populations, and is similarly characterised by ambiguity in terms of the identified characteristics, potential risk factors, and management needs of this population. Like CSEM offenders, the existing literature on the characteristics of online grooming and solicitation offenders has tended to characterise this population in accordance with two extremes (see Seto et al. 2012). At one end of the spectrum it has been suggested that solicitation offenders comprise a new group of sexual offenders whose interactions with children are largely limited to the online space (e.g. Young 2005). Within this perspective, while some solicitation offenders may have histories of online sexual contact with children, many others do not, and this group maintains a comparatively low likelihood of committing contact sexual offences, particularly once their problematic behaviour has been detected and sanctioned through criminal justice intervention. The opposing characterisation holds that online grooming and solicitation offenders are more like CSOs, who avail of new opportunities offered by online technologies for contact with children and for their physical sexual exploitation. According to this position, these solicitation offenders are likely to have had prior sexual contact with children and are similar to contact sexual offenders in terms of their risk of future contact sexual offending (Seto and Hanson 2011).

Briggs et al. (2011) similarly characterised two subtypes of solicitation offender, whose profiles appeared to resolve in accordance with the function of the grooming or solicitation process: *fantasy-driven* offenders, apparently motivated to sexually victimise children in a remote fashion and to use the Internet as a sexual medium for purposes of cybersexual activity and masturbation, and *contact-driven* offenders, for whom the Internet functioned to identify and engage new victims, and to pursue a physical sexual relationship with the child. Of course, it is likely that this continuum is more fluid and dynamic than this rigid dichotomy suggests, and that a range of dynamic factors may affect an individual's positioning between these extremes, for example offence motivation and modus operandi, timing of the offender's detection, the assessor's ability to establish a full offence history, levels of offending skill, and the offender's capacity to recognise and act upon offending opportunities as they arise. Indeed, very recent, empirical findings from a larger and more geographically diverse US sample (n = 200) by DeHart et al. (2017) identified a similar polar distinction between contact- and fantasy-driven types of solicitation offenders, but extended this typology to encompass other, apparently intermediate types that could support additional classifications of solicitation offenders. These authors proposed a typology of online solicitation offenders that encompassed 'cybersex-only' (fantasy-driven) offenders, 'schedulers' (contact-driven offenders), as well as 'cybersex/schedulers' who engaged in cybersexual and contact-offence scheduling activities, and 'buyers' who offered payment for sexual activity with the solicited child.

An important study by Seto et al. (2012) compared solicitation offenders with low-risk CSO and CSEM-only offenders on a range of variables including sociodemographic factors and psychological variables associated with dynamic risk of reoffending. A central objective here was to begin to shed further light on the discrepancies reported in previous studies by (1) identifying the particular characteristics, possible risk factors, and risk management needs of solicitation offenders, and (2) examining how solicitation offenders compared to CSEM-only and low-risk CSO populations. Based on a comparison group comprising 38 CSEM-only, 38 CSO, and 70 solicitation offenders, the authors determined that online (i.e. CSEM-only and solicitation offenders) were identified as being better educated than CSOs, but did not differ significantly on any other measured sociodemographic variable. In so far as psychological characteristics and dynamic risk factors for reoffending were concerned, solicitation offenders exhibited significantly lower capacity for relationship stability, lower levels of sexual preoccupation, and deviant sexual preference than CSEM-only offenders. In terms of their comparability to CSOs, solicitation offenders were also more significantly problematic on measures of sexual preoccupation and capacity for relationship stability, had greater self-reported use of CSEM, and were more likely to report f interests and to have had stranger/unrelated victims. These authors concluded that while more comparison studies are needed, solicitation offenders maintain different profiles of risk for recidivism to CSEM offenders and CSOs and therefore merit differentiated management interventions (albeit these differentiated interventions still require comprehensive development and evaluation).

The Mediating Role of Technology in Offence Commission

Over the last decade, the therapeutic and wider management literature has suggested that the context and meaning of online child sexual offending requires individualised assessment (e.g. Merdian et al. in press; Middleton 2008). However, empirical work to identify criminogenic needs with application in the assessment and management of this cohort has proceeded in a vacuum of empirical information about the contextual or situational factors that influence or impel online offending (e.g. technology choices or modes of application), notably their psychological functions, or their role in offence commission. Here, the suggestion is that the role of the Internet environment, opportunity, and other situational factors may have more importance than previously considered in influencing engagement in offence-related activities. Indeed, the literature increasingly points to the formative influence of the online environment and other contextual features in the manifestation of online child sexual offences (e.g. Babchishin et al. 2014; Carr 2004; Merdian et al. in press). There has been a tendency, both in the literature and in practice, to overlook the offence-specific information that can be gained from online profiles of CSEM offenders, specifically related to the content and function of CSEM accessed and the offence-supportive applications of technology. Little has been published, for example, about the relationship between profiles of image use and online activity in CSEM offenders and the commission of contact offences, although as Glasgow (2010) has pointed out, online activities such as downloading sexual imagery involves a dynamic relationship between available stimulus materials and sexual interest, mediated by sexual and masturbatory fantasy.

Given the dearth of empirical information on these criminogenic needs of CSEM offenders, it is perhaps unsurprising that those involved in their treatment and management report having little insight at their disposal about the characteristics of offending environments or their functions that could serve to inform assessment and management strategies. Indeed, important early research by Quayle and Taylor (2002) identified this factor as a key obstacle to intervention with CSEM offenders in therapeutic and other management settings; here, a range of professionals articulated particular challenges to effective management stemming from an inability to understand the function of the Internet for adults with a sexual interest in children. The requirement for better integration of information on offending contexts with management efforts has been echoed in the broader sex offender management literature by authors such as West and Greenall (2011, p. 144), who argue that knowledge of the (index) offence and the offending context (e.g. crime scene information) is important in understanding the offender and attendant decisions around amenability to treatment, risk of reoffending, and decisions on disposal and discharge, and that any such decision-making may be considerably challenged where there is limited awareness of what the offender has actually done.

The literature has sporadically considered the role of technology in offence commission, and the ways in which it might afford favourable opportunities and conditions for offending, for example in peer facilitation, victim access, and anonymity (Seto 2013). Individuals may respond deliberately or opportunistically to these opportunities, giving rise to variable offence pathways or modus operandi (Taylor and Quayle 2006).

More recently, particular concern has been expressed around the ways in which technology (and other mediating conditions) may inflect offending capacity, for example in the acquisition of offending skills in online grooming scenarios (Quayle et al. 2014). By the same token, a functional analysis of offenders' accounts of their pathways to offending Merdian et al. (in press) examined the role of technology in offence commission and distinguished between situational factors that act as broad, contextual facilitators of the offending behaviour and those that serve as direct precipitators of offending activity. The major contextual facilitator of offending behaviour identified by these authors, the Internet environment, functioned as a 'bubble', a unique environment that provided individuals presenting with offence-related propensities (e.g. sexual interest in children; Seto 2013) with the opportunity and lack of supervision to commit an online offence. The authors' findings were consistent with Wortley and Smallbone's (2006) contention that, in some cases, the Internet creates proximal circumstances that trigger offence-related vulnerabilities, with the effect that individuals behave in ways they would not normally consider; study participants reported 'not recognising themselves' in their offending behaviour. These cognitions (e.g. permission-giving thoughts such as the idea that CSEM is not harmful to children) could be seen as factors that both initiated and maintained the offending behaviour. Sustained online engagement further conditioned gratification and continued to trigger offence-supportive cognitions, subsequently intensifying offending behaviour. These authors also alluded to the sexually arousing influence of the online environment and the attendant reinforcing impact of this state of arousal on their decisionsto access CSEM.

One of the main obstacles to the integration of behavioural information relating to online sex offences in risk assessment is that much of the offence-related behaviour that may be observed in the online space is not readily accessible to traditional risk assessment or case formulation approaches. However, some effort has been made to remedy this situation. For example, Brennan and Hammond (2017), through a large-scale analysis of CSEM search behaviour on peer-to-peer file sharing networks identified that user search behaviours may serve as an indicator of paraphilic interest and may be used as a basis for identifying those with problematic paraphilic profiles, including those with a paedophilic and hebephilic presentation. Similarly, in describing a phenomenon he termed Internet-initiated Incitement and Conspiracy (IIIC) to commit child sexual abuse, Gallagher (2007) suggested that certain categories of online interactions between offending peers could play a significant role in the escalation of offending behaviour from engagement with CSEM to the sexual abuse of children. Moreover, there is some evidence that recidivism for CSEM offending may be predicted by the character of an individual's CSEM collection, specifically the ratio of boy versus girl material maintained by the offender (Eke and Seto 2012). The significance of these early findings is that, at least for a proportion of those who engage with CSEM, other dynamic factors in the offending context may serve to indicate their propensity to commit a contact sexual offence or recidivistic potential in assessment contexts.

New Directions in Risk Assessment and Case Formulation with Online Offenders

A number of standardised risk assessment tools have been developed for contact sex offenders. Generally, these comprise combinations of (1) static (unchanging) risk factors such as a prior criminal record (e.g. Rapid Risk Assessment for Sex Offender Recidivism), (2) dynamic (changeable) risk variables (e.g. Sex Offender Need Assessment Rating), and (3) a combination of both (e.g. the Minnesota Sex Offender Screening Tool Revised). More recently, structured professional risk assessment approacheshave emerged, such as the Sexual Violence Risk-20. Empirically derived actuarial measures appear the strongest predictors of sexual, violent, and general reoffending, followed by structured professional judgement systems (Hanson and Morton-Bourgon 2009).

However, in the case of CSEM users a number of challenges persist which can limit the relevance and utility of these tools for this population. For example, the type of risk being considered in the context of risk assessment needs to be formally established (i.e. CSEM reoffending vs crossover to contact sexual offending), as do risk factors of differential relevance to these judgements, what recidivism base rate exists for these offences, and what risk groups may be differentiated for assessment purposes. While there is limited support for use of risk assessment tools developed for contact sex offender populations with CSEM users (Webb et al. 2007), the majority of studies have found that existing risk assessment tools do not hold predictive accuracy for CSEM users (Wakeling et al. 2011). Furthermore, while there is one actuarial assessment tool specifically developed for CSEM users, the Child Pornography Offender Risk Tool (CPORT; Seto and Eke 2015), its utility for the risk assessment of CSEM-only offenders has not yet been validated. Whilst it significantly predicted reoffending in CSEM users with a previous offence history, it did not do so for non-contact CSEM offenders without a criminal history, consistent with other findings that general antisociality is an essential element in predicting contact sexual offending.

In an effort to address these challenges, Merdian et al. (in press) attempted to integrate existing knowledge of CSEM offending with a comprehensive set of interviews and assessments with self-acknowledged CSEM offenders to develop a preliminary model of pathways to CSEM offending. The resulting model provides a CSEM-specific application of the existing theoretical and empirical work on sex offending pathways, so as to formally integrate this offending population within this theoretical context. In line with their focus on functional analysis, Merdian et al. developed the paradigm as a CSEM-specific case formulation model, based on interviews and psychometric testing of CSEM users at both post-arrest and post-conviction stages (Fig. 5.2). The resulting model identified key stages in an individual's pathway to CSEM offending, integrating offence-related vulnerabilities (including developmental factors, e.g. paraphilias or socio-emotional dysfunction), with situational features of the offence, namely their interaction with the broader online offending context, and the immediate personal circumstances to their offending. Finally, the model attends to the individual's experiences of positive and negative reinforcers of the behaviour, such as the sexual gratification linked to CSEM, which either support or deter future offending behaviour.

This model encompasses the motivational and facilitative components of Seto's (2013) Motivation-Facilitation Model, but extends it by inte-

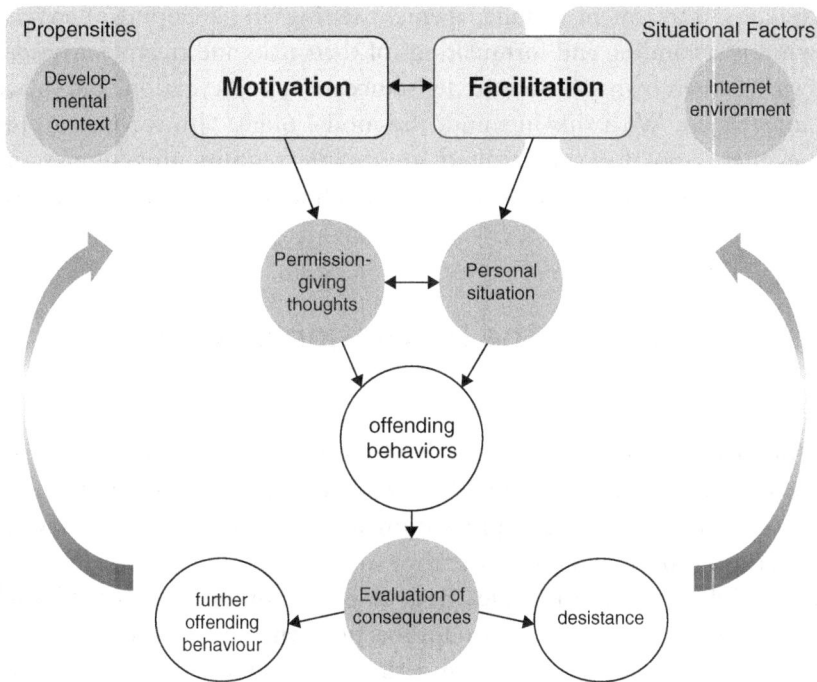

Fig. 5.2 Case formulation model for CSEM users (Merdian et al. 2017) (Reprinted with permission of the authors)

grating the major tenets of Finkelhor's (1984) '*Four Pre-Conditions of Abuse*'—a model used to explain automatic and deliberative decision processes in CSOs. The first two pre-conditions: (1) The thinking (motivational) stage, and (2) Overcoming internal inhibitions (permission-giving) stage, refer to the internal characteristics of the offender. The two remaining pre-conditions: (3) Overcoming external inhibitions (creating opportunity), and (4) Overcoming the victim's resistance, arguably correspond to the characteristics of the environment and offending situation. These authors offer that this model may provide a useful framework for future research as well as an aid to practice-based case formulation, including treatment planning and risk management, when used in conjunction with other sources of information. More specifically, the proposed *CSEM Pathways Model* may be potentially helpful in working with CSEM offenders in treatment and management settings in developing offenders' own understanding and formulations of their risks and treatment needs, as well as their own solutions to desistance, relapse prevention, and social reintegration. With this in mind, the model might also serve as a pre-assessment tool for standardised group intervention programmes, in order to enable group members to focus differentially on the content of the programme.

Current Issues in the Prevention of Online Sex Offending

Efforts to prevent sexual violence before it occurs (i.e. 'primary prevention') are increasingly recognised as a critical and necessary complement to 'secondary' and 'tertiary' prevention strategies, which aim to prevent re-victimisation or recidivism and to ameliorate the adverse effects of sexual violence on victims (DeGue et al. 2014). In the context of CSEM offending, primary prevention approaches generally involve interventions with at-risk populations and the wider public, while secondary and tertiary prevention strategies target detected CSEM users. CSEM offence prevention efforts have also focused on undetected CSEM users, potential victims, and reducing real or perceived opportunities to offend.

Secondary and Tertiary Prevention with Online Sex Offenders

Secondary and tertiary prevention approaches have emphasised 'relapse prevention' with detected online offending populations, largely mediated through criminal justice interventions and associated post-apprehension strategies for offender management. These interventions can vary considerably, and in accordance with a range of factors, including the perceived (or assessed) risk level of the offender in question, the severity of the CSEM offending activity and the availability of requisite resources and supports to meet that individual's management needs at local level.

In some cases, particularly in relation to first-time CSEM-only offenders, alternatives to traditional prosecution may be exercised, whereby CSEM offenders are dealt with 'out of court'. In the UK, for example, CSEM offenders identified as low risk may receive a simple police caution, while in other jurisdictions, such as New Zealand, a diversion agreement may be offered under the police's discretionary powers whereby the offender agrees to comply with a series of agreed conditions (typically involving completion a treatment programme at a prescribed treatment centre) in order to avoid prosecution. In prosecuted cases, secondary and tertiary interventions range from more formal management interventions administered through police, probation, prisons and other statutory agencies, for example sex offender registration, supervision, treatment, and social and housing services, to community-based charitable programmes such as Circles of Support and Accountability, helplines, and psycho-educational interventions, which emphasise reintegration, social inclusion, and self-management in order to prevent reoffending. One psycho-educational programme, InformPlus, provided by an independent child protection charity, the Lucy Faithfull Foundation, is open to anyone who has admitted accessing CSEM, at any stage in the judicial system. InformPlus aims to provide information to aid participants' understanding of their online offending, to encourage them to explore their own involvement in CSEM-related activity, and to consider practical and realistic methods of self-management/control.

Notwithstanding the availability of these interventions, substantial challenges for relapse prevention persist with CSEM offending populations. These have been identified to the authors of this chapter in the context of a two-year consultation with international stakeholders in the management and prevention of online child sexual offending behaviour under the aegis of the International Workgroup for Best Practice in the Management of Online Offending.[1] Whilst in some jurisdictions, a number of interventions are in place, such as risk assessments, access to treatment, psycho-educational interventions and case support, as well as community-based support services, such as helplines, monitoring software 'Circles', typically, offending individuals only receive support once they are arrested, charged or convicted with a CSEM offence. This situation can compromise the potential for suitably motivated, at-risk individuals or undetected offenders to access relevant help to achieve meaningful pre-criminal self-management and control or to desist from offending.

Moreover, and as identified above, there are substantial concerns around the application of risk assessment tools developed for contact sex offenders with CSEM users, especially given the lack of norm data and the differences in observed recidivism rates for this population (Faust et al. 2014; Seto and Eke 2015). At practitioner level, there is a lack of confidence and statistical ability in the assessment of CSEM reoffending, especially in the assessment of those who engage with CSEM exclusively, and do not engage in other forms of offending behaviour. The Kent Internet Risk Assessment Tool (KIRAT) was developed as a decision support instrument for law enforcement investigators and functions to discriminate CSEM offenders with the potential to commit a contact sexual offence against a child on the basis of a series of empirically identified factors such as the number and type of CSEM accessed by the offender, their access to children, or previous criminal history (Long et al. 2013). However, the authors make clear that this is an investigation prioritisation, and not a risk assessment tool in the conventional sense. New generation approaches for the identification of CSEM users who may be at risk of committing a contact offence have been developed which do not require the assessor to access personal and identifying case data (Brennan and Hammond 2017). These provide new possibilities for psychological profiling of CSEM offenders in investigative contexts, based exclusively on online CSEM offence behaviours (i.e. CSEM user searches) where no personal history or characteristics are available to the assessor.

Finally, challenges persist regarding the availability, targeting, and efficacy of treatment programmes for CSEM offenders. In the UK, the governmental intervention programme (i-SOTP: Internet Sex Offender Treatment Programme) was developed based on established dynamic risk factors for contact sex offenders; to date, there has been no systematic evaluation of its treatment outcomes, nor has it been made sufficiently clear if the intervention maps onto the specific risks and needs of CSEM offenders, or if it could be linked to behaviour changes in this population. More broadly, it is still an empirical question whether interventions predicated on more generic sex offender treatment programmes are appropriate for broad-based administration with online sex offenders, or whether this population would be better treated as a distinct group with bespoke treatment needs, as suggested by the findings of Babachishin et al. (2014). For instance, as a group, CSEM-only offenders are frequently classified as low risk; yet psychological research suggests that interventions with low-risk offenders can actually break down protective factors that prevent relapse into offending behaviour (Carter 2014). Furthermore, it has been suggested by several authors that traditional sex offender treatment programmes may unsuitable for CSEM offenders due to the information sharing that may occur between CSOs and CSEM offenders (Quayle et al. 2006). Also, findings from the extensive and successful application of the Risk Need Responsivity principles would suggest that over-treating a generally low recidivism offender group such as CSEM users may be counter-productive, and points to the need for proportionate as well as criminogenically focused interventions.

The Need for Primary Prevention

Given the apparent inefficacy of legal interventions and associated relapse prevention strategies in stemming the growth of CSEM-related offending activity, it has become apparent that a greater emphasis on primary prevention approaches is required—specifically, community-based interventions that focus on behavioural management with undetected offenders and pre-criminal populations. There is some recognition that detected and convicted CSEM offenders are only the 'tip of the iceberg' (Beier et al. 2009), and that primary prevention approaches are required for meaningful CSEM offence management, approaches that complement and extend the prevailing secondary prevention effort with detected offenders. Another important rationale for community-based prevention strategies is that it is now understood that unidentified CSEM behaviours are more prevalent in this population than in officially reported recidivism or law enforcement detection rates (Beier et al. 2015).

Recent primary prevention strategies have largely focused on health-based and educational self-management interventions for offenders, provided in the community. These include, for example, anonymous helplines (e.g. CROGA or the StopitNow! Helpline in the UK) which encourage online sex offenders, those at risk of offending and their associates to recognise problematic thoughts or behaviours as abusive or potentially abusive and to seek help to promote change. In the online space, the UK has introduced 'Splash Pages', landing pages that link from CSEM-related keywords used in online searches; these pages provide information to the searcher about the illegality of accessing CSEM as well as links to the StopitNOW! Helpline. More recently, Europol and an alliance of international law enforcement agencies have launched the Police2Peer initiative, which promotes the sharing of 'fake' CSEM files on Peer-to-peer networks, one of the principal vectors for online CSEM exchange. These 'fake' files have the appearance of CSEM files but do not have content, or indeed the 'fake' files may contain images of police officers, informing the downloader of the risks they are taking in accessing this material. The underlying philosophy with these approaches is to create a situational barrier to offending behaviour (Babchishin et al. 2014; Wortley and Smallbone 2006), and to reduce the anonymity and perceived impunity the Internet provides.

Another important form of intervention in the primary prevention sphere is the rollout of community-based treatment and support programmes for individuals with a self-identified sexual interest in children. For example, the Prevention Project Dunkelfeld (PPD) exists in Germany as a confidential support service for men who wish to manage their sexual interest in children. PPD does not observe mandatory disclosure of CSEM-related crimes to the statutory authorities unless an imminent risk of serious harm towards an identifiable victim is made known to its personnel. In a similar vein, there is some recognition of the fact that adolescents are commonly implicated in sexual crimes against children and therefore warrant similar intervention.

Recent research indicates that adolescents perpetrate between 30% and 50% of all CSA cases, and in a proportion of these cases, these adolescents were motivated by a sexual interest in young children (Finkelhor et al. 2009, 2014). To address this need, members of the Association for the Treatment of Sexual Abusers have undertaken a programme of work to develop Help Wanted, a primary prevention programme for adolescents who have expressed a sexual interest in prepubescent children. The goal of this intervention is to promote self-acceptance and self-esteem while maintaining the message that children must never be sexually touched or harmed (Shields et al. 2015).

These early intervention programmes share the philosophy that sexual interest is (partly) biologically driven, and that individuals need to learn to manage their arousal and their negative emotion as a potential offence trigger in order to enable them to take responsibility for future behaviours. For example, InformPlus has integrated emotional coping skills through the teaching of mindfulness techniques, which has led to significant decreases in depression and anxiety levels in its programme participants (Gillespie et al. 2016).

This preventive philosophy is rationalised by accounts of desistence from offending offered by CSEM offenders themselves. For example, in their study of the offending pathways of CSEM users, Merdian et al. (in press) reported that a number of CSEM users had attempted to access support for their sexual interests using such strategies, but were either led towards online illegal sites, or misunderstood the intent of 'pop up' warning messages. While CSEM users in this sample reported an increase in social accountability as a driving factor for their desistance from CSEM offending, respondents feared the legal consequences of disclosing their sexual interests and reinforced the need for confidential help as a means to prevent their behaviour.

In closing, it should be noted that the lack of public or 'social' engagement with sexual offender reintegration persists as a critical obstacle to the prevention of sexual offending behaviour. Media reporting of sexual crime in particular is cited as a causal factor in the combination of widespread public hostility and press influence on public policy which, in turn, can compromise the reintegration prospects of people with sexual convictions. An important series of observations for a more constructive public response to these issues and to sexual offending more generally, identified by Harper and Hogue (2015), suggested that a more forceful effort is needed from within academia to better engage the public with empirical research findings and the most appropriate responses to sexual offending, as well as debates on policy development.

Notes

1. The International Workgroup for Best Practice in the Management of Online Sex Offending (IWG) is facilitating the development and distribution of a framework for evidence-led practice in the management and prevention of online sex offending behaviour as well as professional knowledge exchange and collaboration across key stakeholders from academic and clinical research, practitioners, and policymakers concerned with the management of online sexual offending.

References

Akdeniz, Y. (2016). *Internet child pornography and the law: National and international responses.* London: Routledge.

Antoniou, A. (2013). Possession of prohibited images of children: Three years on. *The Journal of Criminal Law, 77*(4), 337–353.

Babchishin, K. M., Hanson, R. K., &VanZuylen, H. (2014). Online child pornography offenders are different:A meta-analysis of the characteristics of online and offline sex offenders against children. *Archives of Sexual Behavior.* Advance online publication. doi:10.1007/s10508-014-0270-x.

Beech, A. R., Elliott, I. A., Birgden, A., & Findlater, D. (2008). The internet and child sexual offending: A criminological review. *Aggression and Violent Behavior, 13*(3), 216–228. doi:10.1016/j.avb.2008.03.007.

Beier, K. M., Ahlers, C. J., Goecker, D., Neutze, J., Mundt, I. A., Hupp, E., & Schaefer, G. A. (2009). Can pedophiles be reached for primary prevention of child sexual abuse? First results of the Berlin Prevention Project Dunkelfeld (PPD). *The Journal of Forensic Psychiatry & Psychology, 20*(6), 851–867.

Beier, K. M., Grundmann, D., Kuhle, L. F., Scherner, G., Konrad, A., & Amelung, T. (2015). The German Dunkelfeld Project: A pilot study to prevent child sexual abuse and the use of child abusive images. *The Journal of Sexual Medicine, 12*(2), 529–542.

Brennan, M., & Hammond, S. (2017). A methodology for profiling paraphilic interest in Child Sexual Exploitation Material users on peer-to-peer networks. *Journal of Sexual Aggression, 23*(1), 90–103.

Briggs, P., Simon, W. T., & Simonsen, S. (2011). An exploratory study of internet-initiated sexual offenses and the chat room sex offender: Has the internet enabled a new typology of sex offender? *Sexual Abuse, 23*(1), 72–91.

Buschman, J., Bogaerts, S., Foulger, S., Wilcox, D., Sosnowski, D., & Cushman, B. (2010). Sexual history disclosure polygraph examinations with cybercrime offences: A first Dutch explorative study. *International Journal of Offender Therapy and Comparative Criminology, 54*(3), 395–411.

Carr, A. (2004). *Internet traders of child pornography and other censorship offenders in New Zealand.* Wellington: Department of Internal Affairs.

Carter, A. J. (2014). Sexual offending treatment programs: The importance of evidence-informed practice. In *Responding to sexual offending: Perceptions, risk management and public protection* (pp. 111–127). Hampshire: Palgrave Macmillan.

Cooper, K., Quayle, E., Jonsson, L., & Svedin, C. G. (2016). Adolescents and self-taken sexual images: A review of the literature. *Computers in Human Behavior, 55*, 706–716.

Crown Prosecution Service. (2014). *Violence against women and girls crime report 2013–14.* Retrieved from http://www.cps.gov.uk/publications/docs/cps_vawg_report_2014.pdf

DeGue, S., Valle, L. A., Holt, M. K., Massetti, G. M., Matjasko, J. L., & Tharp, A. T. (2014). A systematic review of primary prevention strategies for sexual violence perpetration. *Aggression and Violent Behavior, 19*(4), 346–362.

DeHart, D., Dwyer, G., Seto, M. C., Moran, R., Letourneau, E., & Schwarz-Watts, D. (2017). Internet sexual solicitation of children: A proposed typology of offenders based on their chats, e-mails, and social network posts. *Journal of Sexual Aggression, 23*(1), 77–89.

Durkin, K. F. (1997). Misuse of the internet by pedophiles: Implications for law enforcement and probation practice. *Federal Probation, 61*(3), 14–19.

Eke, A. W., & Seto, M. C. (2012). Risk assessment of online offenders for law enforcement. In *Internet child pornography: Understanding and preventing online child abuse* (pp 148–168). Devon: Willan.

Eke, A. W., Seto, M. C., & Williams, J. (2011). Examining the criminal history and future offending of child pornography offenders: An extended prospective follow-up study. *Law and Human Behavior, 35*(6), 466–478.

Faust, E., Bickart, W., Renaud, C., & Camp, S. (2014). Child pornography possessors and child contact sex offenders: A multilevel comparison of demographic characteristics and rates of recidivism. *Sexual Abuse: A Journal of Research and Treatment* [OnlineFirst publication]. doi:10.1177/1079063214521469.

Finkelhor, D. (1984). *Child sexual abuse: New theory and research.* New York: Free Press.

Finkelhor, D., Ormrod, R., & Chaffin, M. (2009). *Juveniles who commit sex offenses against minors*. Washington, DC: Office of Juvenile Justice and Delinquency Prevention.

Finkelhor, D., Shattuck, A., Turner, H. A., & Hamby, S. L. (2014). The lifetime prevalence of child sexual abuse and sexual assault assessed in late adolescence. *Journal of Adolescent Health, 55*(3), 329–333.

Frangez, D., Klancnik, A. T., Karer, M. Z., Ludvigsen, B. E., Konczyk, J., Perez, F. R., Veijalainen, M., & Lewin, M. (2015). The importance of terminology related to child sexual exploitation. *Revija za kriminalistiko in kriminologijo, 66*(4), 291–299.

Gallagher, B. (2007). Internet-initiated incitement and conspiracy to commit child sexual abuse (CSA): The typology, extent and nature of known cases. *Journal of Sexual Aggression, 13*(2), 101–119.

Gillespie, A. A. (2010). Legal definitions of child pornography. *Journal of Sexual Aggression, 16*(1), 19–31.

Gillespie, A. A. (2012). *Child pornography: Law and policy*. New York: Routledge.

Gillespie, S. M., Bailey, A., Squire, T., Carey, M. L., Eldridge, H. J., & Beech, A. R. (2016). An evaluation of a community-based psycho-educational program for users of child sexual exploitation material. *Sexual Abuse: A Journal of Research and Treatment*. Advance online publication. doi.org/10.1177/1079063216639591.

Goode, S. D. (2009). *Understanding and addressing sexual attraction to children: A study of paedophiles in contemporary society*. Abingdon: Routledge.

Hamilton, M. (2011). The child pornography crusade and its net-widening effect. *Cardozo Law Review, 33*, 1679–1732.

Hanson, R. K., & Morton-Bourgon, K. E. (2009). The accuracy of recidivism risk assessments for sexual offenders: A meta-analysis of 118 prediction studies. *Psychological Assessment, 21*(1), 1–21.

Harper, C. A., & Hogue, T. E. (2015). The emotional representation of sexual crime in the national British press. *Journal of Language and Social Psychology, 34*(1), 3–24.

Hernandez, A. E. (2000, November). *Self-reported contact sexual offenses by participants in the Federal Bureau of Prisons' Sex Offender Treatment Program: Implications for internet sex offenders*. Presented at the 19th Research and Treatment Conference of the Association for the Treatment of Sexual Abusers, San Diego.

Interagency Working Group on Sexual Exploitation of Children. (2016). *Terminology guidelines for the protection of children from sexual exploitation and sexual abuse*. Retrieved from http://cf.cdn.unwto.org/sites/all/files/docpdf/terminologyguidelines.pdf

Internet Watch Foundation. (2015). *Emerging patterns and trends report #1 online – Produced sexual content*. Retrieved from https://www.iwf.org.uk/sites/default/files/inlinefiles/Onlineproduced_sexual_content_report_100315.pdf

Kimball, K. A. (2011). Losing our soul: Judicial discretion in sentencing child pornography offenders. *Florida Law Review, 63*(6), 1515–1548.

Lee, A. F., Li, N. C., Lamade, R., Schuler, A., & Prentky, R. A. (2012). Predicting hands-on child sexual offenses among possessors of internet child pornography. *Psychology, Public Policy, and Law, 18*(4), 644.

Long, M. L., Alison, L. A., & McManus, M. A. (2013). Child pornography and likelihood of contact abuse: A comparison between contact child sexual offenders and noncontact offenders. *Sexual Abuse, 25*(4), 370–395.

Merdian, H. L., Curtis, C., Thakker, J., Wilson, N., & Boer, D. P. (2013). The three dimensions of online child pornography offending. *Journal of Sexual Aggression, 19*(1), 121–132.

Merdian, H. L., Gresswell, D. M., & Craig, L. A. (2017). Considering parental risk in parenting (child custody) evaluation cases involving child sexual exploitation material. In L. Dixon, D. F. Perkin, C. Hamilton-Giachritis, & L. A. Craig (Eds.), *The Wiley handbook on what works in child maltreatment: An evidence-based approach to assessment and intervention in child protection*. Chichester: Wiley-Blackwell.

Merdian, H. L., Perkins, D. E., Dustagheer, E., & Glorney, E. (in press). Development of a case formulation model for users of child sexual exploitation material. *Archives of Sexual Behaviour*.

Middleton, D. (2008). From research to practice: The development of the internet sex offender treatment programme (i-SOTP). *Irish Probation Journal, 5*, 49–64.

Nair, A. (2010). Real porn and pseudo porn: The regulatory road. *International Review of Law, Computers & Technology, 24*(3), 223–232.

Netclean. (2015). *Eleven unblievable truths: The Netclean Report*. Retrieved from https://www.netclean.com/wpcontent/uploads/2015/10/The_NetClean_Report_2015.pdf

Neutze, J., Seto, M. C., Schaefer, G. A., Mundt, I. A., & Beier, K. M. (2011). Predictors of child pornography offenses and child sexual abuse in a community sample of pedophiles and hebephiles. *Sexual Abuse, 23*(2), 212–242.

Osborn, J., Elliott, I., Middleton, D., & Beech, A. (2010). The use of actuarial risk assessment measures with UK internet child pornography offenders. *Journal of Aggression, Conflict and Peace Research, 2*(3), 16–24.

Phippen, A. (2017). *Children's online behaviour and safety: Policy and rights challenges*. London: Palgrave Macmillan.

Phippen, A., & Brennan, M. (2016). The new normal? Young people, technology & online behaviour. *NOTA News, 80*, 11–12.

Phippen, A., & Brennan, M. (2017). "Doing more" to end sexting – Facts, fictions and challenges in the policy debate on young people's sexting behaviour. *Entertainment Law Review, 28*(3), 91–96.

Powell, A. (2010). Configuring consent: Emerging technologies, unauthorised sexual images and sexual assault. *Australian and New Zealand Journal of Criminology, 43*, 76–90.

Quayle, E. (2008). Online sex offending: Psychopathology and theory. In D. R. Laws & W. T. O'Donohue (Eds.), *Sexual deviance: Theory, assessment, and treatment* (pp. 439–458). New York: Guilford Press.

Quayle, E., & Taylor, M. (2002). Paedophiles, pornography and the internet: Assessment issues. *British Journal of Social Work, 32*(7), 863–875.

Quayle, E., Erooga, M., Wright, L., Taylor, M., & Harbinson, D. (2006). *Only pictures? Therapeutic work with internet sex offenders*. Dorset: RHP.

Quayle, E., Allegro, S., Hutton, L., Sheath, M., & Lööf, L. (2014). Rapid skill acquisition and online sexual grooming of children. *Computers in Human Behavior, 39*, 368–375.

Seto, M. C. (2010). Child pornography use and internet solicitation in the diagnosis of pedophilia. *Archives of Sexual Behavior, 39*(3), 591–593.

Seto, M. C. (2013). *Internet sex offenders*. Washington, DC: American Psychological Association.

Seto, M. C., & Eke, A. W. (2005). The criminal histories and later offending of child pornography offenders. *Sexual Abuse: A Journal of Research and Treatment, 17*(2), 201–210.

Seto, M. C., & Eke, A. W. (2015). Predicting recidivism among adult male child pornography offenders: Development of the Child Pornography Offender Risk Tool (CPORT). *Law and Human Behavior, 39*(4), 416.

Seto, M. C., & Hanson, K. R. (2011). Introduction to special issue on internet-facilitated sexual offending. *Sexual Abuse: A Journal of Research and Treatment, 23*, 3–6. doi:10.1177/1079063211399295.

Seto, M. C., Cantor, J. M., & Blanchard, R. (2006). Child pornography offenses are a valid diagnostic indicator of pedophilia. *Journal of Abnormal Psychology, 115*(3), 610.

Seto, M. C., Reeves, L., & Jung, S. (2010). Explanations given by child pornography offenders for their crimes. *Journal of Sexual Aggression, 16*(2), 169–180.

Seto, M. C., Hanson, K. R., & Babchishin, K. M. (2011). Contact sexual offending by men with online sexual offences. *Sexual Abuse: A Journal of Research and Treatment, 23*, 124–145. doi:10.1177/1079063210369013.

Seto, M. C., Wood, J. M., Babchishin, K. M., & Flynn, S. (2012). Online solicitation offenders are different from child pornography offenders and lower risk contact sexual offenders. *Law and Human Behavior, 36*(4), 320–330.

Shields, R. T., Benelmouffok, A., & Letourneau, E. J. (2015, October). *Help wanted: Lessons on prevention from non-offending young adult pedophiles.* Presented at the 34th Annual Conference for the Association for the Treatment of Sexual Abusers, Montréal, Québec.

Surjadi, B., Bullens, R., van Horn, J., & Bogaerts, S. (2010). Internet offending: Sexual and non-sexual functions within a Dutch sample. *Journal of Sexual Aggression, 16*(1), 47–58.

Taylor, M., & Quayle, E. (2006). The internet and abuse images of children: Search, precriminal situations and opportunity. In R. Wortley & S. Smallbone (Eds.), *Situational prevention of child sexual abuse* (p. 7). New York: Criminal Justice Press/Willan Publishing.

Virtual Global Taskforce. (2015). *2015 VGT child sexual exploitation environmental scan.* The Hague: Europol.

Wakeling, H. C., Howard, P., & Barnett, G. (2011). Comparing the validity of the RM2000 scales and OGRS3 for predicting recidivism by internet sexual offenders. *Sexual Abuse: A Journal of Research and Treatment, 23*(1), 146–168.

Webb, L., Craissati, J., & Keen, S. (2007). Characteristics of internet child pornography offenders: A comparison with child molesters. *Sexual Abuse: A Journal of Research and Treatment, 19*(4), 449–465.

West, A. G., & Greenall, P. V. (2011). Incorporating index offence analysis into forensic clinical assessment. *Legal and Criminological Psychology, 16*(1), 144–159.

Wolak, J., & Finkelhor, D. (2011). *Sexting: A typology.* New Hampshire: Crimes Against Children Research Center.

Wortley, R. K., & Smallbone, S. (2006). *Child pornography on the internet.* Washington, DC: US Department of Justice, Office of Community Oriented Policing Services.

Yeung, T. H., Horyniak, D. R., Vella, A. M., Hellard, M. E., & Lim, M. S. (2014). Prevalence, correlates and attitudes towards sexting among young people in Melbourne, Australia. *Sexual Health, 11*(4), 332–339.

Young, K. (2005). Profiling online sex offenders, cyber-predators, and pedophiles. *Journal of Behavioral Profiling, 5*, 1–18.

6

Risk Management of Youth Who Sexually Offend: The Singapore Experience

Gerald Zeng and Chi Meng Chu

Introduction

Over the past few decades, there has been increasing public panic over how society should deal with offenders who commit sexual crime, which has led to the practice of "populist punitiveness" in some jurisdictions to manage offenders who commit sexual crime, in which punishment of the offender and prevention of recidivism (e.g., indeterminate sentences, sex offender registries) take precedence over treatment (Appelbaum 2009; Birgden 2004; Birgden and Cucolo 2011; Edwards and Hensley 2001). However, there have also been recent judicial shifts towards providing sentencing options that punish the crime, but not the offender (Appelbaum 2009). Such approaches allow for the rehabilitation of offenders who commit sexual crime through comprehensive treatment and reintegration (Appelbaum 2009; Birgden 2004).

G. Zeng • C.M. Chu (✉)
Clinical and Forensic Psychology Service, Ministry of Social and Family Development, Singapore, Singapore

© The Author(s) 2017
H. Kemshall, K. McCartan (eds.), *Contemporary Sex Offender Risk Management, Volume II*, Palgrave Studies in Risk, Crime and Society,
DOI 10.1007/978-3-319-63573-6_6

The management of offenders who commit sexual crime is therefore a contentious issue, with various jurisdictions having to find a balance between the prevention of harm to society again (i.e., treatment as management of offender risk) and the protection and reintegration of the sex offender (i.e., treatment as rehabilitation and addressing the offender's needs) (Birgden and Cucolo 2011). This debate over the management of individuals who sexually offend is also present in Singapore. For example, an increase in sexual offending in recent years (Cheong and Lim 2015) has prompted public discussion on the establishment of a sex offender registry (Phua and Lim 2012). This issue has been raised recently in parliament, with the Minister of Home Affairs noting that legislation already allows for the maintenance and screening (by the Singapore Police Force) of nonpublic records of offenders who have committed serious crime (including sex offences) for Government Agencies[1] that work with sensitive populations (e.g., children, vulnerable youth). In this way, the nonpublic database achieves a balance by mitigating the risk of exposing children to individuals who have committed serious sex offenders, while ensuring that rehabilitation and reintegration is not disrupted by the stigmatisation that a sex offender registry may entail (Ministry of Home Affairs 2017).

However, achieving this balance between prevention of harm to society and the reintegration of the sex offender is particularly crucial when managing youth who sexually offend. Contrary to perceptions that all offenders who commit sexual crime are the same, or that they are "lifelong predators", these offenders differ significantly in terms of the risks, needs, and protective factors that influence their offending, and this affects their assessed risk of recidivism and subsequent treatment (Appelbaum 2009; Birgden 2004). For youth who sexually offend in various stages of psychosocial development, their personal and developmental needs must be taken into account. The way in which youth who sexually offend are managed and treated is therefore crucial to their rehabilitation and reintegration into society.

This chapter will first introduce the juvenile justice system in Singapore, and touch on how the philosophy of restorative justice is applied to youth offending to achieve a balance between deterrence and personal accountability and ensuring that programmes and opportunities for rehabilitation, reintegration, and restoration are provided. The various pathways through which youth who sexually offended can take through the justice system will also be presented. However, the majority of youth who sexually offend in Singapore are served by the Ministry of Social and Family Development, and the chapter will focus on the assessment and management of these youth by the Ministry, particularly through the Clinical and Forensic Psychology Service, which provides specialised assessment and treatment to offenders. After describing profiles of local youth who sexually offend, the chapter will introduce and elaborate upon the implementation of the Risk-Need-Responsivity model and the Good Lives Model (GLM), which form the foundation from which offender assessment and treatment is carried out. The effort to conduct empirically based assessment and treatment via the integration of findings from local research and evaluation will also be detailed, before a final discussion on the future directions of the management of youth who sexually offended in Singapore.

Juvenile Justice in Singapore

Singapore is a sovereign island city-state in South East Asia with a land area of 718 square kilometres and a total population of 5.54 million[2] (Singapore Department of Statistics 2016). Being a multicultural business and trading hub, it is heavily influenced by both Asian and Western cultures. As a former British colony, many statutes in Singapore are based on English common law. Therefore, the way in which offences are defined is similar to that of other commonwealth jurisdictions.

The pathway through the justice system that youth who sexually offended typically take is outlined in Fig. 6.1.

In Singapore, several legislations are pertinent to youth offending. The passing of the Family Justice Act in 2014 led to the creation of the Family Justice Courts, within which the Youth Court (formerly Juvenile Court of Singapore) hears cases for offenders from 7 up to 16 years of age (Family Justice Courts of Singapore 2017a). The Youth Court's jurisdiction is defined by Section 28 of the Children and Young Persons Act (CYPA) of 2001,[3] which directs the Youth Court to consider the welfare

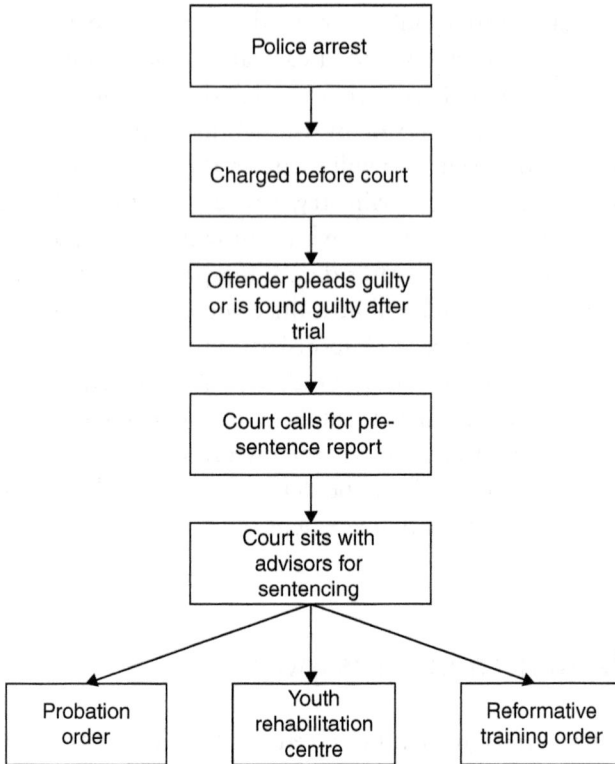

Fig. 6.1 Legal pathways for youth offenders in Singapore

of youth offenders while making judicial decisions (Family Justice Courts of Singapore 2017a; Singapore Statutes 2001).

The Youth Court adopts a philosophy of restorative justice, which seeks to achieve a balance between personal accountability for offences committed, and the rehabilitation of the offender with a view towards reintegration into family and community. The Youth Court seeks to apply such a balance in its sentencing and programming by considering the availability of opportunities for youth to acquire basic life skills, education, employability, and self-sustenance while addressing the underlying causes of their offending. In doing so, the Youth Court seeks to draw on available resources such as the youth's family and community of care, to address problems in a holistic manner and enact meaningful change and reform in the youth[4] (Family Justice Courts of Singapore 2017a).

Importantly, such positive change is achieved through youth offenders taking responsibility for their antisocial or offending behaviour (Family Justice Courts of Singapore 2017a). In recognising the consequences and impact of their actions on victims and the offenders' own life, reparations may then be made to redress their wrongdoings. For example, the Youth Court may direct the offender to attend victim-offender mediation,[5] where the offender is made more acutely aware of the harm caused to the victim, and can also offer an apology or some form of compensation (Family Justice Courts of Singapore 2017a). This process is meant to be both rehabilitative for the offender and restorative for the victim.

In addition to these restorative justice programmes, the Youth Court may issue youth with several orders upon the finding of guilt. The Youth Court first calls for a pre-sentence report to assist in sentencing. For the majority of youth offending cases, this is conducted by the Ministry of Social and Family Development (the Ministry), and considers various circumstances and risk factors such as family, education and/or employment, peers, gang membership, and antisocial attitude and behaviour of the youth. The pre-sentence report is taken into account by the Youth Court when it sits with two Panel Advisors,[6] Court counsellors, and a probation officer prior to sentencing. The Youth Court has a number of options at its disposal, the most common of which are to issue a probation order, to commit offenders to a youth rehabilitation centre, or to undergo training at the Reformative Training Centre.[7] Youth who are placed on probation or ordered to reside in a youth rehabilitation centre are managed by the Ministry, whereas youth who are on reformative training orders are managed by the Singapore Prison Service. However, the majority of youth who sexually offend are generally served with the former two orders, while only a few youth who sexually offend are issued with reformative training orders; therefore, most youth are referred to the Ministry for management and treatment.

In particular, three Services in the Ministry are involved in the rehabilitation of youth who sexually offend—the Probation and Community Rehabilitation Service (which manages the probation of youths and those in youth rehabilitation centres), the Youth Residential Service (which manages youth ordered to reside in the Singapore Boys' Home), and the Clinical and Forensic Psychology Service (CFPS), which provides empirically based assessment and treatment of youth and adults who have offended. With regard to sexual offending, psychologists from CFPS are involved in providing assessments that inform the pre-sentencing report (e.g., assessing the risk of sexual and general recidivism), as well as providing specialised treatment via individual or group treatment programmes after sentencing. Referrals to CFPS may also come from community agencies, child protection services, and from youth residential institutions when current residents commit sexual offending. The youth that are seen by CFPS are thus representative of youth who sexually offend in Singapore.

Profile and Typologies of Youth Who Sexually Offended

The crime rate in Singapore is generally low at 588 crimes per 100,000 population (Department of Statistics Singapore 2017), and similarly the crime rate among youth is low, with youth arrests accounting for approximately 18–19% of all arrests in Singapore from 2011 to 2015 (Department of Statistics Singapore 2017). With regard to sexual offending, the Singapore police encounter an average of 150 sexual assault cases and about 1,200–1,300 cases of molest each year (Seow 2017). For youth, only 168 youth who sexually offended (aged 12–18 years) were referred to the CFPS for psychological assessment of risk of future sexually abusive behaviour in the approximately 14 years from October 2002 to December 2011. None of the youth were female, and the majority of the youth were Chinese (44.3%, 74/167) or Malay (40.7%; 68/167); 12.0% ($n = 20$) were Indian, and 3% ($n = 5$) were of other ethnicities (Zeng et al. 2015a).

In the same sample, the most common type of sexual offending committed by the youth was molestation (81.4%, 136/167), followed by voyeuristic (81.4%, 136/167) and exhibitionistic (81.4%, 136/167) offences.

Only a minority of youth committed penetrative offences of nonconsensual fellatio 14.4% (*n* = 24) and 18.0% (*n* = 30) rape. Furthermore, the majority of youth who sexually offended tended to commit only sexual offending; in a study of 167 youth who sexually offended referred to the CFPS from 2002 to 2012, 33.5% (56/167) of the sample committed nonsexual offences in addition to sexual offences (Zeng et al. 2015a). Among these youth, 18 (32.1%) had committed violent offences (e.g., rioting, robbery, causing harm) and 38 (67.9%) had nonviolent nonsexual offences (e.g., nonviolent theft, fraud, drug abuse). Delving into the typology of criminal diversity among youth who sexually offended, the same study found that youth who offended both sexually and nonsexually were found to have higher risk and criminogenic needs as compared to youth who only sexually offended, specifically in terms of psychosocial functioning, peer relations, and engagement in recreational activities (Zeng et al. 2015a). Findings mirror those of a previous study that found youth who offended both sexually and nonsexually to more likely to reoffend violently, as compared to youth who only offended sexually (Chu and Thomas 2010). Both studies therefore point to a distinction between youth who offended sexually and nonsexually and youth who offended only sexually, and suggest general criminogenic risk and needs may underpin the sexual offending committed by criminally versatile youth, which may result in a higher risk trajectory (Chu and Thomas 2010; Zeng et al. 2015a).

Such results are also consistent with research by Pullman and Seto (2012) suggesting that the risk for sexual and general reoffending among adult offenders who commit sexual crime depends on their levels in two risk dimensions—sexual deviance (e.g., atypical sexual interests) and general antisocial orientation (e.g., antisocial attitudes and beliefs). Offenders who commit sexual crime who are high in either sexual deviance or general antisocial orientation are likely to offend only sexually or generally respectively. However, offenders high in both dimensions will have the greatest likelihood of reoffending (Pullman and Seto 2012). These findings have been taken into account by psychologists in CFPS, who currently include assessments of future risk of nonsexual (general) reoffending (e.g., YLS/CMI) alongside that of sexual reoffending when assessing and treating youth who have past or current nonsexual offending in addition their sexual offending.

Frameworks for Rehabilitation

Two frameworks in particular have played significant and complimentary roles in guiding the assessment and management of youth offenders in Singapore—the Risk-Need-Responsivity (RNR) model, and the GLM. The implementation of both models and application towards the assessment and rehabilitation of youth who sexually offended is described below.

The Risk-Need-Responsivity Framework in Singapore

The Risk-Need-Responsivity (RNR) framework seeks to provide practitioners with accurate information and classification on risk and needs for effective rehabilitation to occur (Andrews and Bonta 2010). The foundation of the RNR framework is the general personality and cognitive social learning theoretical perspective on offending behaviour, which suggests that eight major risk and need factors, also known as the "Central Eight", are implicated in offending behaviour. Having a history of antisocial behaviour, antisocial cognition, antisocial personality patterns, and antisocial associates constitute the "Big Four" major risk factors, while family and marital relationships, poor education and/or employment circumstances, difficulties pertaining to substance use, and the absence of leisure or recreational activities make up the "Moderate Four" (Andrews and Bonta 2010). The influence of the Central Eight on criminal behaviour has subsequently been supported by empirical studies and meta-analyses (e.g., Bonta et al. 1998; Gendreau et al. 1996; Hanson and Morton-Bourgon 2005; Lipsey and Derzon 1998; McGuire 2004).

The accurate identification and assessment of risks and needs such as the Central Eight can help practitioners to make informed decision about the type of risk and needs to focus on, the level of treatment to be provided, and on how to tailor intervention to best suit the offender

(Andrews and Bonta 2010). These are expressed in three principles of the RNR model. The Risk principle states that the intensity of treatment to be provided should match the risk level of the offender. For example, offenders who are assessed to be high risk should receive more intensive supervision and treatment as compared to those who are assessed to be of low risk (Andrews et al. 1990, 2011). The second principle—the Need principle—states that the intervention for each offender should focus on the specific dynamic criminogenic needs implicated in the offending behaviour. Finally, the Responsivity principle states the intervention and its delivery should be tailored to match that of the offender's abilities and learning style. Altogether, these three principles of RNR ensure that resources and service delivery are appropriately and efficiently delivered to offenders in a manner that maximises their learning and rehabilitation (Andrews and Friesen 1987; Andrews and Kiessling 1980; Baird et al. 1979; O'Donnell et al. 1971). Furthermore, research has shown that interventions that incorporated the RNR principles have better outcomes in terms of the reduction in recidivism rates, as compared to interventions that do not employ the RNR principles (Andrews and Dowden 2005).

In order to move towards empirically based assessment and management of offenders in Singapore, the Ministry of Social and Family Development adopted the RNR framework in 2003, and incorporated all three principles across the various Services that provided assessment and treatment services to adult and youth offenders (Chu et al. 2012b). The introduction of the RNR framework led to significant changes in the way that offenders were first assessed and subsequently managed. Key to the implementation was the introduction of the Level of Service instruments, which allowed for structured assessments of the Central Eight risk and need factors to be conducted, and produced risk classifications for targeted intervention and case management. As such, the Youth Level of Service/Case Management Inventory (YLS/CMI—elaborated in the Assessment section below) is currently used for the assessment of all youth offenders seen by the Ministry. Importantly, since its introduction, the RNR framework and the YLS/CMI have been gradually adopted by other government and nongovernment agencies that come into contact with youth offenders.[8] This has created a common language among professionals working with youth offenders, from which risks, needs and responsivity factors can be better understood and communicated (Chu et al. 2012b; Chu and Zeng 2017).

The Good Lives Model for Strengths-Based Rehabilitation

Other than the RNR model, the GLM has also played an integral role in the rehabilitation of youth offenders, and in particular, youth who sexually offended in Ministry of Social and Family Development. Whereas the RNR model focuses on identifying risk factors in order to manage them and alleviate deficits, the GLM was first conceptualised as a strengths-based approach to the rehabilitation of offenders who commit sexual crime that was in contrast to traditional risk management approaches (Willis et al. 2013). Nevertheless, the GLM is complimentary to the RNR model, and has therefore been adopted for use in combination with an RNR-based approach to treat youth who sexually offended in Singapore.

The GLM posits that all human beings value certain states of mind, personal characteristics, and experiences, defined as primary human goods, which they strive to achieve (Willis et al. 2013). There are 11 types of primary human goods: (1) life (including healthy living and functioning), (2) knowledge (how well informed one feels about things that are important to them), (3) excellence in play (hobbies and recreational pursuits), (4) excellence in work (including mastery experiences), (5) excellence in agency (autonomy, power and self-directedness), (6) inner peace (freedom from emotional turmoil and stress), (7) relatedness (including intimate, romantic, and familial relationships), (8) community (connection to wider social groups), (9) spirituality (finding meaning and purpose in life), (10) pleasure (feeling good in the here and now), and (11) creativity (expressing oneself through alternative forms). All these primary goods appeal to individuals in varying magnitudes, but their prioritisation reflects their value to the particular individual, and what the individual strives for in life (Willis et al. 2013). Individuals form a good life plan around these core values and seek to achieve them to live a fulfilled and meaningful life (Chu and Ward 2015; Willis et al. 2013). Attainment of these goods is thus assumed to be associated with increased wellbeing and happiness, whereas the converse is associated with psychological problems (Chu and Ward 2015; Ward and Stewart 2003).

Individuals then engage in secondary or instrumental goods, which represent the approach goals and concrete actions that individuals use to obtain primary human goods (Willis et al. 2013). For example, the primary good of relatedness may be achieved by spending time with family and friends or engaging with social activities. However, when primary goods prove difficult to obtain, individuals may seek to achieve them through harmful secondary goods (which are sometimes also dynamic risk factors) that have been influenced by criminogenic or noncriminogenic needs (Chu and Ward 2015). Therefore, relatedness may be achieved through mixing with antisocial peers (risk factor), or in the case of sexual offending, through molest or criminal intimidation.

Importantly, it is the secondary goods or the manner in which primary goods are obtained that is flawed, and not the primary goods themselves (Willis et al. 2013). There are four different secondary good flaws in the GLM: (1) inappropriate or harmful means to obtain primary goods, (2) a good life plan that is too narrow and excludes other primary goods, (3) experiencing conflict or incoherence between core primary goods and/or secondary goods, and (4) lack of capabilities to satisfy primary goods. The aim of rehabilitation is therefore to address these flaws and criminogenic needs so that primary goods may be sought in nonharmful ways, while reducing the risk of reoffending (Willis et al. 2013). Within the GLM framework, the significance of offenders' primary goods as core values are acknowledged and used to motivate offenders' to cultivate the skills required to craft nonharmful good life plans to achieve their primary goods[9] (Chu et al. 2015a).

The GLM approach was adopted in the assessment and treatment of youth who sexually offended (described below) in 2011 by the Clinical and Forensic Psychology Service to introduce positive criminology approaches to existing RNR approaches[10] (Chu and Ward 2015). Research conducted to describe 168 youth who sexually offended referred to the CFPS revealed that the top primary goods sought by these youth were pleasure (91.1%; 153/168), relatedness (35.7%; 60/168), and inner peace (17.3%; 29/168), reflecting that sensation seeking, connecting with others, and being free from inner turmoil and stress were important goals for adolescents at that stage of life; it was through flaws (e.g., lack of appropriate means, lack of capability) that led them to sexually offend to fulfil these primary goods (Chu et al. 2015a).

Protective Factors

In line with the shift towards incorporating strengths-based and positive criminological approaches with the traditional risk-based RNR framework, assessment and intervention with youth who sexually offended have also come to include protective factors. There is no consistent definition of protective factors. Some conceptualise protective and risk factors as two sides of the same coin, where the absence of a risk factor indicates the presence of protective factors (Borum et al. 2006; Luthar and McMahon 1996); others define protective factors as distinct and complimentary to risk factors, both of which contribute to an overall risk and protection judgement (Borum et al. 2006; Luthar and McMahon 1996). Additionally, the extant literature on the mechanisms though which protective factors influence desistance and recidivism are still unclear. One perspective suggests that protective factors reduce the risk of recidivism independent of risk factors; however, another suggests that protective factors moderate or buffer the impact of risk factors on recidivism (de Vries Robbé and Willis 2017). However conceptualised, it is generally agreed that protective factors may contribute to reducing the risk of recidivism, and should therefore be integrated into the assessment and management of offenders (de Ruiter and Nicholls 2011; Zeng et al. 2015b).

Preliminary examination of protective factors among youth who sexually offended in the Singapore context produced mixed results. The study examined the relationship between protective factors and recidivism among 97 youth who sexually offended referred to the CFPS (Zeng et al. 2015b). It also examined the predictive validity of two measures of protective factors—the Structured Assessment of Protective Factors for Violence Risk (SAPROF—de Vogel et al. 2012), and the Desistance for Adolescents who Sexually Harm (DASH-13—Worling 2013; Zeng et al. 2015b). Scores on both measures of protective factors were inversely related to scores on the ERASOR, indicating that the presence of more protective factors was indeed associated with a lower risk of recidivism. However, scores on the SAPROF and DASH-13 were not found to be related to sexual recidivism, or to possess adequate predictive validity with regard to desistance from sexual recidivism (Zeng et al. 2015b).

Although such findings are not encouraging, a few caveats from the study must be taken into account. First, there was a very low base rate of sexual recidivism of only 7.2% (7/97)[11] during the follow-up period, which may have resulted in difficulty detecting any significant relationships between scores on the SAPROF and DASH-13 and sexual recidivism (Zeng et al. 2015b). Similarly, the accuracy of the predictive validity for desistance may have also been affected. Second, at the time of the study, the SAPROF had only been designed and validated for the assessment of adults; some items were therefore more suited for adults rather than youth,[12] which may have affected ability of the SAPROF to assess youth (Zeng et al. 2015b). Since then, a youth version of the SAPROF (SAPROF-YV) has been developed, which addresses protective factors specific to youth.

Even though initial findings above were not promising, there may still be utility in assessing protective factors for individual case management and intervention. Therapists or case workers can not only obtain a more balanced overview of factors that may encourage rehabilitation and desistance, but also build on identified protective factors to reduce the risk of recidivism, or to buffer other risk factors and criminogenic needs (de Vogel et al. 2012; Lodewijks et al. 2010; Miller 2006). Therefore, the SAPROF-YV was introduced as an assessment tool for youth who sexually offended by CFPS in 2015, following training by the developers of the tool; further evaluation and validation of the new youth version is currently underway.

The Assessment of Youth Who Sexually Offended

The SAPROF-YV is used alongside other measures to provide a comprehensive assessment of the risk, needs, and protective factors that are present for each youth who sexually offended. When these youth are assessed by CFPS, psychologists employ a set of primary assessment and case management tools, supplemented by other tools as necessary.[13] The primary measure used for the evaluation of risk of sexual recidivism is the Estimate of Risk of Adolescent Sex Offense Recidivism (ERASOR—Worling and Curwen 2001). The ERASOR was selected after local research indicated that both its clinical rating and total score possessed adequate predictive validity for sexual recidivism[14] (Chu et al. 2012a).

Correspondingly, the Youth Level of Service/Case Management Inventory (Hoge and Andrews, 2011) was chosen by CFPS (as well as other youth justice agencies in Singapore) as the primary assessment measure of risk factors and criminogenic needs for general and nonsexual recidivism in youth offenders. It was also used as a case management tool (YLS/CMI—Hoge and Andrews 2011). The Level of Service suite of instruments[15] were adopted together with the implementation of the RNR model in Singapore, to introduce greater structure and consistency to the assessment of youth and adult offenders, in contrast to previously unstructured and subjective clinical judgements that were prone to bias and unreliability (Ægisdóttir et al. 2006; Chua et al. 2014; Grove et al. 2000; Hoge and Andrews 2002; Monahan 1981). Being closely aligned with the RNR model, the YLS/CMI consists of eight domains that correspond to the central eight risk and need factors for recidivism, but also contains a section on noncriminogenic needs (e.g., familial history of offending, financial/accommodation problems, poor problem solving skills) to improve responsivity in case management (Hoge and Andrews 2011). Several local studies have established the predictive validity of the instrument for use in assessing risk of general and violent recidivism (Chu et al. 2015b; Chu et al. 2014b; Zeng et al. 2015a). However, it should be noted that predictive validity has not been found for sexual recidivism (Chu et al. 2012a), and the instrument is therefore always used together with a sexual recidivism risk-specific tool such as the ERASOR when assessment is conducted on local youth who sexually offended.

In addition to identifying the risks and needs of youth who sexually offend, a crucial part of assessment also involves determining the youths' good life plans. In order to assess the primary human goods associated with youth who sexually offend, psychologists conduct an open-ended and transparent interview, where the psychologist describes the purpose of the interview in wanting to talk and discover what the youth consider as valuable for a fulfilling life (Chu et al. 2015a; Chu and Ward 2015). The psychologist also explains each primary human good in detail and asks the youth to indicate how meaningful each good is, how the youth currently obtains the good, and discusses whether the method of obtaining the good is positive or negative (Chu et al. 2015a; Chu and Ward 2015). The interview allows for a frank exploration of the youths' good life plan and the flawed approaches or secondary goods that led to their sexual offending (Chu et al. 2015a; Chu and Ward 2015).

Treatment of Youth Who Sexually Offended

After assessment of their risks and needs, strengths and good life plans, youth who sexually offended may also be referred for treatment at CFPS. As with assessment, all group programmes and individual therapy provided by CFPS adopt an integrated strength (GLM) and risk-based (RNR) approach that focuses on relapse prevention while at the same time providing positive goals that youth can achieve (Chu and Ward 2015). To this end, an emphasis on a respectful, collaborative therapeutic relationship that involves the youth owning and constructing their own rehabilitation is crucial (Chu and Ward 2015). The psychologists work together with the youth to openly explore and discuss the youths' risks, needs, and primary human goods, and how they have affected offending behaviour; additionally, internal and external strengths (e.g., good at math) and capabilities (e.g., represents the school for math Olympiad) are also identified (Chu and Ward 2015; Thakker et al. 2014). Intervention strategies and targets are then established, identifying the skills and capacities required to manage or mitigate the assessed risks and needs (internal and external barriers) in order to fulfil the youth's good life plan (Chu et al. 2015a; Chu and Ward 2015). Psychologists then work with the youth to execute the intervention plan, as well as build a strong thera-peutic alliance, which may contribute to better motivation and subse-quent treatment success (Chu and Ward 2015; Thakker et al. 2014).

Notably, CFPS is the main provider of sexual offending-specific group treatment for youth in Singapore. Such treatment is offered through two longstanding but evolving programmes—the Positive Adolescent Sexuality Treatment programme for youth, and the Basic Education and Sexuality Treatment programme for males who have sexually offended with intellectual disability.

The Positive Adolescent Sexuality Treatment (PAST)

The Positive Adolescent Sexuality Treatment (PAST) programme was established in 2000 as the first empirically based specialised treatment group (8–15 participants) programme for adolescent males (13–18 years of age) who have sexually offended. The primary goal of the programme is to provide participants with the knowledge and skills to prevent re-offending. The programme is also heavily influenced by the GLM, and adopts a strengths-based approach towards building participants' capa-bilities to obtain their human goods through nonoffending ways. Through interactive discussions and activities, participants learn to take responsi-bility for their offending, learn about victim impact and issues, identify their offence cycles, develop plans to deal with offending triggers, and cultivate social and life skills. The programme is conducted in an open-group format, whereby participants are able to complete treatment at different time points, allowing them to better pace their progress. The approximate completion time for PAST is 6 months with weekly sessions of 2 hours each.

The PAST programme was evaluated in 2012 based on data from 2008 to 2011.[16] Reliable change indexes were calculated with data from 46 PAST participants who were administered a battery of instruments[17] at pre-treatment and post-treatment, to determine if reliable therapeutic changes occurred after treatment (Chu et al. 2015c). Findings indicated a decrease in the percentage of participants assessed as high (from 28% to 7%) and moderate (from 65% to 35%) risk from pre-treatment to post-treatment; the percentage of participants assessed to be of low risk increased from 6% to 58% from pre-treatment to post-treatment (Chu et al. 2015c). Of the full sample, 67.4% of participants improve in their risk ratings, while 32.6% remained the same; there was no deterioration of risk ratings. Treatment gains were also reflected in terms of improvement in attitudes supportive of sexual entitlement (34.78% of participants) and exhibitionism (63.04%), sexual attitudes towards children (41.3%), sexual harm (39.13%), endorsement of rape and cognitive distortions about women (67.39%), and dating abuse (50.0%)

However, deteriorations were also found among the sample, mostly notably in terms of endorsement of rape (15.22% of participants), attitudes supportive of exhibitionism (8.70%), and dating abuse (28.26%); these findings may have been due to contamination effects from participants higher in risk to those who were low in risk at pre-treatment. The evaluation in 2012 then led to a further evolution of PAST into an empirically based[18] three-phase approach of enhancing engagement, targeting criminogenic needs, and developing self-management plans to achieve fulfilling lives. New psychometric tools that were well-validated for use in youth were also introduced and another round of evaluation is underway.

Basic Education and Sexuality Treatment (BEST)

The Basic Education and Sexuality Treatment (BEST) programme was launched in 2007 to provide individual and group treatment to males (at least 13 years of age) who have sexually offended with special needs or mental disorders, and are assessed to have at least moderate risk of reoffending. Similar to PAST, the programme incorporates the GLM with a cognitive behavioural model of treatment, and seeks to equip participants with skills to prevent re-offending and to achieve meaningful lives through attainment of human goods. The programme was adapted from Professor William Lindsay's treatment programme for offenders who commit sexual crime with developmental disabilities in the UK. However, BEST takes into account the special learning needs of intellectually disabled participants, to bring across content and learning in a more responsive manner. Therefore, strategies such as simplified communication and role-play are employed. The average completion time for BEST is 9–12 months with weekly sessions.

Changes were made to the BEST programme in 2011, to facilitate better understanding and communication for participants (e.g., more role-plays, greater use of images), incorporate the GLM and introduce more behavioural strategies to manage sexual offending behaviours. After further evaluation in 2012, the programme is currently under revision to expand its coverage on emotional regulation strategies and activities to increase self-esteem. Evaluation in 2012 was conducted on data from seven participants who had completed the programme between 2008 and 2011. Reliable change indexes were calculated to detect clinically significant change as measured by a battery of instruments[19] pre- and post-treatment. Results pointed to improvements in distorted cognitions relating to sexual offending, problem solving skills, and emotional regulation.

As with PAST, evaluation of the BEST programme pointed to several limitations, which are addressed in the current revision. In accordance to the responsivity principle of the RNR model, new instruments more suited to participants with intellectual disability were introduced, together with other measures to cover the expanded treatment targets (e.g., victim empathy, social competency, and self-regulation). The redeveloped programme also offers greater therapeutic contact and support for parents and/or caregivers of participants, with the aim of equipping them with parenting and risk management skills.

Future Directions

The regular evaluation and tweaking of treatment programmes such as PAST and BEST is important for the provision of empirically based services to youth who sexually offend. Research and evaluation studies should continue to examine the profiles of these youth in Singapore, validate existing assessment tools for local use, explore new instruments, and regularly evaluate treatment programmes. To this end, research initiatives are underway to conduct in-depth research into youth sexual offending. Notably, a longitudinal study was launched in 2016 to include all youth offenders in Singapore. The study, *Enhancing Positive Outcomes in Youth Offenders and the Community*, is intended as a holistic examination of the interaction between youth offenders' developmental and offending trajectories.[20] The study will examine a broad range of aspects such as risks, needs and protective factors, adaptive and maladaptive functioning, and adverse childhood experiences, so as to deliver insights that can further contribute to clinical and operational work.

At the same time, CFPS is continually exploring interventions that may be more effective not only with youth who sexually offend, but also with children and youth who are at risk of developing problematic sexual behaviour. For example, it is looking at adapting the evidence-based Problematic Sexual Behaviour-Cognitive Behavioural Therapy to specifically target inappropriate sexual behaviours among at-risk youth (Carpenter and Addis 2000; National Institute of Justice 2015). Introducing such programmes, as well as providing specialised training to community agencies that serve low-risk individuals who exhibit sexualised behaviour are part of efforts to place a greater emphasis on early intervention that may prevent further offending and sexual abuse. Additionally, CFPS will continue ongoing programmes of professional training and attachment (to other local and international specialist centres) for its own clinicians in order to keep up to date on the developments in sexual offending management and treatment.

In summary, the assessment and management of youth who sexually offend in Singapore is guided by the principles of restorative justice, the Risk-Need-Responsivity framework and the GLM. Through the application of an integrated strengths- and risk-based approach, youth who sexually offended are able to achieve positive change and reintegration with family and community. At the same time, it is important that the assessment and management of such youth continues to evolve and respond to changes in the youth sexual offending landscape, while integrating increasingly available local research and programme evaluation into practice.

Notes

1. Two Government Agencies that the Singapore Police Force provide such screening for are the Ministry of Education and the Ministry of Social and Family Development. All child-related care and educational institutions in Singapore are registered with or managed by either Ministry.
2. The total population of 5.54 million includes Singapore citizens (61%), permanent residents (10%), and non-residents (29%). The resident population totals about 3.90 million, of whom 74.4% are of Chinese descent, 13.4% are Malay, 9.1% are Indian, and the remaining 3.1% are of other races.
3. In the *Children and Young Persons Act*, a "child" refers to a person who is below the age of 14 years and a "young person" refers to a person who is 14 years of age (or above) and under 16 years old.
4. Family conferences are organised, which bring together all relevant parties (e.g., family, psychologists, case officers, school authorities) to plan, execute, and address issues faced during the youth's rehabilitation and reintegration. Family conferences may also be used to repair or build familial relationships (between family members or with the youth) through counselling.
5. These victim-offender mediation conferences (also termed HEAL—healing, enriching, and linking conferences) focus on victim rehabilitation and restoration through meeting the offender only in circumstances that are comfortable to the victim. Follow-up counselling or restoration can be conducted after the mediation if necessary (Family Justice Courts of Singapore 2017a).
6. Panel Advisors are individuals from the community who have extensive experience in working with youth. Panel Advisors are appointed by the President of Singapore (Family Justice Courts of Singapore 2017b).
7. This option is only provided for youth who are 14–16 years of age.
8. These include Government Agencies such the Ministry of Social and Family Development, the Singapore Prisons Service, the Central Narcotics Bureau, and the Singapore Police Force, as well as non-Government Agencies such as social service organisations. For a comprehensive account of the implementation of the RNR model and the YLS/CMI in Singapore, see Chua et al. (2014), and Chu and Zeng (2017).

9. For case studies on the application of the GLM model, see Thakker et al. (2014) and Chu et al. (2014a).

10. Since then the GLM approach has also been adopted for use by probation officers for the rehabilitation of youth probationers by the Probation and Community Rehabilitation Service, Singapore.

11. The base rate for sexual and nonsexual recidivism was 26.8% (26/97).

12. For example, Item 8: Financial Management; Item 11: Positive Life Goals; Item 14: Intimate Relationship.

13. The core set of assessment measures include the Youth Level of Service/Case Management Inventory, the Estimate of Risk of Adolescent Sexual Offense Recidivism, the Paulhus Deception Scales, the Novaco Anger Scale and Provocation Inventory, and the Youth Self Report. Often times, a personality test or questionnaire relating to interpersonal style is also administered with the youth.

14. In contrast, the same study found that the Juvenile Sex Offender Assessment Protocol-II (J-SOAP-II), another specialised tool for assessing risk of sexual recidivism, failed to predict sexual recidivism.

15. These measures include the Level of Service Inventory (Andrews 1982), the Level of Service Inventory-Revised (Andrews and Bonta 1995), the Level of Service/Case Management Inventory (Andrews et al. 2004), the Level of Service/Risk-Need-Responsivity (Andrews et al. 2008), the Youth Level of Service Inventory (Andrews et al. 1984), and the Youth Level of Service/Case Management Inventory (Hoge and Andrews 2002, 2011).

16. Although PAST started in 2000, it underwent changes in 2008 that included the introduction of new measures or modification of old ones. Therefore, evaluation was only conducted on PAST after the change.

17. Instruments included in the battery were the Basic Empathy Scale, the Social Self-Esteem Inventory, The Hanson Sex Attitude Questionnaire, the Questionnaire on Attitudes Consistent with Sexual Offending, and the Brief Control Scale.

18. Adapted from the Rockwood Psychological Services Primary Programme.

19. Instruments included in the battery were the Dundee Provocation Inventory, Social Problem Solving Inventory—Revised: Short, adapted Barratt Impulsiveness Scale, adapted Sensation Seeking Scale, and adapted Questionnaire on Attitudes Consistent with Sexual Offending.

20. The corresponding author can be contacted for further information on the EPYC study.

References

Ægisdóttir, S., White, M. J., Spengler, P. M., Maugherman, A. S., Anderson, L. A., Cook, R. S., … D., R. J. (2006). The meta-analysis of clinical judgment project: Fifty-six years of accumulated research on clinical versus statistical prediction Stefania Aegisdottir. *The Counseling Psychologist, 34*(3), 341–382. doi:10.1177/0011000005285875.

Andrews, D. A. (1982). *The Level of Supervision Inventory (LSI): The first follow up*. Toronto: Ontario Ministry of Correctional Services.

Andrews, D. A., & Bonta, J. (1995). *The level of service inventory-revised*. Toronto: Multi-Health Systems.

Andrews, D. A., & Bonta, J. (2010). *The psychology of criminal conduct* (5th ed.). New Providence: Anderson.

Andrews, D. A., & Dowden, C. (2005). Managing correctional treatment for reduced recidivism: A meta-analytic review of programme integrity. *Legal and Criminological Psychology, 10*(2), 173–187. doi:10.1348/135532505X36723.

Andrews, D. A., & Friesen, W. (1987). Assessments of anticriminal plans and the prediction of criminal futures aresearch note. *Criminal Justice and Behavior, 14*(1), 33–37. doi:10.1177/0093854887014001004.

Andrews, D. A., & Kiessling, J. J. (1980). Program structure and effective correctional practices: A summary of the CaVIC research. In R. R. Ross & P. Gendreau (Eds.), *Effective correctional treatment* (pp. 439–463). Toronto: Butterworth.

Andrews, D. A., Robinson, D., & Hoge, R. D. (1984). *Manual for the youth level of service inventory*. Ottawa: Carleton University, Department of Psychology.

Andrews, D. A., Bonta, J., & Hoge, R. D. (1990). Classification for effective rehabilitation: Rediscovering psychology. *Criminal Justice and Behavior, 17*(1), 19–52. doi:10.1177/0093854890017001004.

Andrews, D. A., Bonta, J., & Wormith, J. S. (2004). *The level of service/case management inventory (LS/CMI)*. Toronto: Multi-Health Systems.

Andrews, D. A., Bonta, J., & Wormith, J. S. (2008). *The level of service/risk-need-responsivity (LS/RNR)*. Toronto: Multi-Health Systems.

Andrews, D. A., Bonta, J., & Wormith, J. S. (2011). The risk-need-responsivity (RNR) model does adding the good lives model contribute to effective crime prevention? *Criminal Justice and Behavior, 38*(7), 735–755. doi:10.1177/0093854811406356.

Appelbaum, P. (2009). Foreword. In F. M. Saleh, J. Grudzinskas, J. M. B. Albert, & D. J. Brodsky (Eds.), *Sex offenders: Identification, risk assessment, treatment, and legal issues.* New York: Oxford University Press.

Baird, S. C., Heinz, R. C., & Bemus, B. J. (1979). *Project report #14: A two-year follow-up.* Wisconsin: Department of Health and Social Services, Case Classification/Staff Deployment Project, Bureau of Community Corrections.

Birgden, A. (2004). Therapeutic jurisprudence and sex offenders: A psycho-legal approach to protection. *Sexual Abuse: A Journal of Research and Treatment, 16*(4), 351–364. doi:10.1023/B:SEBU.0000043328.06116.ee.

Birgden, A., & Cucolo, H. (2011). The treatment of sex offenders: Evidence, ethics, and human rights. *Sexual Abuse: A Journal of Research and Treatment, 23*(3), 295–313. doi:10.1177/1079063210381412.

Bonta, J., Law, M., & Hanson, K. (1998). The prediction of criminal and violent recidivism among mentally disordered offenders: A meta-analysis. *Psychological Bulletin, 123*(2), 123–142. doi:10.1037/0033-2909.123.2.123.

Borum, R., Bartel, P., & Forth, A. (2006). *Structured assessment for violence risk in youth (SAVRY).* Tampa: Mental Health Institute, University of South Florida.

Carpenter, K. M., & Addis, M. E. (2000). Alexithymia, gender, and responses to depressive symptoms. *Sex Roles, 43*(9–10), 629–644. doi:10.102 3/A:1007100523844.

Cheong, D., & Lim, Y. H. (2015, August 23). Rise in sexual crimes over last four years. *The Straits Times.* Singapore. Retrieved from http://www.strait-stimes.com/singapore/courts-crime/rise-in-sexual-crimes-over-last-four-years

Chu, C. M., & Thomas, S. D. M. (2010). Adolescent sexual offenders: The relationship between typology and recidivism. *Sexual Abuse: A Journal of Research and Treatment, 22*(2), 218–233. doi:10.1177/1079063210369011.

Chu, C. M., & Ward, T. (2015). The good lives model of offender rehabilitation: Working positively with sexual offenders. In N. Ronel & D. Segev (Eds.), *Positive criminology: The good can overcome the bad* (pp. 140–161). Abingdon: Routledge.

Chu, C. M., & Zeng, G. (2017). The assessment and management of youth offenders in Singapore: The implementation of the risk, needs, and responsivity framework. In H. C. O. Chan & M. Y. S. Ho (Eds.), *Psycho-criminological perspective of criminal justice in Asia: Research and practices in Hong Kong, Singapore, and beyond* (pp. 200–218). London: Routledge.

Chu, C. M., Ng, K., Fong, J., & Teoh, J. (2012a). Assessing youth who sexually offended the predictive validity of the ERASOR, J-SOAP-II, and YLS/CMI in a non- western context. *Sexual Abuse: A Journal of Research and Treatment, 24*(2), 153–174. doi:10.1177/1079063211404250.

Chu, C. M., Teoh, J., Lim, H. S., Long, M., Tan, E. E., Tan, A., … Lim, P. L. (2012b). *The implementation of the risk-needs-responsivity framework across the youth justice services in Singapore.* Poster presented at the Australian and New Zealand Association for Psychiatry, Psychology, and Law 2012 Congress, Melbourne, Australia.

Chu, C. M., Ward, T., & Willis, G. (2014a). Practicing the good lives model. In I. Durnescu, & F. McNeill (Eds.), *Understanding penal practice* (pp. 206–222). London: Routledge.

Chu, C. M., Yu, H., Lee, Y., & Zeng, G. (2014b). The utility of the YLS/CMI-SV for assessing youth offenders in Singapore. *Criminal Justice and Behavior, 41*(12), 1437–1457. doi:10.1177/0093854814537626.

Chu, C. M., Koh, L. L., Zeng, G., & Teoh, J. (2015a). Youth who sexual offended: Primary human goods and offense pathways. *Sexual Abuse: A Journal of Research and Treatment, 27*(2), 151–172. doi:10.1177/1079063213499188.

Chu, C. M., Lee, Y., Zeng, G., Yim, G., Tan, C. Y., Ang, Y., … Ruby, K. (2015b). Assessing youth offenders in a non-Western context: The predictive validity of the YLS/CMI ratings. *Psychological Assessment, 27*, 1013–1021. doi: 10.1037/a0038670.

Chu, C. M., Tan, J., Liu, D., Noorahman, N., & Goh, M. L. (2015c). *Programme evaluation compendium: Clinical and forensic psychology branch.* Singapore: Clinical and Forensic Psychology Service, Ministry of Social and Family Development.

Chua, J. R. Z. H., Chu, C. M., Yim, G., Chong, D., & Teoh, J. (2014). Implementation of the risk-need-responsivity framework within the juvenile justice agencies in Singapore. *Psychiatry, Psychology and Law, 21*(6), 877–889. doi:10.1080/13218719.2014.918076.

de Ruiter, C., & Nicholls, T. L. (2011). Protective factors in forensic mental health: A new frontier. *International Journal of Forensic Mental Health, 10*(3), 160–170. doi:10.1080/14999013.2011.600602.

de Vogel, V., de Ruiter, C., Bouman, Y., & de Vries Robbé, M. (2012). *SAPROF: Guidelines for the assessment of protective factors for violence risk* (2nd ed.). Utrecht: Van der Hoeven Stichting.

de Vries Robbé, M., & Willis, G. M. (2017). Assessment of protective factors in clinical practice. *Aggression and Violent Behavior, 32*, 55–63. doi:10.1016/j. avb.2016.12.006.

Department of Statistics Singapore. (2017). *Latest data.* Retrieved 6 March 2017, from http://www.singstat.gov.sg/statistics/latest-data

Edwards, W., & Hensley, C. (2001). Restructuring sex offender sentencing: A therapeutic jurisprudence approach to the criminal justice process. *International Journal of Offender Therapy and Comparative Criminology, 45*(6), 646–662. doi:10.1177/0306624X01456002.

Family Justice Courts of Singapore. (2017a). *Youth court matters.* Retrieved 19 February 2017, from https://www.familyjusticecourts.gov.sg/Common/ Pages/YouthMatters.aspx

Family Justice Courts of Singapore. (2017b). *Youth courts.* Singapore. Retrieved from https://www.familyjusticecourts.gov.sg/QuickLink/Pages/Brochures. aspx

Gendreau, P., Litte, T., & Goggin, C. (1996). A meta-analysis of the predictors of adult offender recidivism: What works! *Criminology, 34*(4), 575–608. doi:10.1111/j.1745-9125.1996.tb01220.x.

Grove, W. M., Zald, D. H., Lebow, B. S., Snitz, B. E., & Nelson, C. (2000). Clinical versus mechanical prediction: A meta-analysis. *Psychological Assessment, 12*, 19–30.

Hanson, R. K., & Morton-Bourgon, K. E. (2005). The characteristics of persistent sexual offenders: A meta-analysis of recidivism studies. *Journal of Consulting and Clinical Psychology, 73*(6), 1154–1163. doi:10.1037/0022-006X.73.6.1154.

Hoge, R. D., & Andrews, D. A. (2002). *Youth level of service/case management inventory (YLS/CMI).* Toronto: Multi-Health Systems.

Hoge, R. D., & Andrews, D. A. (2011). *Youth level of service/case mangement inventory 2.0 (YLS/CMI 2.0): User manual.* Toronto: Multi Health Systems.

Lipsey, M. W., & Derzon, J. H. (1998). Predictors of violent or serious delinquency in adolescence and early adulthood: A synthesis of longitudinal research. In R. Loeber & D. P. Farrington (Eds.), *Serious and violent juvenile offenders: Risk factors and successful interventions* (pp. 86–105). Thousand Oaks: SAGE Publications. doi:10.4135/9781452243740.n6.

Lodewijks, H. P. B., de Ruiter, C., & Doreleijers, T. A. H. (2010). The impact of protective factors in desistance from violent reoffending a study in three samples of adolescent offenders. *Journal of Interpersonal Violence, 25*(3), 568–587. doi:10.1177/0886260509334403.

Luthar, S. S., & McMahon, T. J. (1996). Peer reputation among inner-city adolescents: Structure and correlates. *Journal of Research on Adolescence, 6*(4), 581–603.

McGuire, J. (2004). *Understanding psychology and crime: Perspectives on theory and action.* Berkshire: Open University Press.

Miller, H. A. (2006). A dynamic assessment of offender risk, needs, and strengths in a sample of pre-release general offenders. *Behavioral Sciences & the Law, 24*(6), 767–782. https://doi.org/10.1002/bsl.728.

Ministry of Home Affairs. (2017). Written reply to parliamentary question on the number of child sex offences reported in the past five years by Mr K Shanmugam, Minister for Home Affairs and Minister for Law. Retrieved 30 March 2017, from https://www.mha.gov.sg/Newsroom/in-parliament/written-replies-to-pqs/Pages/Written-Reply-to-Parliamentary-Question-on-the-Number-of-Child-Sex-Offences-Reported-in-The-Past-Five-Years.aspx

Monahan, J. (1981). *Predicting violent behavior: An assessment of clinical techniques.* Beverly Hills: SAGE Publications.

National Institute of Justice. (2015). *Program profile: Children with problematic sexual behavior-cognitive behavioral therapy (PSB–CBT).* Retrieved from https://www.crimesolutions.gov/ProgramDetails.aspx?ID=380

O'Donnell, C. R., Lydgate, T., & Fo, W. S. O. (1971). The buddy system: Review and follow-up. *Child Behavior Therapy, 1,* 161–169.

Phua, A., & Lim, J. (2012, July 14). Is it time for a sex offender registry? *The New Paper.* Singapore. Retrieved from http://news.asiaone.com/News/Latest%2BNews/Singapore/Story/A1Story20120712-358736.html

Pullman, L., & Seto, M. C. (2012). Assessment and treatment of adolescent sexual offenders: Implications of recent research on generalist versus specialist explanations. *Child Abuse and Neglect, 36,* 203–209. doi:10.1016/j.chiabu.2011.11.003.

Seow, B. Y. (2017, February). New one-stop centre for sexual crime victims after review of investigation, court processes: MHA. *The Straits Times.* Retrieved from http://www.straitstimes.com/singapore/courts-crime/new-private-centre-for-sexual-crime-victims-after-review-of-investigation

Singapore Department of Statistics. (2016). *Yearbook of statistics 2016.* Singapore. Retrieved from http://www.singstat.gov.sg/publications/publications-and-papers/reference/yearbook-of-statistics-singapore

Singapore Statutes. (2001). *Children and young persons act.* Singapore. Retrieved from http://statutes.agc.gov.sg/aol/search/display/view.w3p;page=0;query=D

ocId%3A911aba78-1d05-4341-96b7-ee334d4a06f0 Status%3Ainforce Depth %3A0;rec=0

Thakker, J., Ward, T., & Chu, C. M. (2014). The good lives model of offender rehabilitation: A case study. In W. O'Donohue (Ed.), *Case studies in sexual deviance: Towards evidence-based practice* (pp. 79–101). New York: Routledge.

Ward, T., & Stewart, C. A. (2003). The treatment of sex offenders: Risk management and good lives. *Professional Psychology: Research and Practice, 34,* 353–360.

Willis, G. M., Yates, P. M., Gannon, T. A., & Ward, T. (2013). How to integrate the good lives model into treatment programs for sexual offending: An introduction and overview. *Sexual Abuse: A Journal of Research and Treatment, 25*(2), 123–142. doi:10.1177/1079063212452618.

Worling, J. R. (2013). *Desistence for adolescents who sexually harm.* Unpublished document. Retrieved from http://www.erasor.org/new-protective-factors.html

Worling, J. R., & Curwen, T. (2001). Estimate of risk of adolescent sexual offense recidivism (Version 2.0: The "ERASOR"). In M. C. Calder (Ed.), *Juveniles and children who sexually abuse: Frameworks for assessment* (pp. 372–397). Lyme Regis: Russell House Publishing.

Zeng, G., Chu, C. M., & Lee, Y. (2015b). Assessing protective factors of youth who sexually offended in singapore: Preliminary evidence on the utility of the DASH-13 and the SAPROF. *Sexual Abuse: A Journal of Research and Treatment, 27*(1), 91–108. doi:10.1177/1079063214561684.

7

Desistance from Sexual Offending and Risk Management

Joanne L. Hulley

Introduction

Over the last three decades, sexual offending has increasingly become the focus of popular and political discourse (Brown 2005; Rainey 2010), with responses based on the management of risk, harsher sentencing practices and the introduction of legislative measures designed to place controls on sexual offenders (Thomas 2010). Media portrayal of sexual offences implies their widespread prevalence despite the fact that these account for a small proportion of all recorded crime (Office for National Statistics 2017). Convicted sexual offenders consistently demonstrate lower reconviction rates than those evidenced by other types of offenders (Laws and Ward 2011). Sex offenders tend to be uniformly labelled and treated as dangerous psychopaths, irrespective of offence type (Quinn et al. 2004). They are popularly perceived as irredeemable, unamenable to treatment and incapable of change, notions that are perpetuated by

J.L. Hulley (✉)
School of Law, University of Sheffield, Sheffield, UK

© The Author(s) 2017   **175**
H. Kemshall, K. McCartan (eds.), *Contemporary Sex Offender Risk Management,*
Volume II, Palgrave Studies in Risk, Crime and Society,
DOI 10.1007/978-3-319-63573-6_7

politicians and the media alike. Governments have responded to sexual offenders by introducing harsher sentencing practices, greater supervision and a range of civil prevention orders with the overarching aim of public protection via restrictive methods of risk management. Together these factors are argued to hold serious consequences for sexual offenders attempting to desist and reintegrate into society (McAlinden 2010, 2011; Weaver 2014; Weaver and Barry 2014).

Sex offenders have become subject to risk management penal strategies reflective of the "new penology" (Feeley and Simon 1992), which emphasises public protection with a focus on dangerous groups and harsher punishment practices, highlighting the decline of the welfare approach within penology. The context of a contemporary risk society sustains a moral panic which may otherwise subside, and is suggested to, in part, underpin the increasingly restrictive raft of sex offender legislation (Walker 2011).

Desistance from crime has become a key concept within probation practice (e.g., McNeill 2006) and criminological research. Recent decades have witnessed a growth in both empirical research and theorising around desistance from non-sexual offending (e.g., Farrall and Calverley 2006; Giodarno et al. 2002; Maruna 2001; Sampson and Laub 1993), with the current academic consensus acknowledging desistance as a process involving the interaction of both social and structural influences together with internal cognitive processes (e.g., Giodarno et al. 2002; Maruna 2001). Whilst research has focused extensively on desistance from non-sexual offending, desistance from sexual offending has attracted little research attention (with the exception of Kruttschnitt et al. (2000)) until recent years, which have witnessed the publication of several empirical qualitative studies (e.g., Farmer et al. 2012, 2015; Harris 2014), with findings highlighting the significance of employment, sex offender treatment programmes and cognitive transformations resulting in the formation of a new identity.

Drawing on the author's PhD research, which explored desistance from sexual offending in a sample of 15 men convicted of offences involving a child, this chapter focuses on participants' experiences of police supervision and the impact of this upon their desistance.

Defining Desistance

The concept of desistance from crime lacks universal definition and is more complex than simple cessation of offending. Defining desistance raises as many questions as there are answers: Is desistance a reduction in the frequency of offending? Or the seriousness (Bushway et al. 2001)? How many years of non-offending are required until desistance can be assumed (Bushway et al. 2001; Laub and Sampson 2001; Maruna 2001; Piquero et al. 2003)? Or can desistance only be ensured upon death (Elliott et al. 1989; Farrington and Wikström 1994; Maruna 2001)?

Meisenhelder's (1977) early work referred to desistance as "exiting", relating this concept to disengagement from a subjectively recognised pattern of criminal behaviour. Uggen and Kruttschnitt (1998) refer to behavioural desistance, which implies a shift from a state of offending to a state of non-offending and its maintenance. Laub and Sampson (2001: 11) refer to termination as "the time at which criminal activity stops", and desistance as "the causal process that supports the termination of offending", which "maintains the continued state of nonoffending". Indeed, the academic consensus proposes that desistance should be perceived as a gradual process requiring maintenance, rather than simple termination (Kazemian 2007). Maruna and Farrall (2004) identify two forms of desistance—primary and secondary. Primary desistance refers to a lull or a crime free gap in a criminal career, whilst secondary desistance, the type of interest to researchers, is "the movement from the behaviour of non-offending to the assumption of a role or identity of a non-offender" (2004: 175). For the purpose of the current study, desistance is defined as no further self-reported sexual offending since participants' most recent custodial sentence.

Sex Offender Risk Assessment and Management

Risk assessments for sexual offenders in England and Wales attempt to predict both the likelihood of reoffending and the risk of harm to others, through the use of structured assessment tools, such as the Risk Matrix 2000 (RM2000) and OASys (Offender Assessment System) (Criminal

Justice Joint Inspection 2010). Kewley et al. (2015) found that the OASys assessments of 216 individuals convicted of sexual offences often provided little detail of how clients' support networks were developed or utilised, which they felt was "surprising given that prison and probation practice and policy advises practitioners to promote the development of pro-social networks through meaningful community integration" (Kewley et al. 2015: 249). But rather, at the expense of detailed support mechanisms, the use of control mechanisms dominated the risk management plans analysed. Whilst both police and probation services recognised the value of OASys in assessing dynamic risk of serious harm, and of the Structured Assessment of Risk and Need (SARN) reports on sexual offenders who had undertaken Sex Offender Treatment Programmes, OASys was only used by the National Offender Management Service (NOMS) (McNaughton Nicholls and Webster 2014). This overarching focus on risk and the use of control mechanisms reflects a retrospective approach, characterising offenders "primarily by deficiencies to be corrected" (Raynor 2004: 212), rather than providing them with the tools to achieve positive outcomes. In contrast, the Good Lives Model (GLM), a strengths-based offender rehabilitation framework introduced by psychologist Tony Ward (2002), focuses on what can be achieved rather than what must be avoided. Whilst the "GLM is a rehabilitation theory *not* a treatment program" (Laws and Ward 2011: 212), it does have significant practical implications for sex offender assessment and intervention. The GLM's holistic approach is based on the premise that human beings are naturally inclined to seek particular experiences or "primary human goods", in order to achieve a sense of wellbeing. The Model includes 11 primary goods (Willis et al. 2013) which can be secured by "secondary goods"—the means of achieving the primary good, such as work or relationships. Clearly, some individuals will place greater weight on one "good" over another and the model can incorporate this, thus making interventions more individualised. Laws and Ward (2011) proposed an integrated framework of the GLM and Desistance theories (the GLM-D), which holds practice implications for encouraging desistance in sexual offenders. Laws and Ward (2011) propose that the GLM-D model should involve an individualistic focus, with a comprehensive assessment and intervention plan, encouraging offenders to identify social and personal circumstances in their lives with the aim of connecting them with valued social and personal networks to assist them in building more fulfilling lives. Both the theoretical perspectives of the GLM and desistance recognise offenders' value as human agents, and combined, can focus on achieving human goods in socially acceptable ways (Laws and Ward 2011).

The Active Risk Management System (ARMS)

Recently introduced across all police forces in England and Wales (Kewley forthcoming), and used alongside the Risk Matrix 2000 (static assessment), the Active Risk Management System (ARMS) represents an attempt to combine the assessment of both dynamic risk and protective factors in sexual offenders, with the intention of providing "Police and Probation with information to plan management of convicted sex offenders in the community" (McNaughton Nicholls and Webster 2014: i). ARMS represents a strengths-based tool for sex offender assessment and management, which draws upon the desistance literature and the GLM and mirrors developments in sex offender treatment (McNaughton Nicholls and Webster 2014). The authors of the report detailing the ARMS implementation and pilot study acknowledge several papers which underpin the development of ARMS. These highlight the importance of the Risk Need Responsivity principles (RNR; Andrews et al. 1990); the Risk, Need, Strengths and Responsivity approach, which combines the GLM and the RNR principles (Worling and Langton 2012); and Ward et al.'s (2007) paper, which discusses the GLM—Comprehensive (GLM-C) and suggests that assessment should explore the individual's life goals and priorities and how they prioritise primary human goods, rather than concentrating on their vulnerabilities.

ARMS differs from previous models of dynamic risk assessment and includes eight key risk factors and five protective factors within its framework. Risk factors focus on opportunity, offence-related sexual interests, sexual preoccupation, emotional congruence with children, hostile orientation to others, poor self management, negative orientation to rules and anti-social influences. Protective factors focus on a prosocial network, a commitment to desist, an intimate relationship, employment/being busy and citizenship/giving something back (McNaughton Nicholls and Webster 2014). These protective factors reflect both the findings of desistance research and the "primary human goods" within the Good Lives Model. The role of stable employment in desistance from non-sexual offending is widely acknowledged (Farrall 2002; Laub and Sampson 2001; Uggen and Staff 2001; Visher and Travis 2003). In relation to desistance from sexual offending, employment was found beneficial by Kruttschnitt et al. (2000) and McAlinden (2009), whilst Harris's (2014) participants discussed the barriers to obtaining both employment and romantic relationships resulting from a sexual conviction. Farmer et al. (2012) found that a prosocial network was beneficial to desistance from sexual offending. "Giving something back" reflects the concept of generativity, found to be significant in desistance from non-sexual offending (e.g., Healy 2014; Maruna 2001). Generativity, a psychological construct, is a form of prosocial behaviour which promotes psychological wellbeing (McAdams et al. 1997). Generative behaviour involves a concern for others by contributing to positive changes that benefit others and thus contribute to society (McAdams et al. 1997). The GLM recognises "relatedness" as one of the primary human goods, which may be fulfilled by the presence of an appropriate intimate relationship (Willis et al. 2013). "Community", defined as "connection to wider social groups", is also one of the primary human goods within the GLM (Willis et al. 2013) and reflects the concept of citizenship within ARMS.

Within ARMS, Risk factors are rated in accordance with the level of management required (low, medium, high), whilst protective factors are rated for risk management action that is the reverse of the risk factors (low priority when there is strong evidence of the presence of a protective factor).

A pilot evaluation of the ARMS model was undertaken by NOMS in 2012 with a very small sample of 20 officers from three probation trusts and two police forces using the tool as part of their routine supervision of 37 sexual offenders. The small pilot study was said to produce positive results and made several recommendations, including the need for a larger pilot (McNaughton Nicholls and Webster 2014). Despite this small study, ARMS was later recommended as an approach that the police and probation should consider by the College of Policing (Blandford

2014; cited in Bows and Westmarland 2017). However, although ARMS has since been rolled out to police, probation services have been excluded. There is no evidence of further, larger pilots being conducted, or whether other recommendations from the initial small pilot have been addressed. It is unclear why, despite its limited evidence base and lack of randomised control trial, ARMS has been rolled out to police.

Kewley (forthcoming) explored police practitioners' experience of working with the ARMS model, their attitudes towards risk assessment, risk management planning, interviewing clients for the assessment, and their perspective on strengths-based approaches in general. Kewley's findings highlighted that officers perceived sex offenders as dangerous and requiring severe punishment, in support of previous findings (Church et al. 2011; Day 2014; Höing et al. 2016). Johnson et al. (2007) also found police to demonstrate less empathy towards sex offenders than the general public, although these police officers were not those responsible for managing such offenders. Kewley's (forthcoming) participants felt ARMS principles were generally incongruent with traditional policing. Whilst acknowledging their changing role over recent years, participants felt that the implementation of ARMS and its focus on strengths-based factors had changed their role significantly. Participants' new role required them to support the reintegration process rather than one which controls and detects crime; this conflicted with how they viewed their core duties, leading them to become "rehabilitators" rather than "law enforcers". Kewley's findings highlight Nash's (2008: 309) concerns that the public protection agenda of the late nineties resulted in "polibation officers"—"a fanciful name for what has become in reality a public protection officer, who may be a police or probation officer...", whereby the focus on risk resulted in the merging of the work of both police and probation. Nash considers the shift in value bases and conflicts and questions which criminal justice agency changes the most in this "fusion of police and probation roles into one entity 'the polibation officer'" (Nash 1999; cited in Nash 2008: 302).

Indeed, Kewley notes that the negative values held by the specialist police officers conflicted with a role that supports the process of reintegration, a finding also highlighted by several respondents in the current author's research. Kewley's (forthcoming) respondents were able to acknowledge the value of protective factors but felt that they themselves were lacking the skills of other criminal justice agents who may be better placed to support clients, such as probation services, leading to tension regarding ARMS as diluting the enforcement element of their role. Kewley's (forthcoming) findings led her to conclude that police officers responsible for conducting ARMS assessments require further specialist training to attempt to realign their attitudes with strengths-based risk management principles in order to achieve a relationship with clients that is more likely to promote desistance. Kewley (forthcoming: no page) notes that "Debate over whether the role of a police Management of Sexual Offenders and Violent Offenders (MOSOVO) officer should be that of an offender manager is one that needs greater discussion and one that cannot be justified in the limitations of this paper". MOSOVO officers' reluctance to embrace the strengths-based element of the ARMS tool may result from a number of factors: their cultural values typically align with a law enforcement rather than a welfare approach, reflecting not only role clash but also culture clash. "Some officers [in the ARMS pilot] also talked about their general interest in new research and approaches to working effectively with offenders" (McNaughton Nicholls and Webster 2014: 11), however, it is unclear whether these were police or probation officers. Thus, a failure to understand desistance perhaps also underpins police officers' reluctance to engage with the strengths-based element of the ARMS tool.

Research Methodology

The findings discussed in this chapter are drawn from a PhD study at the University of Sheffield exploring desistance from sexual offending in a sample of 15 men convicted of sexual offences involving a child. All had served prison sentences and had been living in the community for periods ranging between 1 and 15 years at the time of interview. One of the project's aims was to explore respondents' experiences of police supervision in the community and the effect of this upon desistance.

Whilst the existing literature finds that probation supervision may more enabling for desistance if a participatory approach is adopted (e.g.,

Digard 2010; Healy 2012; Weaver 2014), a focus on the police approach to management from a sexual offender's perspective appears to have been largely neglected. Wood and Kemshall (2007) found that Multi-Agency Public Protection Arrangments (MAPPA) offenders valued and benefitted from attention paid to their social and personal problems, rather than a rigid enforcement approach. However, this research focused on MAPPA management as a whole, rather than a sole focus on the input provided by the police.

The sample comprised a heterogeneous group of 15 adult male child sex offenders who had received convictions for contact offences, which involved both intra- and extra-familial victims, and non-contact offences. Contact offences included sexual assault, whilst non-contact offences included distributing pornographic images of children and grooming offences. Participants provided informed consent and were assigned pseudonyms to ensure anonymity.

Respondents were not specifically asked regarding their level of assessed risk, although some volunteered this. One participant (Ian) claimed to be a "*MAPPA 2*" and was thus presumably deemed high risk and subject to supervision by several agencies. Two participants claimed to be currently assessed as low risk, whilst a further participant (Adam) stated that upon leaving prison (27 months prior to interview) he was assessed as being very high risk. The nature of respondents' offences indicates that the majority were likely to be considered low risk.

The 15 men (100% white) had an average age of 50.6 years (range = 28–79). The most recent custodial sentence length was on average 58 months (range = 9 months–12 years) for various sexual offences involving a child. The majority of participants (n = 14) responded to an advertisement seeking participants placed through Unlock (reformed offender association), and self-reported that they had not committed a further sexual offence since their most recent prison release. As with any research exploring desistance, one cannot be certain of desistance until death (Maruna 2001: 23); an issue which is magnified in relation to sexual offences, given that a large amount of these are likely to remain undetected. With the exception of participant one, Alan, to whom access was obtained via his local police force, it was not possible to verify participants' conviction records. Despite this, as Farmer et al. (2015: 324) note:

"the low re-offending rate amongst sexual offenders actually means that statistically the likelihood of interviewing a desisting sex offender is far larger than interviewing an active or persisting one".

Risk Management and Implications for Desistance

Representatives of the police responsible for managing sex offenders in the community are referred to in this study as Public Protection Officers (PPOs), officers based in public protection units within the police service where the responsibility for sex offender management is located (Nash 2016)—given that this is how they referred to themselves in previous research conducted by the current author (Hulley 2011). It is acknowledged that other studies refer to these criminal justice professionals as police Offender Managers (Nash 2016) and MOSOVO officers (Kewley forthcoming). Individuals in receipt of a conviction for a sexual offence become subject to the terms and conditions of the Sex Offender Register (SOR), which includes unannounced visits by PPOs to registrants' homes, with the frequency of such visits dictated by assessed risk level. PPOs are the officers with whom participants had contact in relation to both the SOR and any Sexual Offence Prevention Orders (SOPOs)[1] to which they were subject.

As Nash (2016) notes, the police service are often the agency involved in sex offender supervision for lengthy periods due to the length of time individuals can spend on the SOR. Within MAPPA, the management of sex offenders in the community is often solely the role of police PPOs, given that the input of probation will more often than not cease when the individual's licence period expires, unless the individual is deemed as greater risk and thus requiring input from more than one criminal justice agency.

As previously noted, whilst research has explored probation supervision and desistance more broadly (e.g., Digard 2010; Healy 2012), the role of PPOs in sex offender desistance has been largely neglected. Healy's (2012) study highlighted two types of probation supervision operating in Ireland; these she termed the "welfare" versus the "surveillance" model.

Healy found that participants receiving the surveillance approach spoke of their experiences less positively than those in receipt of the practical assistance associated with the welfare approach.

Weaver and Barry (2014) explored the MAPPA supervisory process as experienced by both service users (sexual and violent offenders managed at MAPPA levels 2 and 3) and the professionals responsible for managing them (both police and probation). The majority of supervisees felt that supervision was more oriented to control, focused on monitoring and enforcement rather than support. The majority of police and probation practitioners also saw their role as primarily to manage the risks posed by such offenders in order to protect the public. As such, their focus was primarily on preventative practices and on securing compliance rather than co-operation and change. It is well-documented that "control oriented, preventative practices predominate over change focused, participatory approaches" (Weaver and Barry 2014: 278) to the management of sexual offenders; such approaches are less likely to promote service users' active engagement and thus, perhaps, less likely to encourage secondary desistance.

Digard (2010), whilst not focusing on probation services' influence in sex offender desistance but the procedural fairness of the criminal justice system and its likely impact on desistance in those recalled to prison, found that respondents perceiving legitimacy deficits were disinclined to comply with state sanctions in the future and to display animosity towards their probation officer. Similar findings emerged in the present study, in which two types of desistance were identified. Respondents in receipt of support from their PPOs were more likely to demonstrate internal change associated with secondary desistance (Maruna and Farrall 2004), including the development of a new prosocial identity, whilst those in receipt of a control and enforcement approach lacked any evidence of internal change and tended to display desistance which was purely deterrence based. The approach of PPO's varied both across and within police forces, with some adopting the traditional enforcement role whilst others took a more flexible, supportive role, thus broadly aligning with Healy's (2012) findings of the surveillance versus welfare approaches of probation officers.

Differing Approaches to Management

Several respondents noted that different PPOs adopted different approaches. Pete, released from prison for almost 15 years at the time of interview, had experienced management by several PPOs, and noted that his previous PPO was *"obnoxious"*, whilst his current officer was particularly helpful and supportive.

Simon, convicted of incest offences, commented on the different approaches taken by PPOs, stating that he had developed a good working relationship with the first PPO responsible for his supervision, and had found him an invaluable source of support. Should this officer visit while Simon was out, the officer would simply ring to enquire where he was and call on another occasion. However, Simon claimed that his current PPO had made more of an issue of him being unavailable, such that he had lost two days pay through taking time off work to wait in for her. He contrasted the differences between officers:

> ...the chap that I first saw here, I was comfortable, if I had anything that I needed to talk to him about I could ring him up...and we'd sit and chat. The person at the moment, if I was to turn around and say "this and this", I guarantee she'd be at the door enforced with back up and all that sort of stuff, and they'd be searching the place and they'd be doing this and doing that, when all I want is some support. So...I have nothing to do with her other than what the law requires me to, you know.

Simon believed that the supportive approach taken by his previous PPO had been particularly beneficial to his progress. In contrast, Simon's narrative demonstrates that the inflexible approach of some PPOs is unlikely to encourage co-operation and engagement.

Kewley's (forthcoming) respondents saw their role as law enforcers, a role clearly adopted by John's PPO who appeared to take an inflexible approach to the management of risk, one which failed to consider the significance of protective factors, such as employment, in achieving desistance from sexual offending. Since release from prison, John had managed to obtain a job which involved Internet use both at his place of work and his work from home. His PPO had informed John that it was necessary to speak to his employer to inform them of his conviction:

> …*well that's not fair because you know, I've just managed to get past the criminal record nonsense, now you're saying that if I use any of their computers you're gonna come in and check them?, "yes that's right". So I went to court, erm and they said nope they're [police] not allowed in your place of work while you're at work unless there's evidence of a crime, so you know. The SOPO which says I can't delete Internet history only applies outside of the work environment, if it's on work computers they will have their own protection and that I have a right to work. They [police] didn't like that. So they said "well we're gonna tell your boss unless you tell them", so I was put in that position.*

John, convicted of Internet pornography offences, expressed animosity towards the police and the fact that they were able to intrude in his daily life. He made reference to PPOs' management as a constant threat, apparent in the following excerpt from his narrative: "*it's just having that sort of 'sword of Damocles'*[2] *above your head*". In common with some of the other participants' comments, he noted differences in the approaches of PPOs:

> *it is absolutely horrific having them [PPOs] come and visit all the time, and you can't ever sort of get peace and depending on what mood they're in…I mean some of the officers are really nice, some of them are really horrible, you know.*

Similarly, Adam was astounded at the different approaches to management his PPOs had taken. His SOPO prohibited unsupervised contact with under sixteens unless their parent/guardian was aware of his conviction. He developed a passion for playing chess whilst in prison and had devoted much of his time to this since release (27 months at the time of interview). Given that he was unemployed, such constructive activity served to occupy his time and provided a meaningful and fulfilling hobby, which also prevented excessive Internet use, the source of his sexual conviction. Whilst his first PPO had been happy with his engagement in chess tournaments despite the potential of under sixteens being present, his current PPO was described by Adam as "*…a nightmare*":

I went to chess club and the police were aware of it and the MAPPA were aware of it and I started going, when my curfews were less I could go and play some one day competitions so I did that and it was all fine. And then when I moved to this new area they [the police] came to see me to do a risk assessment and I just mentioned…I didn't wanna not say about it, it's a big part of what I do, so I said "look, I go and play chess" and I explained to them "yes there's sometimes under sixteens there, sometimes I have to play one occasionally" and you know, she like hit the roof about it, this police officer. I said "the contact is only playing a game, shake hand at beginning, shake hand at the end" and when I said about shaking their hand, the way she looked at me, she looked at me like "you do what?! Shake their hand?!" And she had a big problem with it…caused me big problems.

The PPO prevented Adam from participating in chess tournaments, as she felt that this breached his SOPO terms. He recognised that chess served to occupy his time constructively, thus taking his mind off any thoughts of reoffending:

…and you'd think the police would've known that, but they just wanted…well unrealistic and take it away from me… I mean I can just see how different it can be just from one area to the other. In some ways it's remarkable, or even just different officers…

Perceptions of Legitimacy

Previous research such as Digard's (2010), has found that perceptions of sanctions as legitimate are significant in encouraging service users' engagement. In the current study, respondents' perceiving their sanctions as unfair were more likely to provide negative accounts of their PPOs, demonstrate a lack of engagement, and experience antagonistic relationships with them. This finding corresponds with Robinson and McNeill's (2008) dynamic model of compliance with community supervision in which perceived legitimacy deficits aligned with formal compliance—behaviour which reflects compliance with the legal rules. Alternatively, substantive compliance is more likely to involve perceived legitimacy (of the community order). This type of compliance is underpinned by different mechanisms and involves the co-operation and active engagement of the individual with the requirements of their community order, and may also involve the individual's genuine desire to change (Robinson and McNeill 2008).

Alan, released from prison 13 years prior to interview, claimed to have received no support from his PPOs, and referred on numerous occasions to the police *"constantly hounding and harassing"* him. He was dissatisfied with the way he had been dealt with by the legal system and although he accepted that his prison sentence was warranted, he felt that indefinite sex offender registration constituted an additional punishment by providing the police with the powers to visit him regularly:

> ...*if you go into prison and you're being punished in accordance with the law and at the end of the day you're released and you're left alone... maybe the police keep an eye on you for a year or two, fair enough, can't argue with that. But to be hounded and harassed continually after you come out...*

He articulated quite different views to other participants in relation to the police and their aims:

> ...*if anything, they try to drive me to reoffending [the police]. They'll never succeed...they're hounding and harassing in an attempt to force me to reoffend... the only job of police is to arrest somebody, get 'em convicted and that's brownie points on their record for their promotion...so they go out of their way to arrest as many people as they can...*

Alan's defiance (contra Sherman 1993[3]) is presented as underpinning his desistance, claiming that police want him to reoffend and therefore, he will not. He failed to demonstrate any of the internal changes associated with secondary desistance. The police appeared to serve as a deterrent to Alan's desistance from further sexual offending, although his health had deteriorated over the previous two years, such that the opportunity for further contact sexual offending was prevented.

Similarly, Mike believed that the police had treated him badly and adopted an antagonistic approach to interactions with them. His narrative was replete with animosity towards his PPO. Convicted of collecting online images, Mike had begun a relationship with a woman with three children and claimed that, despite her knowledge of his conviction and desire to continue their relationship, his PPO demanded that contact cease. Mike claimed this resulted in his depression together with additional mental health problems, which led him to quit his job. His anguish surrounding these events meant that he felt that the formation of new relationships was too complicated, thus eliminating two potentially protective factors. A SOPO was then imposed, prohibiting Mike's contact with under sixteens. Thus, although Mike's conviction required sex offender registration for 10 years, which had, at the time of interview, expired, the imposition of the lifetime SOPO meant that he must remain on the SOR indefinitely. Mike was particularly bitter about this and felt it to be an unfair sanction. He failed to understand the purpose of PPOs visits and adopted an obstructive attitude to interactions with the police, claiming that they failed to focus on or believe in rehabilitation.

Perpetuating the "Label"

The SOR and civil orders such as SOPOs represent late modern society's "tough on crime" politics, which Garland (2000) argues have resulted in distinctive punitive policies which convey public sentiment and as such, punishment and denunciation are paramount. Strategies of punitive segregation including lengthy prison sentences and a "monitored existence" once released, are apparent in both the SOR and SOPOs as a source of "penal marking" (Garland 2000: 350), which serve to enhance and perpetuate stigmatisation and "othering". Such "penal marking" may serve to perpetuate labelling, likely to delay or prevent the construction of a reformed identity and one that is worthy of redemption. Lacombe (2008: 59) found that sex offender treatment programmes seek to encourage (self-) control, rather than cure, via the discourse of "once a sex offender always a sex offender", a theme which also extends to sex offender management via PPOs.

It was clear that a number of PPOs supervising respondents in the present study held the popular view shared by the media and the public alike, that sexual offenders have a lifelong propensity for reoffending and are unlikely to change (Laws and Ward 2011). This was highlighted by Mike:

> *They don't believe in it [rehabilitation]. I've even had them [PPOs] saying a sex offender is never rehabilitated, once a sex offender always a sex offender because you always have that interest so therefore you'll always be a risk and they say that's why we give people lifetime SOPOs…*

This lack of belief in the potential of sex offender reform reinforces stigma and may lead to internalisation of the "sex offender" label, reflecting Becker's (1963) concept of the "master status", which is unlikely to encourage significant change or redemption (Lacombe 2008).

Mike also felt that he could never say the "right thing", as his words were interpreted to imply increased risk:

> *If I tell 'em, "I haven't got this interest in boys and I haven't got this interest in anyone who's pre-pubescent" they always turn around and say, "come on you're in denial".*

The theme of risk assessment and its focus on sexual fantasies and deviant sexual interest found in prison treatment programmes by Lacombe (2008), is thus recurrent in sex offender management. This approach is likely to prove counter-productive by encouraging offenders' deception in their attempts to reduce their perceived risk, supporting Digard's (2010) assertion that the management of sexual offenders often employs mechanisms which may exacerbate risk. Mike also found their repeated questioning intrusive:

> *…all they ask me over and time and time again is, "how often do you masturbate?" You know "what do you think of?" They can be quite obtuse at times. It just goes round and round, they will not move on…*

The retrospective approach of Mike's PPOs persistently reinforces "an erroneous perception of the offender as someone permanently at risk of re-offending, who is unable to change and who must be managed" (Kemshall 2008, cited in Weaver 2014: 17).

Despite being 11 years post-prison release at the time of interview, Mike found the retrospective focus of PPOs questions to be detrimental to his progress. He displayed little internal change and seemed to have given up hope, his adult daughter being his only *"reason to keep going"*, although he was unable to see her regularly due to their geographical distance and the financial difficulties created by Mike's unemployment. The retrospective nature of treatment programmes for sex offenders has been articulated by Raynor (2004: 212) as a "deficit model" "which sees offenders as characterised primarily by deficiencies to be corrected"; a model which seems to be reflected in sex offender management. Such an approach fails to provide individuals with the tools to achieve positive outcomes by focusing persistently on what must be avoided rather than what can be achieved. Indeed, Laws and Ward (2011: 33) argue that interventions with sex offenders:

> ...should reflect a concern to enhance their ability to achieve lives they want while ensuring that inevitable restrictions are ethically justified and proportional to the assessed level of threat or risk.

Russ, convicted of Internet offending, had been living in the community for around 2 years at the time of interview. His comment implies that the approach of some PPOs may actually be criminogenic, indeed Sherman (1993: 445) suggests that "...crime might be reduced more by police and courts treating all citizens with fairness and respect than by increasing punishments". Russ described his current PPO as:

> *...a nightmare, really difficult...it's almost like they're looking for a reason [to return him to prison]...it doesn't really help...it's a very adversarial sort of thing rather than a supporting thing, you know and that's gonna, you know, for some people that might tip them more towards reoffending...*

For this reason (and echoing Mike's comment previously), Russ claimed to exercise caution during interactions with his PPO, afraid of "saying the wrong thing". It seems that the new penology's (Feeley and Simon 1992) emphasis on public protection takes precedence, for some criminal justice practitioners, over the promotion of desistance and reintegration (Barry 2007).

Participants were acutely aware of the "pain induced by being labelled a sex offender" (Ievins and Crewe 2015: 486) and were keen to attempt re-labelling. The labelling associated with stigmatised groups such as convicted sex offenders presents barriers not only to reintegration, but also to identity construction. Respondents felt that such labelling was perpetuated by both treatment and management approaches, which encourage the individual to internalise the "sex offender" label and focus retrospectively on offending behaviour. This presents difficulties for the individual to establish an identity as anything other than a sex offender, when in fact convicted sex offenders have "…multiple identities and characteristics besides the label of sex offender" (Hudson 2005: 56).

Kevin articulated concerns reflecting the labelling assigned to convicted sex offenders:

…the problem is, society encourages them [sex offenders] to reoffend. Because whenever, for example, anyone is referred to in the press or whatever, it doesn't matter whether I was convicted for an indecent assault in 1980 that's long since spent…it's now 2013 so we're talking 33 years ago, yet I'm still a sex offender. If I am an offender, I am an offender because of what I am doing now. And if I am not offending right now I cannot possibly be an offender, let alone a sex offender.

Similar concerns were emphasised by Simon:

*There's no such thing as an ex [sex] offender, there's no such thing as being able to move forward, you've gotta tread water for the rest of your life, as far as the officials are concerned. There certainly has to be more done in this country to help people to ditch the offender, erm, title, because not all of us **are**. Not all of us are ever gonna go down that path again.*

Balancing Risk and Rehabilitation

The accounts of 2 respondents in the current study highlight the possibility of balancing risk and rehabilitation in sex offender management. Both Adam and Russ applied for alterations to the conditions of their SOPOs and were successful in achieving these. Adam, discussed in a previous section of this chapter, recognised that attending chess tournaments was important to his desistance and appealed for changes to his SOPO conditions. These changes meant that Adam was able to utilise his time constructively to pursue his hobby. He acknowledged the role of this in the prevention of reoffending:

> Now I've got my chess it makes me really happy, but if I didn't have my chess and if I didn't have my gym and I was just at home all the time with nothing, then what would I have? Other than my family, you know, what would I have? I'd have nothing, I'd just be thinking well, I might as well just be in prison.

The changes to Adam's SOPO reflect the potential of flexibility within the criminal justice system and the fact that discretion may be exercised when a particular activity is deemed beneficial to the individual's desistance. This reflects the "governmentality gap" identified by McNeill et al. (2009), within which governmental rationalities often differ from penal practice in actuality, which is "often renegotiated, restructured and even potentially softened in practice" (Ievins and Crewe 2015: 485).

Russ was in receipt of an indefinite SOPO prohibiting unsupervised contact with under sixteens. However, following a protracted process with social services, this was amended so that his baby daughter was able to live with him and his girlfriend. The potential flexibility of the system is highlighted in both Adam's and Russ's narratives. The possibility of appealing the conditions of their SOPO and their success in achieving this may have provided Adam and Russ with a sense of legitimacy, likely to reinforce their continued desistance. This appears to be possible when individuals have demonstrated their ability to acquire social capital (protective factors) and thus reduce their dynamic risk (as risk assessment tools recognise that enhanced social capital is beneficial in aiding desistance). The rigid enforcement practices typical of the new penology's preoccupation with the management of risk (Feeley and Simon 1992) can therefore be balanced with a desistance enabling approach.

The management of Adam and Russ illustrate examples of how formal social controls can adapt to support and build upon the informal social controls. Success in achieving changes to SOPO terms acts as a form of "de-labelling", described as the "certification" stage of desistance by Meisenhelder (1977: 329), within which "Some recognized member(s) of the conventional community [...] publicly announce and certify that the offender has changed...". Thus, Adam and Russ's desistance is likely to have been encouraged by the display of trust and belief in their steps towards reform acknowledged by the criminal justice system in the relaxed terms of their SOPOs. The fact that the criminal justice system, as a symbol of authority, recognised that Russ and Adam had made progress potentially reinforced to them that they were worthy of redemption and served to reinforce their desistance. Furthermore, the fact that both Adam and Russ recognised the protective factors necessary to their desistance and exercised agency in their efforts to change the terms of their SOPOs demonstrates their own self-belief and internal locus of control, beneficial to desistance.

Conclusion

Findings from the present study reinforce the claims of numerous others (e.g., Kemshall 2008; Weaver 2014; Weaver and Barry 2014; Kewley forthcoming) in arguing for an approach to risk management which blends public protection with reintegrative practices and strategies for developing internal change. Retrospective approaches continually reinforce to the individual what he cannot do and provide little opportunity to develop a more positive alternative (Weaver 2014). Strengths-based approaches to both treatment and management may also serve to enhance their perceived legitimacy, also significant to the achievement of substantive desistance.

Of course, the approaches of PPOs here are provided by the service users themselves, thus, it should be remembered that the PPOs to whom respondents refer may provide rather different accounts of their management approaches to the service users. However, as Digard (2010: 58) notes:

> the voice of the offender has been privileged in this article in order to understand and give credence to the experiences of a traditionally

invalidated group. By engaging offenders in a discussion regarding their treatment we can begin to understand how and why they might respond to their management—when they might comply, when they might resist, when they stand to suffer disproportionately. This knowledge may be used to inform the successful management of offenders as they both enter and leave prison.

Two types of desistance were identified in the present study, one which was underpinned by deterrence; a desire to avoid a return to prison and the belief that police management (through the terms and conditions of the SOR) was likely to detect any further offending. These individuals failed to acknowledge the harm caused by their offending, or demonstrate any desire to change. These men were more likely to view their sanctions as lacking in legitimacy, and to have experienced a pure crime control approach from their supervising PPOs. Whilst it could be argued that cessation of offending is sufficient (and I had no reason to believe that any respondents were continuing to offend), it may be questionable that this type of desistance is sustainable in the longer term. However, several respondents demonstrating deterrence-based desistance had been released for lengthy periods (ranging from 27 months to 13 years).

The second type of desistance identified in the present study involved identity change, thus aligning with Maruna and Farrall's (2004) definition of secondary desistance. The men in the present study who had experienced some element of support from their PPOs, or the "certification of desistance" (Meisenhelder 1977) from the criminal justice system were more likely to demonstrate cognitive transformations and identity change (the latter being a particularly protracted process). Respondents who demonstrated internal change had found meaning (and made investments in) sources of informal social control and were able to view their old offending identity as one no longer associated with their emerging new identity. The journey towards identity change, however, was clearly a complex and protracted process, hindered by the stigmatisation and exclusion experienced by those with a conviction for a sexual offence.

Whilst this study is not without its limitations, perhaps significantly the self-selecting sample with the potential of some inherent bias, the fact that its findings support those previously found in relation to the approaches of probation officers (e.g., Digard 2010; Healy 2012) and in relation to MAPPA offenders (Wood and Kemshall 2007), arguably adds further weight to the call for an approach to the management of sex offender risk which encompasses a focus on protective factors and the strengthening of these, in an attempt to encourage desistance from sexual offending. A retrospective focus fails to provide individuals with the belief that they can achieve, and is more likely to promote reoffending. Alternatively, if individuals with a sexual conviction can build a new life with sources of meaning in which they can invest, desistance is more achievable.

The recent implementation of the ARMS model, which includes the assessment of both dynamic risk factors and protective factors, across all police forces in England and Wales (Kewley forthcoming), highlights a welcome development. It is hoped that this model will ultimately assist those attempting to desist from further sexual offending with the tools to equip them with the confidence and agency to develop the protective factors necessary to desistance, with the aim of reduced re-victimisation. However, Kewley's (forthcoming) findings highlight that the success of ARMS is dependent upon the ability of police officers to adapt their traditional law enforcement role to one which is more flexible and able to balance risk management with rehabilitation.

Acknowledgements This research was funded by the Economic and Social Research Council, award ES/J500215/1

Notes

1. The Sexual Offences Prevention Order, a civil order introduced via the Sexual Offences Act 2003, can prohibit the individual from participating in particular activities outlined in the order, in the interests of public protection. These were replaced by Sexual Harm Prevention Orders and Sexual Risk Orders via the Anti-Social Behaviour, Crime and Policing Act 2014. Participants in the present study were interviewed prior to the 2014 Act and some were therefore subject to SOPOs, rather than the recently introduced civil orders.

2. The "Sword of Damocles" refers to the legend in which Damocles had to sit at a meal at the court of Dionysius with a sword hanging by a single hair above his head. It is therefore a phrase employed to refer to "an extremely precarious situation", which symbolises constant threat and imminent danger (Oxford Learner's Dictionaries 2016).
3. Sherman's defiance theory proposes that the legitimacy of punishment is essential for the achievement of deterrence, whilst "punishment perceived as unjust can lead to unacknowledged shame and defiant pride that increases future crime" (1993: 445).

References

Andrews, D. A., Bonta, J., & Hoge, R. D. (1990). Classification for effective rehabilitation: Rediscovering psychology. *Criminal Justice and Behavior, 17*, 19–52. doi:10.1177/0093854890017001004.

Barry, M. (2007). *Effective approaches to risk assessment in social work: An international literature review.* Edinburgh: Education information and analyticalservices, scottish executive [online]. http://www.scotland.gov.uk/Resource/Doc/194419/0052192.pdf. Last accessed 18 Jan 2017.

Becker, H. (1963). *Outsiders: Studies in the sociology of deviance.* New York: The Free Press.

Bows, H., & Westmarland, N. (2017). Older sex offenders – Managing risk in the community from a policing perspective. *Policing and Society* [forthcoming]. Available at: http://www.tandfonline.com/doi/full/10.1080/10439463.2016.1138476

Brown, S. (2005). *Treating sex offenders: An introduction to sex offender treatment programmes.* Cullompton: Willan Publishing.

Bushway, S. D., Piquero, A. R., Broidy, L. M., Cauffman, E., & Mazerolle, P. (2001). An empirical framework for studying desistance as a process. *Criminology, 39*, 491–515.

Church, W. T., Sun, F., & Li, X. (2011). Attitudes towards the treatment of sex offenders: A SEM analysis. *Journal of Forensic Social Work, 1*(1), 82–95.

Criminal Justice Joint Inspection. (2010). *Restriction and rehabilitation: Getting the right mix. An inspection of the management of sexual offenders in the community. Joint inspection by her majesty's inspectorate of probation and her majesty's inspectorate of constabulary.* London: CJJI. http://www.justiceinspectorates.

gov.uk/probation/wp-content/uploads/sites/5/2014/03/Sex_Offenders_ Report-rps.pdf. Accessed 10 Apr 2017.

Day, A. (2014). Professional attitudes to sex offenders. Implications for multiagency and collaborative working. *Sexual Abuse in Australia and New Zealand,* 6(1), 12. http://search.informit.com.au/documentSummary;dn=775756308 532845;res=IELNZC. ISSN: 1833–8488. Accessed 10 Apr 2017.

Digard, L. (2010). When legitimacy is denied: Offender perceptions of the prison recall system. *Probation Journal,* 57(1), 43–61. doi:10.1177/ 0264550509354672.

Elliott, D. S., Huizinga, D., & Menard, S. (1989). *Multiple problem youth: Delinquency, substance use, and mental health problems.* New York: Springer-Verlag.

Farmer, M., Beech, A., & Ward, T. (2012). Assessing desistance in child molesters: A qualitative analysis. *Journal of Interpersonal Violence, 27*(5), 930–950. doi:10.1177/0886260511423255.

Farmer, M., McAlinden, A-M., & Maruna, S. (2015). Understanding desistance from sexual offending: A thematic review of research findings. *Probation Journal,* 62(4), 320–335. doi:10.1177/0264550515600545. Available at: http://pure.qub.ac.uk/portal/files/15408452/Understanding_Desistance_ from_Sexual_Offending_Final_accepted_and_version_April_2015.pdf. Accessed 10 Apr 2017.

Farrall, S. (2002). *Rethinking what works with offenders: Probation, social context and desistance from crime.* Cullompton: Willan Publishing.

Farrall, S., & Calverley, A. (2006). *Understanding desistance from crime. Theoretical directions in resettlement and rehabilitation.* Maidenhead: Open University Press.

Farrington, D. P., & Wikström, P.-O. H. (1994). Criminal careers in London and Stockholm: A cross national comparative study. In E. Weitekamp & H.-J. Kerner (Eds.), *Cross-national longitudinal research on human development and criminal behavior.* Dordrecht: Kluwer Academic.

Feeley, M. & Simon, J. (1992). The New Penology. Notes on the emerging strategy of corrections and its implications. *Criminology, 30*(4), 449–474. Available at: http://scholarship.law.berkeley.edu/facpubs/718. Accessed 10 Apr 2017.

Garland, D. (2000). The culture of high crime societies: Some preconditions of recent 'law and order' policies. *British Journal of Criminology, 40*(3), 347–375.

Giodarno, P., Cernkovich, S. A., & Rudolph, J. L. (2002). Gender, crime and desistance: Toward a theory of cognitive transformation. *The American*

Journal of Sociology, 107(4), 990–1064. Available at: http://citeseerx.ist.psu.edu/viewdoc/download?doi=10.1.1.468.7272&rep=rep1&type=pdf. Accessed 10 Apr 2017.

Harris, D. A. (2014). Desistance from sexual offending: Findings from 21 life history narratives. *Journal of Interpersonal Violence, 29*(9), 1554–1578. doi:10.1177/0886260513511532.

Healy, D. (2012). Advise, assist and befriend: Can probation supervision support desistance? *Social Policy and Administration, 46*(4), 377–394. doi:10.1111/j.1467-9515.2012.00839.x.

Healy, D. (2014). Becoming a desister: Exploring the role of agency, coping and imagination in the construction of a new self. *British Journal of Criminology, 54*(5), 873–891. doi:10.1093/bjc/azu048.

Höing, M. A., Petrina, R., Hare Duke, L., Völlm, B., & Vogelvang, B. (2016). Community support for sex offender rehabilitation in Europe. *European Journal of Criminology, 13*(4), 491–516. doi:10.1177/1477370816633259.

Hudson, K. (2005). *Offending identities: Sex offenders' perspectives on their treatment and management.* Cullompton: Willan Publishing.

Hulley, J. L. (2011). *Police opinions on the sex offender register and 'Sarah's Law' in the UK* (Unpublished MA thesis). Sheffield Hallam University.

Ievins, A., & Crewe, B. (2015). 'Nobody's better than you, nobody's worse than you': Moral community among prisoners convicted of sexual offences. *Punishment and Society, 17*(4), 482–501. doi:10.1177/1462474515603803.

Johnson, H., Hughes, G. J., & Ireland, J. L. (2007). Attitudes towards sex offenders and the role of empathy, locus of control and training: a comparison between a probationer, police and general public sample. *The Police Journal, 80*(1), 28–54. http://citeseerx.ist.psu.edu/viewdoc/download?doi=1 0.1.1.979.8562&rep=rep1&type=pdf. Accessed 10 Apr 2017.

Kazemian, L. (2007). Desistance from crime: Theoretical, empirical, methodological and policy considerations. *Journal of Contemporary Criminal Justice, 23*(1), 5–27. doi:10.1177/1043986206298940.

Kemshall, H. (2008). *Understanding the community management of high risk offenders.* Maidenhead: Open University Press.

Kewley, S. (forthcoming). Policing people with sexual convictions using strengths based approaches. *Journal of Criminal Psychology, 7*(3).

Kewley, S., Beech, A., Harkins, L., & Bonsall, H.(2015). Effective risk management planning for those convicted of sexual offending. *Journal of Aggression, Conflict and Peace Research, 7*(4), 237–257. http://www.open-access.bcu.ac.uk/1336/. Accessed 10 Apr 2017.

Kruttschnitt, C., Uggen, C., & Shelton, K. (2000). Predictors of desistance among sex offenders: The interaction of formal and informal social controls. *Justice Quarterly, 17*(1), 51–87. http://users.soc.umn.edu/~uggen/Kruttschnitt_Uggen_Shelton_JQ_00.pdf. Accessed 10 Apr 2017.

Lacombe, D. (2008). Consumed with sex: The treatment of sex offenders in risk society. *British Journal of Criminology, 48*, 55–74. doi:10.1093/bjc/azm051.

Laub, J. H., & Sampson, R. J. (2001). Understanding desistance from crime. *Crime and Justice, 28*, 1–69. http://www.press.uchicago.edu/presssite/metadata.epl?mode=synopsis&bookkey=34093

Laws, D., & Ward, T. (2011). *Desistance from sex offending: Alternatives to throwing away the keys*. New York: The Guilford Press.

Maruna, S. (2001). *Making good: How ex-convicts reform and rebuild their lives*. Washington, DC: American Psychological Association.

Maruna, S., & Farrall, S. (2004). Desistance from crime: A theoretical reformulation. *Koelner Zeitschrift fuer Soziologie und Socialpsychologie, 43*, 171–194.

McAdams, D., Diamond, A., deSt Aubin, E., & Mansfield, E. (1997). Stories of commitment: The psychosocial construction of generative lives. *Journal of Personality and Social Psychology, 72*(3), 678–694. https://www.scholars.northwestern.edu/en/publications/stories-of-commitment-the-psychosocial-construction-of-generative. Accessed 10 Apr 2017.

McAlinden, A.-M. (2009). *Employment opportunities and community reintegration of sex offenders in Northern Ireland*. Belfast: Northern Ireland Office.

McAlinden, A.-M. (2010). Vetting sexual offenders: State over-extension, the punishment deficit and the failure to manage risk. *Social and Legal Studies, 19*(1), 25–48. http://www.google.co.uk/url?url=http://www2.uwe.ac.uk/faculties/HLS/research/Documents/vetting-sexual-offenders.pdf&rct=j&frm=1&q=&esrc=s&sa=U&ved=0ahUKEwjz_fGM55nTAhXrKMAKHVXNB7sQFggUMAA&usg=AFQjCNG4QAKVUi8dj25J6HIl_P0ajKsDnw. Accessed 10 Apr 2017.

McAlinden, A.-M. (2011). From a 'risks-' to a 'strengths-based' model of offender resettlement. In S. Farrall, M. Hough, S. Maruna, & R. Sparks (Eds.), *Escape routes: Contemporary perspectives on life after punishment*. Abingdon: Routledge.

McNaughton Nicholls, C., & Webster, S. (2014). *Sex offender management and dynamic risk: Pilot evaluation of the active risk management system (ARMS)*. London: NOMS. Available at: http://socialwelfare.bl.uk/subject-areas/

services-activity/criminal-justice/ministryofjustice/162318sex-offender-management-and-dynamic-risk.pdf. Accessed 10 Apr 2017.

McNeill, F. (2006). A desistance paradigm for offender management. *Criminology and Criminal Justice*, *6*(1), 39–62. doi:10.1177/1748895806060666.

McNeill, F., Burns, N., Halliday, S., Hutton, N., & Tata, C. (2009). Risk, responsibility and reconfiguration: Penal adaptation and misadaptation. *Punishment & Society*, *11*(4), 419–442. http://eprints.gla.ac.uk/39482/1/39842.pdf. Accessed 10 Apr 2017.

Meisenhelder, T. (1977). An exploratory study of exiting from criminal careers. *Criminology*, *15*(3), 319–334. doi:10.1111/j.1745-9125.1977.tb00069.x.

Nash, M. (2008). Exit the polibation officer? Decoupling police and probation. *International Journal of Police Science and Management*, *10*(3), 302–312. doi:10.1350/ijps.2008.10.3.86.

Nash, M. (2016). 'Scum cuddlers': Police offender managers and the sex offenders' register in England and Wales. *Policing and Society*, *26*(4), 411–427. doi:10.1080/10439463.2014.942855.

Office for National Statistics. (2017). *Crime in England and Wales: Year ending Sept 2016* [online]. https://www.ons.gov.uk/peoplepopulationandcommunity/crimeandjustice/bulletins/crimeinenglandandwales/yearendingsept2016#csew-sexual-offences-unchanged-and-rise-in-police-recorded-offences-slowing. Last accessed 15 Feb 2017.

Oxford Learner's Dictionaries. (2016). Oxford University Press [online]. http://www.oxfordlearnersdictionaries.com/definition/english/sword. Last accessed 17 May 2016.

Piquero, A., Farrington, D. P., & Blumstein, A. (2003). The criminal career paradigm. In M. Tonry (Ed.), *Crime and justice: A review of research*. Chicago: University of Chicago Press.

Quinn, J., Forsyth, C., & Mullen-Quinn, C. (2004). Societal reaction to sex offenders: An overview of the origins and results of the myths surrounding their crimes and treatment amenability. *Deviant Behavior*, *25*(3), 215–232. doi:10.1080/01639620490431147.

Rainey, B. (2010). Dignity and dangerousness: Sex offenders and the community – Human rights in the balance? In K. Harrison (Ed.), *Managing high-risk sex offenders in the community*. Cullompton: Willan Publishing.

Raynor, P. (2004). Rehabilitative and integrative approaches. In A. Bottoms, S. Rex, & G. Robinson (Eds.), *Alternatives to prison: options for an insecure society*. Cullompton: Willan Publishing.

Robinson, G., & McNeill, F. (2008). Exploring the dynamics of compliance with community penalties. *Theoretical Criminology, 12*(4), 431–449. http://eprints.gla.ac.uk/6235/1/6235.pdf. Accessed 10 Apr 2017.

Sampson, R. J., & Laub, J. H. (1993). *Crime in the making. Pathways and turning points through life.* Cambridge, MA: Harvard University Press.

Sherman, L. W. (1993). Defiance, deterrence and irrelevance: A theory of the criminal sanction. *Journal of Research in Crime and Delinquency, 30*(4), 445–473. doi:10.1177/0022427893030004006.

Thomas, T. (2010). The sex offender register, community notification and some reflections on privacy. In K. Harrison (Ed.), *Managing high-risk sex offenders in the community.* Cullompton: Willan Publishing.

Uggen, C., & Kruttschnitt, C. (1998). Crime in the breaking: Gender differences in desistance. *Law and Society Review, 32*(2), 339–366. http://users.soc.umn.edu/~uggen/Uggen_Kruttschnitt_LSR_98.pdf. Accessed 10 Apr 2017.

Uggen, C., & Staff, J. (2001). Work as a turning point for criminal offenders. *Corrections Management Quarterly, 5*(4), 1–16. http://users.soc.umn.edu/~uggen/Uggen_Staff_CMQ_01.pdf. Accessed 10 Apr 2017.

Visher, C. A., & Travis, J. (2003). Transitions from prison to community: Understanding individual pathways. *Annual Review of Sociology, 29,* 89–113. http://canatx.org/rrt_new/professionals/articles/VISHER-PRISON%20TO%20COMMUNITY.pdf. Accessed 10 Apr 2017.

Walker, B. (2011). Deciphering risk: Sex offender statutes and moral panic in a risk society. *Baltimore Law Review, 40,* 184–212. Available at: http://scholarworks.law.ubalt.edu/ublr/vol40/iss2/2. Accessed 10 Apr 2017.

Ward, T. (2002). Good lives and the rehabilitation of offenders: Promises and problems. *Aggression and Violent Behavior, 7,* 513–518. https://ccoso.org/sites/default/files/import/WArd-2002.pdf. Accessed 10 Apr 2017.

Ward, T, Mann, R., & Gannon, T. (2007). The good lives model of offender rehabilitation: Clinical implications. *Aggression and Violent Behaviour, 12*(1), 87–107. https://www.ccoso.org/sites/default/files/import/Ward-Mann-Gannon-2007.pdf. Accessed 10 Apr 2017.

Weaver, B. (2014). Control or change? Developing dialogues between desistance research and public protection practices. *Probation Journal, 61*(1), 8–26. doi:10.1177/0264550513512890.

Weaver, B., & Barry, M. (2014). Managing high risk offenders in the community: Compliance, cooperation and consent in a climate of concern. *European Journal of Probation, 6*(3), 278–295. doi:10.1177/2066220314549526.

Willis, G., Yates, P., Gannon, T., & Ward, T. (2013). How to integrate the good lives model into treatment programmes for sexual offending. An introduction and overview. *Sexual Abuse: A Journal of Research and Treatment, 25*(2), 123–142. doi:10.1177/1079063212452618.

Wood, J., & Kemshall, K. (2007). *The Operation and experience of multi-agency publicprotection arrangements (MAPPA)*. London: Home Office. Available at: http://www.dmu.ac.uk/documents/health-and-life-sciences-documents/research/rdsolr1207.pdf. Accessed 10 Apr 2017.

Worling, J., & Langton, C. (2012). Assessment and treatment of adolescents who sexually offend: Clinical issues and implications for secure settings. *Criminal Justice and Behaviour, 39*, 814–841. doi:10.1177/0093854812439378.

8

Reframing the Sex Offender Register and Disclosure: From Monitoring and Control to Desistance and Prevention

Kieran McCartan, Hazel Kemshall, and James Hoggett

Introduction

Sexual harm is a high-profile issue, both nationally (UK Office of the Children's Commissioner 2015) and internationally (UNICEF 2014), with the number of perpetrators entering and being managed by the Criminal Justice System continually increasing. These increases in the sexual offender population are the result of a 'perfect storm' created by increased social and traditional media reporting; increased visibility of the offences; increased trust in the criminal justice system to take victims seriously and respond appropriately; the impact of celebrity as well as historical cases; and related government policies, practices, and strategies. The ever-increasing sex offender population places additional pressure on

K. McCartan (✉) • J. Hoggett
University of the West of England, Bristol, UK

H. Kemshall
De Montfort University, Leicester, UK

© The Author(s) 2017
H. Kemshall, K. McCartan (eds.), *Contemporary Sex Offender Risk Management,*
Volume II, Palgrave Studies in Risk, Crime and Society,
DOI 10.1007/978-3-319-63573-6_8

existing risk management services (i.e., Police, Probation, Prison, etc.) already under financial, political, and practical strain (Simon Bailey, Norfolk Police Chief Constable, has called for a rethink on how low-risk sex offenders and viewers of indecent imagery should be managed; *Guardian* Newspaper, 28 February 2017). Such strain ultimately means that sex offender risk management becomes about bureaucracy, cost saving, risk aversion, and an audit culture rather than innovation and adaption. This chapter will consider the implications of this growing offender population and its impact on the current risk management system, posing the questions: Are we looking at this from the correct perspective and are we getting the most out of the existing system?

The Purpose of Risk Management: Control, Protection, or Audit?

In the UK, currently, there are 49,322 registered sex offenders in England and Wales (College of Policing 2016), 1,465 registered sex offenders in Northern Ireland (PPANI 2016), and 4,787 registered sex offenders in Scotland (Scottish Government 2016). This population is only going to increase given current criminal justice policies (Crown Prosecution Service 2016) and organisational and institutional inquires (e.g., Football Association, BBC, Care homes, Independent Inquiry into Child Sexual Abuse & the Office for the Children's Commissioner's report into CSA in the Family Environment). This means that sexual harm in the UK, as well as internationally poses a significant public protection, risk management, public policy, and public relations issue. How do you manage an increasing population that communities do not want to be there while balancing structural, procedural, and logistical strain on the criminal justice system?

Sex Offenders, especially Child Sexual Abusers, are misperceived and fearfully received by the public (McCartan 2010; Harper and Bartels 2016; Harper et al. 2017; Harris and Socia 2014) making them an ostracised population in modern society (Silverman and Wilson 2002; Kitzinger 1999; McCartan et al. 2015) and, therefore a significant challenge to the Criminal Justice System (Kleban and Jeglic 2012). This challenge increases exponentially when you consider public attitudes towards sex offenders sexual abuse is a social construction informed by its high-profile media coverage, political currency, and public concern (see Tabachnick and McCartan 2017 as well as Williams in Vol 1 for a further discussion). Hence, to understand the most effective policy for responding to this child sexual abuse we must recognise that societal discourses are as heterogeneous as the offending population they describe.

The high level of public, media and political attention that sexual offending has received since the 1990s has focused attention on their management post release from custody. Risk management failures are political, public relations failures as well as failures resulting in harm. For example, the murder of Naomi Bryant by Anthony Rice whilst on licence, and the 'cumulative failure' outlined by Her Majesty's Inspectorate of Probation (HMIP 2006) and the subsequent media and Parliamentary scrutiny that followed (Hansard, HC Deb, 10 May 2006, c25WS). Against this backdrop, public understandings of sex offenders, their aetiology, offending behaviour, treatment, and reintegration are mixed at best (Kleban and Jeglic 2012; McCartan and McKenzie 2014), and public perceptions of policy impact can be cautious (see Schiavone and Jeglic 2009 on public perceptions of the effective impact of Megan's Law). The public will often state that they do not have trust in the criminal justice system to manage these offenders despite not having a clear idea what the role of the criminal justice system is or what 'management' looks like (McCartan 2013). Consequently, the UK has moved through a series of high-profile child sexual abuse policies and legalisations in recent years (Kemshall et al. 2012), often in a reactionary and punitive manner (Rogers and Ferguson 2011). These policy changes are often in response to changing societal dynamics around sexual offences prefaced by high-profile media stories, high-profile child victims, and published failings in the existing state systems (Davidson 2008; Levenson and D'Amora 2007). As a result, the public are periodically reawakened to the reality of child sexual abuse, with the result that pre-emptive or ill-advised policy and legislative responses can ensue (Maddan 2008), and policy development is either reactionary or lacks a sound evidential base (Bierie 2015; Terry 2015).

The result of such legislative and policy developments has been increased regulation, surveillance, control, and bureaucratisation of sex offender management, particularly across the Anglophone jurisdictions (Lieb et al. 2011; McAlinden 2012). An extensive net of penal sanctions including a greater emphasis upon preventive sentencing, increased community regulation and a growth in post release civil sanctions have also developed (see Thomas 2016 for a full review). Paralleling these policy and legislative developments there has been increased practitioner guidance (e.g., the National Police Improvement Agency guidance to UK police officers 2010); and the development of regulatory standards for risk assessment and risk management of sexual offenders (see, e.g., Risk Management Authority 2016a).

These developments in the UK have resulted in a largely centralised approach to the management of sexual offenders within the three legal jurisdictions (England and Wales; Scotland; and Northern Ireland), with each jurisdiction having its own sex offender register, community disclosure procedures, differing risk assessment tools, varying multi-agency risk management policies and procedures, and differing systems of accountability. For example, in England and Wales the National Offender Management Service (NOMS) continues to oversee Multi-Agency Public Protection Panels (MAPPA), issues guidance (MAPPA Guidance 2016), and the development of risk assessment tools for probation and MAPPA. However, Police have pursued an alternative tool, The Active Risk Management (ARMS) assessment (McNaughton Nicholls and Webster 2014; see Hulley 2017, Chap. 7, this volume for a full discussion). In Scotland, assessment tools are approved by an independent body, The Risk Management Authority (2016b), although MAPPA is overseen by the Scottish Government Justice Department. Within Northern Ireland multi-agency work is overseen by the Public Protection Arrangements Northern Ireland (PPANI), and joint training and joint selection of risk assessment tools has been done by Probation Board of Northern Ireland and Police Service Northern Ireland. Therefore, whilst some general legislative and policy developments have been pursued in common, implementation and practice can and do differ considerably.

The Sex Offenders Register and the Management of Offenders

Sexual offending is an ongoing life-course issue for the offender, which is more about rehabilitation and reintegration than punishment and exclusion. However, there are still important public safety and social order concerns around sexual offender release and management. One of the main mechanisms for monitoring and managing sexual offenders in the community is the sexual offenders register, which exists throughout a number of countries internationally (Thomas 2010; SMART office 2016) but does not exist across countries (i.e., there is no international or global sex offenders register) apart from through data sharing agreements and transnational police communications (Thomas 2010). In countries where a sex offender's register exist it tends to come about via one of three approaches (Thomas 2010);

1. calls from practitioners (UK, Canada, Australia, South Africa, Kenya);
2. a reaction by governments to societal concerns surrounding the uncovering of sexual abuse networks (Republic of Ireland, France, Jersey, Pitcarian Island, Kenya, Jamaica); and
3. high-profile cases linked to problems with the current Criminal Justice System (USA, Republic of Ireland, South Africa).

The USA was the first country to develop a sex offender's register, with its biggest supporter, California, introducing the 1st state-wide law in the early 1900s. By the end of the 1980s a further 11 states introduced registers and by the mid-1990s another 12 states had adopted registers and a national sex offender register (the wetterling act, 1994) had been developed. Each piece of legislation around sex offender registration has become more punitive introducing the idea of 'civil commitment', community notification, residence restrictions and parkland rezoning (see McCartan 2014 for a further discussion of these issues). As the 1990s progressed more legislation was passed that developed a national sex offenders database with a mandate that all states and the federal government maintain relevant websites relating to the sex offenders register and the development of the Sex Offender Registration and Notification Act (SORNA) which would be monitored at a federal level by the SMART office. The SORNA set national, minimum standards for sex offender registration and notification; research into the effectiveness of SORN policies is challenging, given state-wide variants, studies show that the success of these policies is ambiguous and at worst counter-productive, with little discernible effect on recidivism with reoffending rates varying from 4% to 24% (Tewksbury et al. 2012; Przybylski 2015). Additionally, individual offenders stop engaging with the registration process resulting in them going 'underground' which has a massive impact on their reintegration, especially in respect to employment, housing, and social support (Levenson and Cotter 2005; Mercado et al. 2008; Tewksbury and Lees 2006; Thomas 2011). In the USA the Byrne Formula Grant Funding enforces that a sex offenders register be created and maintained in each state, but if it was not the relevant states would lose 10% of their crime control budget; however, there has been state resistance with some states willing to have the 10% reduction in funding. Internationally, a range of countries have researched and implemented a national sex offender's register with international differences in the way in which different countries implement this policy; therefore, suggesting a loose 'worldly' infrastructure for sex offender management (Thomas 2010).

In the UK the sex offenders register came as a result of a call from professionals for stronger public protection and more information on the whereabouts of these offenders (Thomas 2010; McCartan et al. 2016). The UK, like many western and European countries, is a strong supporter of the register (Thomas 2010; Smart office 2016) with the register being a central component of the community management of sexual offenders. It was introduced in England and Wales as part of the 1997 Sex Offenders Act; which was a period of heightened 'Populist Punitiveness' (Bottoms 1995), especially towards child sexual abusers, with a number of high-profile cases coinciding with the policies introduction (Thomas 2010). This increased 'Populist Punitiveness' towards sex offenders across the 1990s and onwards was not limited to sex offenders as a distinct population but was indicative of public and political attitudes to all types of high-risk offenders (including violent offenders, mentally ill offenders, and drug users) (Garland 2001; Kemshall 2003).

The result was a paradoxical approach to understanding and responding to risk which on one hand is punitive and conservative, regardless of political perspective, while at the same time therapeutically orientated. In other words, there has been a sustained demand for tougher punishments and longer in sentences (Brayford and Deering 2012) while at the same time introduced more restorative justice and community reintegration programmes (McKenize and McCartan 2014) for sex offenders (McAlinden 2008).

The UK sex offender's register contains the details of anyone convicted, cautioned, or released from prison for a sexual offence against a child or adult since its inception in September 1997; however, it is not retroactive so does not include anyone convicted before this date. The register, run by the police, requires individuals to register within 72 hours of release into the community. Initially, in England and Wales the register required convicted sex offenders, for a specified period, to notify the police of their whereabouts and circumstances, with sanctions applied to those failing to comply (Home Office 1997). The length of time that a person spends on the register depends upon the offence that they committed and their sentence, with offences covering the full spectrum of sexual offences and sentencing parameters:

- A prison sentence of more than 30 months for sexual offending is placed on the register indefinitely.
- A prison sentence of between 6 and 30 months remains on the register for 10 years, or 5 years if they are under 18.
- A prison sentence of 6 months or less is placed on the register for 7 years, or 3 ½ years if under 18.
- A caution for a sexual offence is put on the register for 2 years, or 1 year if under 18.

In part the register, both in the USA and UK, was designed to be a tool used by police to keep sex offender records accurate, up to date, and centralised, which was made more significant given that information collection and sharing within as well as across police forces was problematic. In the UK, the Bichard Inquiry (2004), which followed the murder of Holly and Jessica Wells in Cambridge in the UK by Ian Huntley (See discussions around 'The Soham Murders' for further information), discovered that even though all UK police forces had a sex offender's register, this information was not very well connected with different forces recording, storing, and passing on information from the register in inconsistent ways. To enable the police in particular to better manage sex offenders in the community, especially in terms of using the register more effectively in risk management and public protection, there has been a new overarching system introduced in recent years called Violent and Sex Offenders Register (ViSOR) (Edwards 2003). ViSOR is a new intelligence database that was developed to better manage and preserve the register in England and Wales (ViSOR National User Group 2013). ViSOR helps police identify, track, and share information about known sex offenders in their area and the crimes for which they have been placed on the register (ViSOR National User Group 2013). ViSOR was rolled out to all UK police forces by mid-2005 and although, the police are responsible for ViSOR it can now be accessed and used by the National Probation Service and HM Prison Service as well. Despite the centrality of ViSOR to the management of sex offenders until recently there had not been an in-depth evaluation on its utility, effectives, and impact (O'Sullivan et al. 2016).

Recent research on police attitudes towards and use of the sex offender register in England and Wales (O'Sullivan et al. 2016;) found that police officers were generally supportive of the register and the corresponding data management system, ViSOR. However, the research also suggested that officers believe that a number of logistical, operational, and multi-agency issues were affecting its use in practice. A common issue identified from the research was that greater investment, in terms of staffing, training and raising professional and public awareness was needed to enable the register to fulfil its potential in terms of aiding the management of sex offenders in the community. In particular, multi-agency use of ViSOR and the variation in quality and quantity of information recorded on it were issues that were believed to be hindering its effectiveness. These information issues were identified as being of detriment to sex offender managers gaining and sharing a more holistic understanding of the offenders they worked with, their offending motivations and what may help or hinder their rehabilitation.

Community Notification of the Sex Offender Information and Offender Management

Whilst initially posed as an aid to law enforcement, the sex offender register quickly became associated with public notification, particularly following the Sarah Payne case in the UK (Jenkins 1998; Thomas 2010, 2016). The USA in its increasingly restrictive and risk aversive approach to sex offender management introduced 'Megan's law' which required state-level sex offender registration and made the whereabouts of those deemed as 'high risk' available to the public (Thomas 2010). Community notification of sex offender information was subsequently extended to federal legislature, requiring all states to notify the public of 'dangerous' sexual offenders (Ackerman et al. 2012). However, public notification in the UK actually takes a number of different forms, ranging from full active public disclosure, to limited disclosure based on levels of risk with the onus on the public to make an application (see Kemshall 2008 for a full discussion).

In the UK full public disclosure was initially rejected on public protection grounds, amidst fears of sexual offenders going 'underground' (Kemshall et al. 2012). Critical to such resistance was the practical difficulties associated with offender transience foreseen by the Home Office (2007). Additionally, they were concerned by empirical evidence of Megan's law; specifically, public disclosure's lack of efficacy and myriad unintended consequences (Fitch 2006; Home Office 2007; Kemshall and Weaver 2012). Finally, in 2008 the Home Secretary announced a pilot of the Child Sexual Offender Disclosure Scheme (CSODS) should be instituted (Kemshall et al. 2010), to enable members of the public to make an inquiry about a person in order to determine whether that person had previous convictions for sexual offending against a child. The scheme is not a USA community notification scheme and is actually quite limited (Kemshall et al. 2010). An enquiry must be made via the police, about a named person, the person must be in contact with or have access to a child or children, and the person inquiring will only be told something if the subject of the inquiry meets certain criteria of risk, and has previous convictions for sexual offences against children.

In essence, the scheme has three stages, stage one an enquiry to the police; if this meets the criteria it is processed as a formal application; and if risk levels and previous conviction requirements are met then a disclosure is made.

On 15 September 2008 a 12-month pilot study commenced across 4 police force areas in England. Expected take-up and potential disclosure rates across the 4 pilot areas were anticipated to be around 2,400 based on population size of the police force area, known number of Registered Sex Offenders in the area, known offence rates for sexual offending, and significant media campaigning for disclosure (Silverman and Wilson 2002; Thomas 2011). However, evaluation of the pilots identified low take-up against projections (only 585 enquiries from members of the public against the projected 2,400). Of these only 315 inquiries actually met police criteria and were processed, while the number of members of the public actually disclosed to was only 21 across 4 pilot areas (Kemshall et al. 2010). Despite this, the Home Secretary announced the scheme would be nationally implemented at the pilot's mid-point: 18 further forces joined in March 2010, with the rest following suit in August that year (Kemshall and Weaver 2012). Monitoring of the CSDCOC by the Association of Chief Police Officers shows application and disclosure rates continue to be low. By December 2013 UK wide figures (England, Wales, and Scotland) identified that 4,754 applications had been made, resulting in 700 disclosures, at an average of 1:7 (Wall 2012). The College of policing figures from 2015/16 showing that there were 1,252 applications resulting in 192 disclosures, from across 21 police forces in England and Wales (College of Policing 2016), demonstrating a significant reduction in the volume of applications as well as disclosures. The development of ViSOR (Edwards 2003) in addition to assisting with the creation and maintenance of the sex offenders register also enables sex offender information to be disclosed, either through official channels or the CSODS, in the most accurate and up-to-date way.

Building on national and international research, policy, and practice which have examined sex offender community notification schemes (e.g., Thomas 2010, 2016; Harris et al. 2016) recent research from

England and Wales has looked at police officer and sex offender manager attitudes towards the Child Sexual Offender Disclosure Scheme (O'Sullivan et al. 2016;). This research identified that offender managers (OM's) had a positive attitude towards the scheme when it was used effectively and within reason as it enabled the public to become more aware of sex offenders in their communities and thus make appropriate decisions to safeguard children. However, OM's also suggested that the scheme could problematic if misunderstood by those who were applying for disclosure. For example, if disclosed information was not kept confidential it could create risk and management issues for sex offenders in the community. Additionally, it was suggested that the public may not fully understand the information that they are given and that this would make them more fearful and risk sensitive and may result in them taking the law into their own hand. Finally, responding officers argued that the scheme can take up a lot of their time that could be better spent in the community managing offenders. Officers identified that while currently demand for disclosure was manageable, potentially due to lack of public awareness of the scheme evidenced by its poor take-up, if awareness and demand increased then it may have a detrimental impact on their ability to manage offenders in the community and protect the public.

The version of CSDOC implemented in Northern Ireland is identical to the England and Wales version. The provisions, contained in the 2015 Justice Act, which came became operational on 14 March 2016 have been added to existing methods of disclosing conviction information under the public protection arrangements (PPANI). At the time of writing the scheme has been in place for three months and there has been less than 50 applications made. Whereas the Scottish version of CSDOC is identical in every respect the England and Wales version apart from the fact that it is administered through *Stop It Now Scotland*, not the police. Stop It Now Scotland meet with the applicants, process the applications through the police for them and make any disclosures to said applicants. The CSODS scheme does not currently exist in the Republic of Ireland (Smart Office 2016).

The Role of the Register and Disclosure in Understanding Sex Offenders Reoffending/ Desistance

Recently in the UK there has been a shift in the way that we think about sex offender risk management with the introduction of a new, all-inclusive tool called ARMS (Active Risk Management System) (National Offender Management Service 2014; Sheppard 2015; McNaughton Nicholls and Webster 2014). ARMS is designed to be an active tool designed to measure, in real time, the risk proposed by certain offending groups in the community to help police and probation manage offenders better (National Offender Management Service 2014). Preliminary research, based on a small-scale representative sample, suggests that ARMS has been accepted by portions of the risk management community in the UK (McNaughton Nicholls and Webster 2014). This reflected a larger study of police officers in England who believe that using the ARMS tool helped them in their day-to-day working, that the new tool is an inclusive and adaptive one that considers all aspects of the offender's behaviour, psychology as well as practices (O'Sullivan et al. 2016). The introduction of ARMS seems to support a wider move towards a preventive and public health approach to sexual offending rather than simply a reactive criminal justice approach (McCartan et al. 2015; Tabachnick et al. 2016). A public health approach (McCartan et al. 2015) aims to prevent sexual abuse through three prevention categories (for a comprehensive review of public health approaches to child sexual abuse see the chapter by Brown in Vol 1 2017), including;

- **Primary Prevention:** Approaches that take place before sexual violence has occurred in order to prevent initial perpetration or victimisation, which includes societal level interventions like public education campaigns, educational programmes, professional/public engagement and bystander intervention education.
- **Secondary Prevention:** Approaches that work with 'at risk populations' who will be impacted by the abuse, including potential victims and/or potential perpetrators.

- **Tertiary Prevention**: Approaches that work with offenders and victims to limit the negative impact of the abuse and prevent reoffending, these can include restorative justice programmes, Circles of Support and Accountability, sex offender treatment programmes, and risk management programmes.

Sex offender risk management is a tertiary prevention programme that supports the offender and works to prevent reoffending; however, it can and should be able to contribute to primary and secondary prevention as well.

The Sex Offender Register, ViSOR, and the Child Sexual Offender Disclosure Scheme are primarily mechanisms for controlling access to and information about sex offenders. The primary aim being to enable agencies such as police and probation to manage sex offenders in the community more effectively and to fulfil their accountability roles back to central government. In this sense, they have a key role in the offender management of sexual offenders in the community, and in supporting the information exchange, risk assessment and risk management requirements of the various multi-agency procedures across the UK. More recently, commentators have argued that this regulatory function outweighs the effective reintegration and rehabilitation of sexual offenders, and that the present management tools of registration, restrictions, ViSOR, and community disclosure do not enable practice to focus on clinical needs, reintegration and positive development, or self-risk management (Laws and Ward 2011). An alternative focus on desistance and living a good life (the 'Good Lives Model', see Hulley 2017, Chap. 7, this volume) has gained increased attention, particularly focusing on the question as to whether our current risk management strategies enable or discourage self-risk management and desistance. Certainly, in terms of the service user voice, sex offenders are not engaged with by professionals and practitioners in the same way that non-sex offending populations within the criminal justice system are. Research into why sexual offenders desist from sexual offending is a growing area of study (Laws and Ward 2010; Harris 2017) with research indicating that the large proportion of sexual offenders stop offending (Farrall and Calverley 2006; Göbbels et al. 2012; Hanson et al. 2014; Harris 2014; Harris and Cudmore 2015; Laws and Ward 2011). Evidence indicates that offenders desist because of a multiple of explanations including individual (e.g., age, motivations, aspirations, self-perceptions and self-efficacy), relational (e.g., relationships, marriage, parenthood and social as well as faith-based groups) and structural (e.g., housing, finances, employment) (Weaver and Barry 2014). These factors interact differently for each offender and no one single explanation of desistance encompasses all offenders (Maruna 2001; Laws and Ward 2011; Weaver and Barry 2014). Desistance from sexual offending incorporates all of these factors (Laws and Ward 2011; Weaver and Barry 2014; Harris 2017) and is supported, in part, through treatment (Risk Need Responsivity; Good Lives Model; Sex Offender Treatment Programme), social support (Circles of Support and Accountability) and risk management organisations (MAPPA, Probation). This raises the question of whether we should be looking at the sex offender register and CSODS scheme in the UK as a means for facilitating desistance, as we have done with MAPPA (Weaver and Barry 2014), and a means to understand prevention better, as is being done elsewhere (Harris 2017).

Multi-disciplinary/multi-agency approaches can be effective in work with individuals, with England and Wales leading the way in MAPPA work with high-risk sexual offenders. One reconviction study (Peck 2011) comparing an offender cohort pre the introduction of Multi Agency Public Protection Arrangements in England and Wales with a cohort post implementation found a reduction in recidivism rates. Offenders released from custody between 2001 and 2004 (i.e., after the implementation of MAPPA) had a lower one-year reconviction rate than those released between 1998 and 2000; which also remained true at the two-year follow-up point for this cohort. The one-year reconviction rate had been declining before 2001, but fell more steeply after MAPPA was implemented. Whilst the study did not fully meet the requirements of a long term reconviction study, and had some limitations in constructing fully comparable cohorts, it does represent the first evaluative study of MAPPA impact on reconviction rates for sexual and violent offenders. In a more recent analysis, Bryant et al. 2015 found that:

• The one-year proven reoffending rate amongst Category 2 violent and other sexual offenders decreased from 26% in 2000 (pre-implementation of MAPPA) to 23% in 2004. It has remained relatively stable since, fluctuating between 22% and 24% from 2004 to 2010.

• The one-year proven reoffending rate amongst Category 1 registered sexual offenders decreased from 13% in 2000 to 10% in 2004. It has gradually increased back to 13% in 2010.

• For each year between 2000 and 2010, Category 1 registered sexual offenders had a lower proven one-year reoffending rate than Category 2 offenders.

• Amongst new MAPPA eligible offenders assessed as having a high risk of reoffending there was a 20% (17 percentage points) reduction in one-year proven reoffending between 2000 and 2010, with the reoffending rate falling from 83% to 66%.

• Between 2000 and 2010, the one-year serious reoffending rate of the highest risk of reoffending group decreased by 45% (13 percentage points), with the reoffending rate falling from 29% to 16%.

However, determining exactly how MAPPA is having this impact on reoffending rates is more difficult to establish. This makes replicating best practice challenging. However, interviews with offenders managed by MAPPA found that they valued and benefited from attention to their personal and social problems, and to their personal goals, needs and desires. Offenders were more likely to comply with external conditions that were explained to them, which they saw as legitimate and fair (Wood and Kemshall 2007). These findings were echoed by Weaver and Barry (2014), who found that engaging offenders more extensively in the change process resulted in increased benefits.

In an evaluation of supervision strategies for high-risk offenders under MAPPA, Wood et al. (2007) identified that probation practice which promoted reintegration and balanced the promotion of internal controls as well as external ones was the key to effective risk management. Engagement and the promotion of compliance were seen as critical to success. Such strategies have been described as 'protective integration' and seek to offer a more balanced and holistic approach to risk management (Kemshall 2008). Arguably, community protection and reintegration do not have to be mutually exclusive, although policy makers and media have traditionally presented them as such.

One important area (that crisscross police, probation, prisons, MAPPA and other relevant organisations) which may help facilitate understanding of desistance and thus aid better prevention is empowering those that manage sex offenders to capture and use evidence from their everyday work and blend it with existing research-based evidence to aid in the development of practice (Sherman 2013). With increasing sex offender populations and management caseloads, together with budget cuts and drives for efficiency the pressure on those involved in the management of sex offenders has risen dramatically. A turn towards evidence-based practice, particularly within policing as a means to counter such pressure, has long been argued for (Sherman 1998). One of the reasons that development and take-up of evidence-based policing practice has been slow or inconsistent amongst police organisations and their officers is that traditionally decision making in such professions has been based on experience and gut feeling rather than scientific evidence about what works best, how and why (Lum 2009). Compounding this slow take-up is the sense of threat or challenge to established ways of working that evidence-based policing brings, with its perceived focus on top-down outside in rather than bottom-up inside out development of knowledge and practice (Bullock and Tilley 2009). In terms of the management of sex offenders and understanding desistance to better aid prevention it is precisely this bottom-up inside out approach to developing evidence-based practice that offers new opportunities. Capturing offender manager's views as well as empowering them to capture the views of those they manage would provide a wealth of data that could be used to develop knowledge and thus inform practice; since it's the offender managers that are engaging with the sex offenders from the start of this process. As research by Telep and Lum (2014) identified, while officers typically value experience more than research they recognise the importance of working with researchers to address issues relating to offenders and crime and show willingness to engage in the development and use of research methodologies. This is important as through such a process officers can come to see themselves and be seen by others as both a source of knowledge and as treatment providers who use this knowledge to reduce reoffending (Wood et al. 2014). Moves to encourage and increase engagement of offender managers in the research process may thus act as a tipping point (Sherman

2015) in cementing the use of evidence-based practice within the management of sex offenders. Such an approach will in turn aid our understanding of desistance and increase practitioners ability to reduce reoffending through development of evidence-based prevention (Fig. 8.1).

SEX OFFENDER RISK MANAGEMENT

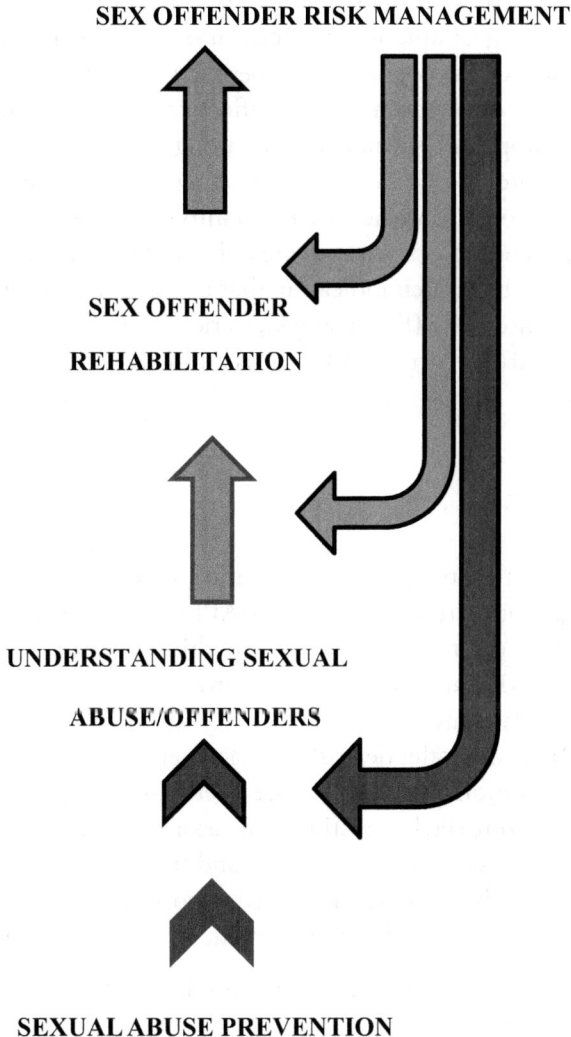

SEX OFFENDER

REHABILITATION

UNDERSTANDING SEXUAL

ABUSE/OFFENDERS

SEXUAL ABUSE PREVENTION

Fig. 8.1 The relationship between risk management, desistance and prevention

Research on the recidivism rates of sexual offenders indicates that they have one of the lowest recidivism rates of any offending population (Levenson et al. 2007), although that is contested by some authors (Bierie 2015), but the Criminal Justice Systems fear of sex offender recidivism is high and that is what drives risk management as well as the sex offenders register (Brierie 2014; Thomas 2010). This raises the question whether there is something unique to this population and their offending that creates a paradox and cognitive gap between their reoffending behaviours, likelihood of offending and/or effective risk management procedures? What stops sex offenders reoffending, themselves, the state or society? Therefore, are we enabling desistance in sex offenders through our risk management strategies? Research into why sexual offenders desist from sexual offending is a growing area of study (Laws and Ward 2010; Harris 2017) with research indicating that the large proportion of sexual offenders stop offending (Farrall and Calverley 2006; Göbbels et al. 2012; Hanson et al. 2014; Harris 2014; Harris and Cudmore 2015; Laws and Ward 2011).

Conclusions

Sex offender risk management is a significant proportion of the work done by police, probation, prison and MAPPA at local as well as regional levels in the UK; given the current climate this workload is only going to increase (CPS 2016) and potentially become unmanageable in its current form, as recently stated by Simon Bailey (*Guardian* Newspaper, 28 February 2017). Sex offender risk management needs to focus on the skills used by the offender (or 'service user') in managing their sexual offending or in completely desisting from sexually abusive behaviour; the key to better understanding the offender and their self-management tools are the professionals and practitioners who work with them.

Professionals across the risk management spectrum should be;

- Recording the risk management procedures being used by individual offenders;
- Identifying what works and what does not work with different types of offenders;

- Reflecting upon their experience of risk management and desistance in sex offenders;
- Listening and translating into practice the desistance and risk management narratives of offenders;
- Thinking about how working with post-conviction/post release sex offenders helps us understand offenders in the community;
- Recognising and listening to the sex offender 'service user' and realising that the best person to help us understand, as well as prevent, sexual abuse is the offender; and
- Recognising that narratives surrounding desistance and risk management can help us engage with and support sexual harm prevention.

The sex offender register, ViSOR, CSODS, and MAPPA offer a real insight into the risk management of offenders, both in terms of offenders and state influences, all of which can be used to develop as well as maintain effective primary, secondary, and tertiary prevention. Sex offender practice and working is a multi-disciplinary field with many of the organisations, as well as the individuals, who are involved in risk management/relapse prevention also being involved in the emerging sexual violence prevention movement therefore providing a perfect opportunity for tertiary prevention to tie directly into primary and, especially, secondary prevention.

References

Ackerman, A., Levenson, J., & Harris, A. (2012). How many sex offenders really live among us? Adjusted counts and population rates in five US states. *Journal of Crime and Justice, 35*(3), 464–474. doi:10.1080/0735648X.2012.666407.

Bichard Inquiry. (2004). *The Bichard inquiry report*. London: The Stationery Office. Available at: http://dera.ioe.ac.uk/6394/1/report.pdf. Accessed 4 Apr 2017.

Brierie, D. M. (2014). Are the collateral consequences of being a registered sex offender as bad as we think? A methodological research note. *Federal Probation, 78*(1), 28–31.

Bierie, D. M. (2015). The utility of sex offender registration: A research note. *Journal of Sexual Aggression, 22*(2). doi:10.1080/13552600.2015.1100760.

Bottoms, A. (1995). The philosophy and politics of punishment and sentencing. In C. Clarkson & R. Morgan (Eds.), *The politics of sentencing reform*. Oxford: Clarendon Press.

Brayford, J., & Deering, J. (2012). Media influences on public perceptions of sex offenders: Impact on policy and practice. In J. Brayford, F. Cowe, & J. Deering (Eds.), *Sex offenders: Punish, help, change or control?: Theory, policy and practice explored* (pp. 52–68). Oxon: Routledge.

Brown, J. (2017). Public health, prevention and risk management. In K. McCartan & H. Kemshall (Eds.), *Perceptions of sex offender risk management*. Palgrave, chapter 2. London: Palgrave.

Bryant, S., Peck, M., & Lovbakke, J. (2015). *Reoffending analysis of MAPPA eligible offenders*. Ministry of Justice Analytical Series. London: The Stationary Office. https://www.gov.uk/government/uploads/system/uploads/attachment_data/file/407139/reoffending-analysis-of-mappa-eligible-offenders.pdf. Accessed 4 Apr 2017.

Bullock, K., & Tilley, N. (2009). Evidence-based policing and crime reduction. *Policing, 3*(4), 381–387.

College of Policing. (2016, April 3). *Current figures on sex offender registration and CDOSD usage*. Private communication.

Crown Prosecution Service. (2016). *Violence against women and girls: Crime report 2015–16*. Crown Prosecution Service. http://www.cps.gov.uk/publications/docs/cps_vawg_report_2016.pdf. Accessed 3 Sept 2016.

Davidson, J. (2008). *Child sexual abuse: Media representations and government reactions*. Abingdon: Routledge-Cavendish.

Edwards, D. (2003). ViSOR—Violent and sex offender register. *Criminal Justice Matters, 51*, 28.

Farrall, S., & Calverley, A. (2006). *Understanding desistance from crime: Theoretical directions in resettlement and rehabilitation*. Maidenhead: McGraw-Hill Education, Oxford University Press: Crime and Justice Series.

Fitch, K. (2006). *Megan's law: Does it protect children? (2) An updated review of evidence on the impact of community notification as legislated for by Megan's law in the United States*. London: NSPCC.

Garland, D. (2001). *The culture of crime control: Crime and social order in contemporary society*. Oxford: Oxford University Press.

Göbbels, S., Ward, T., & Willis, G. (2012). An integrative theory of desistance from sex offending. *Aggression and Violent Behavior, 17*, 453–462. doi:10.1016/j.avb.2012.06.003.

Guardian Newspaper. (2017). *Number of child sexual abuse claims overwhelming police, says lead officer*. Theguardian.com. https://www.theguardian.com/

society/2017/feb/28/child-sexual-abuse-claims-overwhelming-police-says-lead-officer. Accessed 8 Mar 2017.

Hansard, HC Deb. (2006, May 10). c25WS. Available at: https://www.theyworkforyou.com/wms/?id=2006-05-10d.25WS.0. Accessed 27 Feb 2017.

Hanson, R. K., Harris, A. J. R., Helmus, L. M., & Thornton, D. (2014). High-risk sex offenders may not be high risk forever. *Journal of Interpersonal Violence, 29*, 2792–2813. Available at: https://floridaactioncommittee.org/wp-content/uploads/2014/12/HighRiskOffenders_MayNotBeHighForever_Hanson_Harris_Helmus_Thornton.pdf. Accessed 4 Apr 2017.

Harper, C. A., & Bartels, R. M. (2016). Implicit theories and offender representativeness in judgments about sexual crime. *Sexual Abuse: A Journal of Research and Treatment.* doi:10.1177/1079063216658019.

Harper, C. A., Hogue, T. E., & Bartels, R. M. (2017). Attitudes towards sexual offenders: What do we know, and why are they important? *Aggression and Violent Behavior.* ISSN 1359-1789. doi:10.1016/j.avb.2017.01.011.

Harris, D. A. (2014). Tales from the trenches: Zooming in on the process of desistance from sexual offending. In K. McCartan (Ed.), *Responding to sexual offending: Perceptions, Risk management and public protection.* Palgrave, chapter 9.

Harris, D. A. (2017). *Desistance.* London: Palgrave.

Harris, D. A., & Cudmore, R. (2015). Desistance from sexual offending. In *Oxford handbook of criminology and criminal justice* (pp. 1–15). New York: Oxford University Press.

Harris, A. J., & Socia, K. M. (2014). What's in a name? Evaluating the effects of the 'sex offender' label on public opinions and beliefs. *Sexual Abuse: A Journal of Research and Treatment, 28*, 660–678. doi:10.1177/1079063214564391.

Harris, A. J., Levenson, J. S., Lobanov-Rostovsky, C., & Walfield, S. M. (2016). Law enforcement perspectives on sex offender registration & notification: Effectiveness, challenges, and policy priorities. *Criminal Justice Policy Review.* Online first.

Her Majesty's Inspectorate of Probation. (2006). *An independent review of serious further offence case: Anthony Rice.* London: Home Office. Available at: http://www.justiceinspectorates.gov.uk/probation/wp-content/uploads/sites/5/2014/03/anthonyricereport-rps.pdf. Accessed 27 Feb 2017.

Home Office. (1997). *Sex offenders act 1997.* London: Home Office.

Home Office. (2007). *Review of the protection of children from sex offenders.* London: Home Office.

Hulley, J. (2017). Desistance from sexual offending and risk management. In H. Kemshall & K. McCartan (Eds.), *Contemporary sex offender risk management.* Basingstoke: Palgrave, chapter 7.

Jenkins, P. (1998). *Moral panic: Changing concepts of the child molester in modern America*. New Haven: Yale University Press.

Kemshall, H. (2003). *Understanding risk in criminal justice*. Maidenhead: Open University Press.

Kemshall, H. (2008). *Understanding the community management of high risk offenders*. Maidenhead: Open University Press.

Kemshall, H., & Weaver, B. (2012). The sex offender public disclosure pilots in England and Scotland: Lessons for 'marketing strategies' and risk communication with the public. *Criminology and Criminal Justice, 12*, 549–565. http://journals.sagepub.com/doi/abs/10.1177/1748895811433190

Kemshall, H., Kelly, G., & Wilkinson, B. (2012). Child sex offender public disclosure scheme: The views of applicants using the English pilot disclosure scheme. *Journal of Sexual Aggression, 18*(2), 164–178. doi:10.1080/1355260 0.2011.552987.

Kemshall, H., Wood, J., Westwood, S., Stout, B., Wilkinson, B., Kelly, G., & Mackenzie, G. (2010). *Child Sex Offender Review (CSOR): Public disclosure pilots, a process evaluation*. London: Home Office.

Kitzinger, J. (1999). The ultimate neighbour from hell?Stranger danger and the media representation of paedophilia. In B. Franklin (Ed.), *Social policy, the media and misrepresentation* (pp. 207–221). London: Routledge.

Kleban, H., & Jeglic, E. (2012). Dispelling the myths: Can psychoeducation change public attitudes towards sex offenders? *Journal of Sexual Aggression, 18*(2), 178–193. doi:10.1080/13552600.2011.552795.

Laws, D. R., & Ward, T. (2010). *Desistance from sexual offending: Alternatives to throwing away the keys*. New York: The Guilford Press.

Laws, D. R., & Ward, T. (2011). *Desistance from sexual offending: Alternatives to throwing away the keys*. New York: Guilford Press.

Levenson, J. S., & Cotter, L. P. (2005). The effect of Megan's law on sex offender registration. *Journal of Contemporary Criminal Justice, 21*(1), 49–66. doi:10.1002/bsl.770.

Levenson, J. S., & D'Amora, D. A. (2007). Social policies designed to prevent sexual violence: The emperor's new clothes? *Criminal Justice Policy Review*, 168–199. doi:10.1177/0887403406295309.

Levenson, J. S., Brannon, Y. N., Fortney, T., & Baker, J. (2007). Public perceptions about sex offenders and community protection policies. *Analyses of Social Issues and Public Policy, 7*(1), 137–161. doi:10.1111/j.1530-2415.2007.00119.x.

Lieb, R., Kemshall, H., & Thomas, T. (2011, May–Jun). Post-release controls for sex offenders in the US and UK. *International Journal of Law and Psychiatry, 34*(3), 226–232. doi:10.1016/j.ijlp.2011.04.006. Epub 2011 May 8.

Lum, C. (2009). *Translating police research into practice*. Washington, DC: Police Foundation (Ideas in American Policing, Series No. 11).

Maddan, S. (2008). *The labelling of sex offenders. The Unintended consequences of the best intentioned public policies*. New York: University Press of America.

MAPPA Guidance. (2016). https://mappa.justice.gov.uk/connect.ti/MAPPA/view?objectid=23797349. Accessed 27 Feb 2017.

Maruna, S. (2001). *Making good: How ex-convicts reform and rebuild their lives*. Washington, DC: American Psychological Association.

McAlinden, A. M. (2008). Restorative justice as a response to sexual offending – Addressing the failings of current punitive approaches. *Sexual Offender Treatment, 3*(1). Available at: http://www.sexual-offender-treatment.org/1-2008_03.html. Accessed 5 Apr 2017.

McAlinden, A.-M. (2012). The governance of sexual offending across Europe: Penal policies, political economies and the institutionalization of risk. *Punishment and Society, 14*(2), 166–192. doi:10.1177/1462474511435573.

McCartan, K. (2010). Media constructions and reactions to, paedophilia in modern society. In K. Harrison (Ed.), *Managing high-risk sex offenders in the community: Risk management, treatmentand social responsibilities* (pp. 249–268). Cullompton: Willan Publishing.

McCartan, K. (2013). From a lack of engagement and mistrust to partnership? Public attitudes to the disclosure of sex offender information. *International Journal of Police Science and Management, 13*, 219–236. Available from: http://eprints.uwe.ac.uk/22246.

McCartan, K. F. (2014). *Responding to sexual offending: Perceptions, risk management and public protection*. Basingstoke: Palgrave.

McCartan, K. F., & McKenzie, N. (2014). Restorative justice, community action and public protection. In S. Maile & D. Griffiths (Eds.), *Public engagement and the role of social science*. Bristol: Polity Press.

McCartan, K. F., Kemshall, H., & Tabachnick, J. (2015). The reality of community understandings of sexual violence: Rethinking public, practitioner and policy discourses. *Journal of Sexual Aggression, 21*, 100–116. doi:10.1080/13552600.2014.945976.

McCartan, K. F., Hoggett, J., & O'Sullivan, J. (2016). Police officers attitudes to sex offender registration and disclosure in England. UWE.

McNaughton Nicholls, C., & Webster, S. (2014). *Sex offender management and dynamic risk: Pilot evaluation of the active risk management system (ARMS)*. London: NOMS. https://www.gov.uk/government/uploads/system/uploads/attachment_data/file/308159/sex-offender-management-and-dynamic-risk.pdf. Accessed 5 Apr 2017.

Mercado, C. C., Alvarez, S., & Levenson, J. S. (2008). The impact of specialized sex offender legislation on community reentry. *Sexual Abuse: A Journal of Research and Treatment, 20*(2), 188–205. http://journals.sagepub.com/doi/abs/10.1177/1079063208317540

National Offender Management Service. (2014). *Sex Offender management and dynamic risk: Pilot evaluation of the Active Risk Management System (ARMS).* London: Ministry of Justice Analytical Series.

National Police Improvement Agency. (2010). *Guidance on protecting the public: Managing sexual offenders and violent offenders, second edition, version 2.* London: National Policing Improvements Agency.

O'Sullivan, J., Hoggett, J., Kemshall, H., & McCartan, K. F. (2016). Understandings, implications and alternative approaches to the use of the sex offenders register in the UK. *Irish Probation Journal, 13,* 84–101.

Office of Sex Offender Sentencing, Monitoring, Apprehending, Registering, and Tracking. (2016). *Smart summary: Global survey of sex offender registration and notification systems. Office of sex offender sentencing, monitoring, apprehending, registering, and tracking.* https://smart.gov/pdfs/global-survey-2016-final.pdf. Accessed 8 Mar 2017.

Office of the Children's Commissioner. (2015). *Protecting children from harm: A critical assessment of child sexual abuse in the family network in England and priorities for action.* Retrieved from https://www.childrenscommissioner.gov.uk/sites/default/files/publications/Protecting%20children%20from%20harm%20-%20full%20report.pdf. Accessed 1 Feb 2017.

Peck, M. (2011). Patterns of reconviction among offenders eligible for Multi-Agency Public Protection Arrangements (MAPPA). London: Ministry of Justice Research Series 6/11. Available at: https://www.gov.uk/government/uploads/system/uploads/attachment_data/file/217373/patterns-reconviction-mappa.pdf

PPANI. (2016, May 20). *Number of sex offenders on the sex offenders register in Northern Ireland.* Private communication.

Przybylski, R. (2015). *Recidivism of adult sex offenders, sex offender management assessment and planning initiative.* Available at: http://www.smart.gov/pdfs/RecidivismofAdultSexualOffenders.pdf. Accessed 4 Apr 2017.

Risk Management Authority. (2016a). *Updated standards and guidelines for risk managementpublished.* http://www.rmascotland.gov.uk/news-and-information/latest-news/updated-standards-and-guidelines-risk-management-published/. Accessed 27 Feb 2017.

Risk Management Authority. (2016b). *Risk assessment tools evaluation directory (RATED).* http://rated.rmascotland.gov.uk/. Accessed 27 Feb 2017.

Rogers, D. L., & Ferguson, C. J. (2011). Punishment and rehabilitation: Attitudes toward sex offenders versus nonsexual offenders. *Journal of Aggression, Maltreatment & Trauma, 20*(4), 395–414. doi:10.1080/1092677 1.2011.570287.

Schiavone, S. K., & Jeglic, E. L. (2009, December). Public perception of sex offender social policies and the impact on sex offenders. *International Journal of Offender Therapy and Comparative Criminology, 53*(6), 679–695. doi:10.11 77/0306624X08323454. Epub 2008 Aug 26.

Scottish Government. (2016, May 20). *Number of sex offenders on the sex offenders register in Scotland.* Private communication.

Sheppard, D. (2015). *A discussion about the development and implementation of the Active Risk Management System (ARMS) in the UK.* Sajrt blog. http://sajrt. blogspot.co.uk/2015/11/a-discussion-about-development-and.html. Accessed 8 Mar 2017.

Sherman, L. W. (1998). *Evidence-based policing.* Washington, DC: Police Foundation (Ideas in American Policing, Series No. 2).

Sherman, L. W. (2013). The rise of evidence-based policing: Targeting, testing, and tracking. In M. Tonry (Ed.), *Crime and justice: A review of research* (Vol. 42, pp. 377–451). Chicago: University of Chicago Press.

Sherman, L. W. (2015). A tipping point for "totally evidenced policing" ten ideas for building an evidence-based police agency. *International criminal justice review, 25*(1), 11–29.

Silverman, J., & Wilson, D. (2002). *Innocence betrayed: Paedophilia, the media and society.* Cambridge: Polity Press.

Tabachnick, J., McCartan, K. F., & Janson, P. (2016). Changing course: From a victim/offender duality to a public health perspective. In R. Laws & W. O'Donohue (Eds.), *Treatment of sex offenders: Strengths and weaknesses in assessment and intervention.* New York: Springer.

Tabacknick, J., & McCartan, K. F. (2017). Public education and risk management. In K. McCartan & H. Kemshall (Eds.), *Perceptions of contemporary sex offender risk.* Palgrave, chapter 3.

Telep, C. W., & Lum, C. (2014). The receptivity of officers to empirical research and evidence-based policing: An examination of survey data from three agencies. *Police Quarterly, 17*(4), 359–385.

Terry, K. (2015). Sex offender laws in the United States: Smart policy or disproportionate sanctions? *International Journal of Comparative and Applied Criminal Justice, 39*(2), 113–127. doi:10.1080/01924036.2014.973048.

Tewksbury, R., & Lees, L. (2006). Perceptions of sex offender registration: Collateral consequences and community experiences. *Sociological Spectrum, 26*, 309–334.

Tewksbury, R., Jennings, W. G., & Zgoba, K. M. (2012). A longitudinal examination of sex offender recidivism prior to and following the implementation of SORN. *Behavioral Sciences and the Law, 30*, 308–328. doi:10.1002/bsl.1009.

Thomas, T. (2010). Sex offender register, community notification and some reflections on privacy. In K. Harrison (Ed.), *Managing high-risk sex offenders in the community* (pp. 61–78). Cullompton: Willan.

Thomas, T. (2011). *The registration and monitoring of sex offenders: A comparative study*. London: Routledge.

Thomas, T. (2016). *Policing sexual offences and sex offenders*. London: Palgrave Macmillan.

UNICEF. (2014). *Hidden in plain sight*. Retrieved from http://files.unicef.org/publications/files/Hidden_in_plain_sight_statistical_analysis_EN_3_Sept_2014.pdf. Accessed 5 Apr 2017.

ViSOR National User Group. (2013). *ViSOR standards: Version 3.1. ViSOR product management team*. http://library.college.police.uk/docs/college-of-policing/VISOR-standards-2013.pdf. Accessed 5 Dec 2016.

Wall, L. (2012). *Child sex offender disclosure scheme: 18 months on. Understanding public perceptions, media framing, and risk policy formation conference*, probation HQ, Birmingham. http://www1.uwe.ac.uk/hls/research/sexoffenderpublicdisclosure/outputs.aspx. Accessed 2 Jan 2017.

Weaver, B., & Barry, M. (2014). Risky business? Supporting desistance from sexual offending. In K. McCartan (Ed.), *Responding to sexual offending: Perceptions, risk management and public protection*. Basingstoke: Palgrave, chapter 8.

Wood, J., & Kemshall, H. (2007). *The operation and experience of Multi-Agency Public Protection Arrangements (MAPPA)*. London: Home Office. http://www.dmu.ac.uk/documents/health-and-life-sciences-documents/research/rdsolr1207.pdf

Wood, J., Sorg, E. T., Groff, E. R., Ratcliffe, J. H., & Taylor, C. J. (2014). Cops as treatment providers: Realities and ironies of police work in a foot patrol experiment. *Policing and Society, 24*, 362–379. doi:10.1080/10439463.2013.784292.

Index[1]

---

[1] Note: Page numbers followed by "n" denote notes.

© The Author(s) 2017
H. Kemshall, K. McCartan (eds.), *Contemporary Sex Offender Risk Management,
Volume II*, Palgrave Studies in Risk, Crime and Society,
DOI 10.1007/978-3-319-63573-6

Printed by Books on Demand, Germany